CRY OF CASSANDRA

The Resurgence of European Anti-Semitism

by Simon Epstein

translated by Norman S. Posel

A Zenith Edition
National Press, Inc.
7508 Wisconsin Ave.
Bethesda, Md 20814
(301) 657–1616

Library of Congress Cataloging-in-Publication Data

Epstein, Simon, 1947-
    Cry of Cassandra.

    Translation of: L'Antisémitisme français, aujourd'hui
et demain.
    Bibliography: p.
    1. Antisemitism--France. 2. Jews--France--History--
20th century. 3. France--Ethnic relations. I. Title.
DS146.F8E6713 1985   944'.004924   85-10644
ISBN 0-915765-13-6
ISBN 0-915765-14-4 (pbk.)

Contents

Foreword

Zola's Smile

The year is 1898. The Dreyfus Affair reaches a fever-pitch after Emile Zola publishes his *J'accuse* (I accuse) on January 13th. A wave of anti-Jewish demonstrations rolls across France. In Nantes, on January 17th, several hundred youths run through the streets to the cry of "Long live the army! Down with Zola! Down with the Jews!" They throw stones at Jewish stores and demolish the gate to the synagogue. A crowd prevents the police from interfering with the agitators. In an outbreak the same day in Marseille, rioters jeer at Jews and smash Jewish shops. In Nancy, they lay siege to the synagogue. Similar scenes take place in Rennes, Lyon, Clermont-Ferrand, Rouen. . . .

The next day, students in Marseille demonstrate once again outside Jewish establishments, all closed now for fear of violence. In Bordeaux, the demonstrators who attempt to reach the synagogue are dispersed by the police. Other demonstrations are reported in Caen and Montpellier. On January 19th, gangs of students attack Jewish stores in Lille and Angers.[1] The disturbance continues and, in the days that follow, spares not a single city of the land.

On January 22, 1898, a large antisemitic meeting takes place in Alger. There Max Regis proposes to "water the tree of liberty with Jewish blood." The lawyer Langlois declares: "The Jews have dared to hold their heads high; they must be forced down." The crowd then marches towards the Jewish quarter but gives up when it finds it guarded by troops. The pogrom properly speaking takes place the next day. Jewish self-defense is hastily organized in order to repel the aggressors. An anti-Semite, a mason named Cayrol, is killed. The crowd invades the streets of Bab Azoum and Bab el Oued. Jewish homes and shops are pillaged, and some are set on fire.

5

Many Jews are wounded. Returning from Cayrol's funeral, rioters mercilessly beat two Jews and assássinate a third. "Out of 513 people arrested during these disturbances, there were 42 Jews, guilty of having defended themselves, 175 French Catholics, 184 Arabs and 112 foreigners," writes Reinach, who also notes: "Fire, at first set in Alger, soon spreads through the rest of the country into Constantine and Oran. Everywhere, the cheering crowd cudgels Jews, steals and destroys, invades the synagogues . . . and tears the scrolls of the Law to pieces."[2]

The fervor continues into February, during Zola's trial. On the 11th, rioters march in Paris on boulevard Sebastopol. Shots are fired at one Jewish shop, stones thrown at others. The demonstrators take rue de Turbigo, march down place de la Republique and stomp up boulevard Voltaire, attacking Jewish shops.[3] Repeatedly, in many localities, Jews are abused in the streets, and Jewish schoolchildren are taunted by their classmates. The demonstrations redouble in intensity in the provinces. Campaigns to boycott Jewish merchants are launched almost everywhere. Synagogues are guarded. Prominent Jews and "Dreyfusards" are protected by the police.

The gravity of this event is perceived abroad. A cross-Atlantic periodical, *The American Monthly Review of Reviews* offers its readers an accurate summary, in its March 1898 issue, of the situation in France.[4] Three representative personalities are interviewed, one after the other. Edouard Drumont, the anti-Jewish agitator. Max Nordau, the Zionist leader. Emile Zola, champion for human rights. Who are they, and what do they say about these events?

Drumont is the fanatic leader of French antisemitism. When he completes *La France Juive* in 1885, he has great difficulty finding a publisher.[5] His book nevertheless becomes one of the most popular French books of the nineteenth century. Brought out in new editions several dozen times, it outsells even the great popular novels of the day. Its publication marks the birth of a vast mass movement linked with Drumont's name. "The idea behind *La France Juive* was well received, not on account of its elegant style, but because it was in the air, haunting our minds and intellects, so that all Frenchmen, apart from the representatives of the Jewish Republic, thought as I did," the author will explain.[6]

The most widely read pamphleteer in France also sees himself as a visionary. "As far as I'm concerned, I am just the modest spokesman for the curious events that approach. Insulted, slandered, and ignored, perhaps I will die (although I do not believe it) before witnessing the things I proclaim as virtually certain to occur. So what! I will have completed my task and fulfilled my life's work. Each event now but confirms the precision of my predictions," writes Drumont in *La France Juive*.[7]

Anti-Jewish hatred is growing everywhere, he asserts a little later in *La France juive devant l'opinion*. In all countries and throughout all social classes, "The great organizer who will draw together these grudges, this anger, this suffering, will have accomplished a deed that will have repercussions throughout the world."[8] He revives the theme in *la dernière bataille*, in 1890: "When the Jews were all-powerful and no one dared to challenge them, I spoke to them as one speaks to implacable oppressors. Today I speak to them with a sort of gentleness and pity, as one speaks to the condemned. . . ."[9]

"When its time has come, the idea becomes deed. The Jews will not prevent this hour from approaching. What must be done will be done," writes Drumont in *le testament d'un antisémite* in 1891. At this time he is nevertheless discouraged by the anti-Semites' defeat in the municipal elections of 1890. He goes on to specify the meaning of the title of his work: "This book is purely and simply the personal testament of an anti-Semite, a journal of the thoughts and struggles of a man who was the initiator of a great movement in France, and who realizes that the inevitable execution will probably be carried out by others, rather than by himself."[10] After the onset of the Dreyfus Affair in 1894, he regains his optimism. On January 22, 1898, after the first mass demonstrations, he exults in his journal, *La Libre Parole:* "Listen to the cry which rises from all over France: Down with the Jews!" It is the cry of the past, no doubt, but it is also the cry of the future. . . ."[11]

He is then truly euphoric when the journalist Valerian Gribayedoff goes up to his Paris apartment to interview him for the *Review of Reviews* on January 23, 1898. Drumont does not hide his joy and repeats his warnings: "The Jews are singularly blind to the realities of their own social and political situation. . . . Never was this mental blindness more apparent than it is today. Half the Jews you meet will tell you even at this hour that anti-Semitism is a transitory mania, confined to a weak but loudmouthed minority. . . . Nothing seems to open their eyes to the danger threatening their very race."

While showing the journalist to the door, Drumont gives him a final statement. "Whatever you say, do not forget to lay stress on the blindness of the Jews in this crisis—that is the most dramatic element of the situation—it is almost pathetic!"

The second interviewee, Max Nordau, could hardly be classified among the blind. A brilliant essayist, a non-conformist, and a renowned psychiatrist, this Hungarian Jew living in Paris is among the first to support Theodore Herzl.

Before the Zionist Congress, assembled in Bale in 1897, Nordau outlines the situation of the Jewish people. In the East, they suffer material misery. In the West, in the countries of Emancipation, they suffer from spiritual misery. Above all, "anti-Semitism, weary in the past 30 to 60 years, has risen with new fury from the depths of society. The bullied Jew has been reminded of his true situation, which he had meanwhile forgotten. . . . The Jewish question demands a solution."

The new anti-Semitism arises in France and Germany, precisely the countries in which the Jews have been emancipated for the longest time. This disturbing fact nourishes strongly felt fears throughout the whole Zionist movement, since it clearly indicates that the ancient evil has not disappeared, and has even adapted itself to modern times. The Dreyfus Affair, Nordau tells the Second Zionist Congress in 1898, "is a warning and a lesson to all those Jews who think they have been fully admitted into the nations in which they live . . . this is what gives the Affair particular significance in Jewish history, bestowing upon it the instructive value of an alarm, a warning and a chastisement."

At the Third Zionist Congress of 1899, Nordau details the three possible solutions to the Jewish problem. One is a radical change of human nature. Another is that the Jews cease to be Jews. The first is utopian, the second is unacceptable. "The third way is to regather the Jews in their historic homeland," he declares to the applause of the delegates.[12]

Interviewed by Robert H. Sherard in 1898, Nordau promptly gives free rein to his fears, aggravated by the recent anti-Semitic demonstrations. "We are quite simply marching in France toward a new Saint Bartholemew's Eve, to a massacre which will only be limited by the number of Jews whom the Catholics can find and knock on the head." If the government were to relax its vigilance, this would lead to a "general slaughter of Jews throughout the country." Nordau alludes to the persecutions and expulsions of Jews in medieval times. "In France, as in every other country, the history of the Jews is a record of blood and suffering."

He insists before again affirming Dreyfus' innocence: "In the meanwhile, the energetic attitude of the government inspires us with some confidence. But the extermination of the Jews has already begun. . . ."

★

Emile Zola. On January 13, 1898, *L'Aurore* publishes his letter to the president of the Republic. "I accuse General Mercier of having made himself an accomplice (due to weakness of spirit, at the very least) to one of the greatest injustices of the century . . . I accuse General Billot of having had in his hands definite proofs of Dreyfus' innocence, and of having knowingly suppressed them . . . I accuse General de Boisdeffre and General Gonse of having been accomplices to the same crime . . . I am not unaware that I am placing myself under the provision of articles 30 and 31 of the law of July 29, 1881, which punishes defamation offenses. And I put myself at risk voluntarily . . . I wait." I accuse, I risk, I wait. The strategy is remarkable. It will crack the conspiracy of silence. But the act is reckless. It concentrates enemy fire on Zola.

The writer pays the price for his courage. Condemned at his trial, he takes refuge in London, from whence he will return only after a long exile. Caricaturists, journalists and politicians bombard him with insults and drag his name through the mud. Crowds in the streets clamor "Down with Zola!" and "Death to the Jews!" during the great anti-Jewish demonstrations that reach their zenith with Zola's appearance in court before the judges in February, 1898.

Some time earlier, when questioned by the same Robert H. Sherard, he insisted on the impracticability of anti-Semitism. "It must be rather disheartening to Drumont and all the rest of his school to see that after all their efforts to incite the mob against the Jews, not a single pane of glass in the windows of any Jewish home in France has been broken. That is why I speak of this anti-Semitic movement in France as an imbecilic one, and imbecilic because impotent."

But now, in 1898, much more than windows are being broken. Sherard, on behalf of the *Review of Reviews,* quotes to Zola the remarks made by Max Nordau earlier that same afternoon about an eventual massacre of the Jews. Zola is relaxed: ". . . he smiled with real amusement when I related to him the substance of the conversation I had had that afternoon with Max Nordau. He certainly did not share the doctor's gloomy anticipations," writes Sherard. "The *Droits de l'Homme* is a universally accepted creed," Zola decides. Nordau's catastrophism is unjustified. Anti-Semitism is on the way out. The extermination of the Jews is unthinkable.

In 1898, Drumont sneers, Nordau panics, but Zola smiles. The immediate future will favor him over the other two men. The anti-Jewish wave subsides at the beginning of the twentieth century in Germany as in France. Anti-Semitism then takes refuge in Russia, bearing out the comforting theory that links anti-Semitism to archaic obscurantism, thus assuring its disappearance with the progress of liberal ideas, the evolution of minds and the transformation of human society.

The end of anti-Semitism will be declared in 1900 by the head Rabbi of Algeria, who answers before a parliamentary inquest: "We scarcely hear the cry 'Down with the Jews' any longer, and the Israelites can travel about and work freely."[13] It will be proclaimed by Narcisse Leven before the general assembly of the Alliance Israélite Universelle in Paris, in 1903: "France has regained her self-control, she has stood up against anti-Semitism, she has struck it a blow, and I would like to say that she has overcome it. If this is not yet so, is it not true that, with the new century, we are at least entering a new phase?"[14]

Drumont will die in 1917, an isolated and obscure figure. He had known the homage and adoration of crowds, had seen the growth of anti-Semitism and had also seen its decline. Until the end, however, he never ceased to voice his sinister prophecies, though people had long since ceased to pay attention to him.

Nordau will live until 1923. From 1898 on, Zionism progressed considerably. In the countries of Exile, it was well represented in every Jewish community. The Balfour Declaration of 1917 and the League of Nations' mandate laid the legal foundation for its practical fulfillment. The results, however, were slow. By the end of the century, Palestine numbered some tens of thousands of Jews. At the beginning of the 1920's they still numbered just 85,000. By 1933, 250,000 Jews are living in their country. Their community is dynamic, pioneering and structured and it knows how to defend itself. It already exhibits all of the characteristics of the statehood it seeks. But numerically it gathers only a very small part of the 16 million Jews living in the world at the beginning of the thirties. Zionism had grown, but not fast enough. In the dramatic race against anti-Semitism, it was gradually losing ground.

In 1902, Zola will die tragically, by asphyxiation, under mysterious circumstances. He will have the opportunity to welcome Dreyfus back from l'Ile du Diable and express his gratitude and admiration, but not to celebrate his complete rehabilitation in 1906. He had proven that Jews were not alone facing intolerance and prejudice. He reinforced, by his actions and courage, the certitude that anti-Semitism could be resisted and conquered. For Jews all around the world, Emile Zola helped relieve the anxiety generated by the resurgence of anti-Semitism at the end of the nineteenth century. His smile rekindled people's spirits.

Hence, our three interviewees lived through the advance wave of antisemitism at the end of the nineteenth century, but they did not live to see the devastating tidal wave that it foreboded. They will not witness the extermination of six million Jews. Although unable to guess the time or geographical location, to imagine the means or to fathom the scope, Drumont and Nordau had dimly foreseen it. One with rejoicing, the other with dread. But Zola had perceived neither the potential force, nor the possible results of the movement he opposed. He had overestimated the capacity of democratic societies to resist.

★

Can anti-Semitism be fought? Can antisemitism be foreseen? These two questions will be our guidelines. This book will deal both with the future of French anti-Semitism and with the destiny of the French Jews by the late twentieth century. The author's sympathies, as one will have gathered, will not be with Drumont, but will not linger on Zola. Beyond Nordau, his sympathies will extend to the Zionist builders and fighters, the architects of the Jewish renaissance and the return of Israel to its homeland.

Part One

Can Anti-Semitism Be Fought?

Chapter One

Jews and Non-Jews, United!

On the night of October 3, 1980, a bomb explodes before the synagogue on rue de Copernic in Paris. "The synagogue's stained glass windows collapsed. Outside, three people, one woman among them, had been killed instantly, and a dozen wounded were lying among the burnt carcasses of four cars and two motor bikes. Stores and apartment buildings adjoining the synagogue were shaken," writes the *Bulletin de l'Agence Télégraphique Juive.*[1]

The incident comes at the end of a somewhat active month of September. August 31st is marked by the desecration of 72 tombs in the old Jewish cemetery of Forbach. Jews in Nice receive death threats. The community center of Montpellier is plundered. Anti-Semitic inscriptions appear on Jewish storefronts in Belfort. An anti-Jewish tract of the Fascist organization FANE, which had just been outlawed by the government, is destributed underground in Paris. "Happy New Year, Yids!" During the night of September 21st, a Jewish shop is burned in Paris. Another attempt takes aim at Henri Noguéres, president of the League of Human Rights. In the early morning of Friday the 26th, automatic weapons are fired at the facades of four Jewish establishments: the synagogue on rue de la Victoire, the Memorial of the Unknown Jewish Martyr, the Lucien-de-Hirsch School and a day nursery. A protest demonstration is organized by the various Jewish organizations. CLESS (a union of socialist zionist students) organizes a meeting at the Mutualité. "Anti-Semitic graffiti has appeared in different localities in the capital. Certain Jewish shops in the Market of Saint-Ouen have been marked with anti-Semitic inscriptions and skulls. Anti-Semitic publications have been distributed at the Saint-Lazare train station. Incidents have occurred on rue Saint-Denis and there have been numerous reports of anonymous menacing telephone calls," the *Bulletin* also reports.[2]

The bombing on October 3rd is perceived at that moment as the culmination of a dangerous progression and as a potential starting point for worse events to follow. "Times of sorrow and courage have returned, but also times of lucidity and determination," proclaims CRIF (Representative Council of Jewish Institutions in France) the night of October 4th.[3] All day Saturday, demonstrations concurrently organized by the MRAP, the Renouveau juif, and, at night, by CLESS, are on the march in the capital. Their slogans sometimes concur, but often diverge. However, the strong emotions felt by the Jewish community and by all French people blur their differences on this great day.

"Hundreds of thousands of Parisians in solidarity with the Jewish community" the *Bulletin* headlines. Tuesday, October 7, at the call of the syndicates, the antiracist movements and political parties from every side, impressive mass demonstrations are organized throughout the country. Three hundred thousand demonstrators are counted in Paris, 8,000 in Lyon, 10,000 in Nice, and 3,000 in Valence.[4] Declarations of support, and statements of protest abound everywhere. "The huge demonstrations of October 7th in Paris will make history in the struggle against racism," concludes Albert Lévy in *Droit et Liberté.*[5]

★

Analyzing the popular reaction, Annie Kriegel commends "the health of the French social body." She adds: "Nothing compares with Germany in the thirties, gangrenous down to the bone."[6]

After the announcement of the murder, 200,000 gather in the streets of the capital, which are all draped with the tri-colored flag of the Republic. The workers and the middle class unite in a common front against the assassins and demand punishment for the guilty. The crime is condemned by the press and public opinion. Politicians multiply their protest speeches. Expressions of solidarity are innumerable. Repression against the extreme Right gathers strength. Tuesday, the entire nation rises up. There are 50,000 in Breslau, 150,000 in Munich, 50,000 in Essen, and hundreds of thousands on the Lustgarten in Berlin.

Now we are in Germany in the twenties. It is Tuesday, June 27, 1922. Walter Rathenau, a Jew and a liberal, the Weimar Republic's

Minister of Foreign Affairs, has just been assassinated in the wake of a particularly virulent anti-Semitic campaign. "They hated him because he was Jewish," writes the *Vorwärts,* voice of the Social-Democratic Party, which also describes the formidable "human wall" formed by demonstrators.

On July 4th, a second series of marches is organized throughout the country. This time, there are 100,000 in Breslau, 60,000 in Dusseldorf, 50,000 in Konigsberg, 40,000 in Kiel, and nearly a million in Berlin.[7] "Not since the assassination of Abraham Lincoln has the death of a statesman so shaken a whole nation," a contemporary writes. "Stupendous processions, such as Germany had never witnessed, marched in order under the Republican flag through all the cities of the land."[8] Public reaction is so strong that in October 1922 the great nationalist party, the Deutsch-Nationale Volkspartei, distances itself from the racist and anti-Semitic elements within its own ranks. Excluded members leave to rejoin, or to found, a few marginal splinter groups.

The *Israelitisches Familienblatt,* an important Jewish paper published in Hamburg, applauds the "unanimity of the condemnation" that was expressed in Parliament, in the demonstrations, and in the national and foreign press. It amply cites declarations by the Chancellor of the Reich, Wirth, and those of numerous politicians. "Rathenau was struck down as a Jew," declares Dr. Karrell at the time of the Reichstag commemoration. The same Karrell is enthusiastically endorsed when, before an assembly of Liberal youths in Berlin, he calls upon all to fight anti-Semitism "with our fists." In sessions with the Jewish community of Prussia, the government representative takes up the same theme: Rathenau was not just struck down as a Liberal but also as a Jew.[9]

"We accuse!" headlines the *C.V. Zeitung,* the Central Verein mouthpiece. With its 70,000 adherents spread out over more than 600 local sections, Central Verein is the most powerful political organization of German Judaism. It was founded in 1893 in response to the anti-Semitic wave of the late nineteenth century. The June 30th editorial violently denounces the organizations of the extreme Right, demanding that the necessary measures be taken. "We, German Jews, lay claim to no special rights, but we demand with the utmost firmness that the existing laws and provisions be applied to protect us, as much as they protect our fellow-countrymen." The *C.V. Zeitung* dwells on Rathenau, who was a "true German and a true Jew." It prints excerpts from the press proving the extreme Right's responsibility for the assassination.[10] "Is the danger over?"

asks the paper in July. It describes the injuriousness of antisemitic hatred and calls upon Jews to mobilize for action. The *C. V. Zeitung* comments favorably on the instructions given by the Minister of Education: the educators must warn all their students about anti-Jewish agitation.[11]

In September, Curt Burger asks: "Is the fight against anti-Semitism hopeless?" He recalls ancient anti-Semitism and its renewal in the nineteenth century in Germany and France. He warns against ignoring the significance of the danger. His conclusion, a militant one, suggests that anti-Semitism will one day be liquidated. They will carry it away on a "tip-cart."[12]

Meanwhile, Rathenau's two assassins are dead. One is killed by the police on July 17, the other commits suicide. The accomplices' trial takes place in Leipzig. The accused, all very young, declare that the Minister was an "Elder of Zion," planning to subject Germany to worldwide Jewish domination. The lesson of all this is clear, writes the *C. V. Zeitung*. No anti-Semitic attack will be taken lightly, and the Central Verein will do its part.[13] "The lessons of the Rathenau trial" are delineated on October 19, 1922, by Arthur Schweriner, who addresses himself to German Jews: "To be a Jew is to be a fighter!"[14]

The formula will be repeated in Paris in 1979, after the criminal attempt against a Jewish university restaurant: "To be a Jew is to fight," declares a tract of one Jewish organization.[15]

★

"The popular reaction was extremely harsh. These demonstrations mark a historic turning point in relations between the Jews of France and the French nation," writes Richard Marienstras after Copernic.[16]

"Solidarity of the Polish proletariat. The Polish workers of Radom and Byalistock are united in the strike." Thus states the front page of the *Naie Folkszeitung,* the Yiddish daily of the Bund in Warsaw, on March 16, 1936. Several days earlier a band of fascists attacked the Jewish community of Pshitik, and killed several people. The police arrested the aggressors and the Jewish defenders who opposed them indiscriminately, which only heightened the emotion provoked by the pogrom. The great Jewish socialist party thus set March 17th as a day of action, strike, and protest throughout the country. Word goes out to Jewish workers, employees, intellectuals and artisans; very quickly, however, Polish union organizations in many towns join the movement. The editorial of the 16th exults: "We have on our side the sympathy and solidarity of the entire Polish proletariat."[17]

"For our honor! For our right!" The Bund reports, on March 17th, that in many places "the Polish workers are going on strike with their Jewish comrades." In Kalisz, the local section of the Socialist Party (PPS) and other non-Jewish organizations proclaim in the same vein: "The Jewish working class can be assured that we will always be on its side."[18] Reports printed in the paper's subsequent issues under the rubric "The Historic Tuesday" make a case for massive participation by non-Jews in the strikes, marches and anti-fascist meetings that are held in hundreds of towns of the land. In Pietrikov, after an enormous rally against anti-Semitism in which both Jews and non-Jews participate, the crowd intones the Bund hymn, the hymn of the Polish workers, and the International.[19]

The "day of combat" (in Yiddish: *Kampftug*) on the 17th is especially evident in the capital. Factories and stores are closed. "Warsaw is transformed," writes the *Naie Folkszeitung*. Zamenhof, Nalevki and many other streets are filled with tens of thousands of people of all ages who have come to protest. Schoolchildren are restless in class: "Down with the pogroms! We are on strike." The Jewish schools end classes early so the pupils can gather in the streets. Everywhere prevails a "festive atmosphere which expresses courage, force, and faith in victory."[20]

The central meeting unfolds in the great Hall of Fama. "The time has passed when one could carry out pogroms against the Jews with impunity" asserts Zygelboim. Alter, another leader of the Bund, calls upon the Jews to fight, while praising the response of the Polish proletariat. Two Polish anti-Fascists state that they have come not only to express their solidarity, but because they consider the fight against anti-Semitism to be their own.[21] Outside, for the thousands of militants who could not find room inside, a second meeting assembles under the open sky. "Only a closed front of Jewish and Polish workers, only a common fight, will bring an end to anti-Semitism, to terrorism, and to barbarism which are the expressions of fascism." Erlich, one of the most prestigious leaders of the Jewish worker's movement in Poland, receives prolonged applause from the crowd. At the end, a resolution is passed. "A sea of raised hands proclaimed a life and death combat against anti-Semitism and fascism," writes the Bund newspaper.[22] Three days later, Alter writes his assessment of the demonstrations of March 17, 1936, after emphasizing the importance of the Polish workers' rallying: "We have opened a new chapter in the general battle against anti-Semitism . . . and we are sure of victory."[23]

Richard Marienstras will draw similar conclusions regarding the marches of October 7, 1980, in Paris. "Symbolically, a new contract has been established between the Jews of France and the society ... it seems to me that the Jewish community will never again be isolated."[24]

★

"We are not alone," Guy de Rothschild, president of the FSJU (United Jewish Social Foundation) also declares, basing his view on expressions of support offered after the rue de Copernic attack.[25]

In 1933, Bernard Lecache hails the huge protest demonstrations against the first anti-Jewish exactions of the Hitler regime. "A veritable mobilization of conscience is in operation against anti-Semitism. One saw, during the magnificent demonstrations in New York, London, Antwerp, and Poland, representatives of all the Churches, and leaders from all parties, mingling with the sons of Israel. We are not alone." And again: "We are not alone. All of France is with us." *Le Droit de Vivre* describes the great meeting of April 3, 1933, at Salle Wagram in Paris: 8,000 inside, 10,000 outside. A procession marches toward the German Embassy. "On the top of rue Solferino, they were stopped by police blockades and, under the sympathetic gaze of their fellow Parisians, retraced their steps to the cry of 'Down with Hitler!' repeated a thousand times. In summary, a splendid demonstration which proves once again to what extent the people of Paris are with us."[26] Another march takes place in Marseille. Mass meetings are organized in every town in France.[27]

In 1934, during a meeting in Paris, a socialist, Jean Longuet, proclaims anew that the Jews are not alone. Indeed, "they have with them millions of fighters determined to struggle."[28] His encouraging belief will be reinforced by the great anti-Fascist assemblies of 1936. In February, *Le Droit de Vivre* praises the "living wall" formed by demonstrators after an attack by the Camelots du Roy against Léon Blum.[29] As the great Bastille Day parade of July 14 approaches, Bernard Lecache calls upon Jews to participate: "Together, with our Non-Jewish brothers! Together with the people of Paris!"[30] Numerous antiracist banners are brandished by the demonstrators, according to an account of the procession in the LICA journal.[31]

On Sunday, June 7, 1936, Socialist cabinet ministers of the Popular Front, just recently formed, address the people. "Twenty five thousand people crowded into the vast enclosure. Tens of thousands of others filled boulevard de Grenelle and the adjacent streets, where loudspeakers allowed them to hear the speeches," reports *Le Populaire*. "How to describe the crowd which formed last evening on boulevard de Grenelle? It was a virtual flood, a human torrent which gathered and swelled and filled the neighboring streets, submerging everything in its path . . . Revolutionary chants surged forth with vibrancy and enthusiasm."[32] Among the speakers, Marius Moutet gives a moving speech devoted to racism, which he brands with ignominy.

The emotion of Bernard Lecache is thus comprehensible: "More than 100,000 Parisians applauded Marius Moutet, Minister of the Colonies, last Sunday, when he forcefully denounced racism. The next time, we will be a million strong in Paris, and millions more in all of France, to celebrate our common victory. Together we have suffered. Together we have struggled. Together we have triumphed. It is together that we must, Jews and non-Jews, fortify our will to cleanse the country of all the monarchist-fascist scum. Outlaw racism! And quickly!"[33]

To help locate this great assembly of June 7, 1936, we have one specific indication (the crowd gathers on boulevard de Grenelle) and one general assumption (not many halls able to contain tens of thousands of people existed at that time in Paris: we must look for a stadium). It is at the Vélodrome d'Hiver that Marius Moutet launches, in June 1936, his antiracist appeal before thousands of militant liberals. Originally constructed for sports competitions, the site is converted, on special occasions, to host political meetings.

No elaborate preparations were made, on the other hand, for the 7,000 Jews, of whom almost 4,000 are children from 2 to 15 years old, who are incarcerated there for a week in July 1942. During the day it is quite hot, as the sun beats down upon the windows. The air is thick with dust, water is in short supply, and food is scarce. The toilets rapidly overflow and the atmosphere becomes unbearable. What do these imprisoned Jews do? Some attempt to commit suicide, others scream and weep. Some lie prone on the ground while others go mad. At night, they sleep beneath the arches, without covering. This time, there is no room for doubt. The Jews are alone. They were not alone *before*, but they are *now*.

★

What happened to all the liberals? In 1934, Edouard Herriot, former Council President, leader of the Radical party, does not mince words. "If the reactionaries ever again dare to raise the question of race again in France, as they did on the tragic day of the Dreyfus Affair, we of the Left are ready to give them a severe lesson, to demonstrate to them in a definitive way that there is no place in France for anti-Semitism . . . we will not stand for the sabotage of democratic principles. . . . The Jews are an integral part of the nation. To persecute them is to harm the sovereignty of the people of France.

This must not occur."[34] In 1936, Herriot, President of the Chamber of Deputies, rages against an anti-Semitic parliament member who insults Léon Blum, the new Head of Government after the victory of the Popular Front.

Vallat—For the first time, this old Gallo-Roman country will be governed. . . .
Herriot—Watch your words, Mr. Vallat.
Vallat—By a Jew.
Herriot—Mr. Xavier Vallat, it is my unpleasant task to inform you that you have just pronounced words which are inadmissible before a French rostrum.[35]

In 1939, in Lyon, before an enthusiastic audience, he is even more outspoken. "The danger of racist doctrines is that they pervert humankind."[36]

But in 1940, the antiracist Herriot has other worries on his mind. We hear him say: "In her distress, our nation has gathered around Marshal Pétain, with the veneration which his name inspires in us all. We take care not to interfere with the accord that was established under his authority."[37] On July 9, the Chamber of Deputies, convoked in Bordeaux under his presidency, votes to revise the constitution.

After taking separate votes, the Chamber and the Senate meet jointly as the National Assembly on July 10 and proceed with the revision. The text put to vote includes a unique article. "The National Assembly gives all power to the Government of the Republic, under the authority and signature of Marshal Pétain, to the end of promulgating, by one or more acts, a new constitution for the French State. This constitution must guarantee the rights of labor, family, and homeland. It will be ratified by the nation and applied by the Assemblies it will have created." The vote is conclusive. For: 569. Against: 80. The text is adopted by an overwhelming majority. The French have given themselves a new political system.

How did the Socialists vote on that day, barely four years after those great enthusiastic marches of 1936, where, side by side, fraternally linked, Jewish and non-Jewish brothers and sisters expressed their common hatred for fascism? The SFIO includes 168 parliamentarians, of whom 132 participate in the July 10 vote. 90 vote for, 36 against, 6 abstain. The Socialist sellout is slightly less marked than that of other liberals, radicals, and various centralist factions. But the Socialist Bloc voted for Pétain by a clear majority, 90 out of 168. Entire sections of the party will participate, to differing degrees, in the collaboration or will adopt a "wait and see" policy. After the

Liberation, 12 former Socialist Ministers will be excluded from the party because of their vote on July 10, or for their attitude during the war. Only five will be retained, among them Blum, Moutet, and Moch.[38]

★

The Communists are irreproachable antiracists until August 1939. Partisans of a steadfast policy against French or foreign fascism, resolute adversaries of compromise, they forcefully denounce anti-Semitism. Jacques Duclos, one of the principal leaders of the party, attends every meeting organized by the LICA. In November 1938, at the Mutualité, beside Marx Dormoy, Georges Bidault, René Cassin, Pierre Cot, Gaston Monnerville and Rabbi Kaplan, he declares: "Jews! We are with you. We are with all those who understand that to stop barbarism, one should not offer one's back to receive the blows, but rise up to bar the door to fascism."[39] In June 1939, at the Cirque d'Hiver with Victor Basch, Bernard Lecache, Georges Bidault, Léo Lagrange and many others, he exclaims over the applause: "We swear to remain united so that our country will never know the disgrace of the triumph of racism."[40]

But from September 1939 on, the Communist's anti-fascism undergoes an astonishing metamorphosis. The new line is taken after the signing of the Hitler-Stalin pact, at the end of a short period in which the French party is still undecided about which course to pursue. In a sudden shift, the leaders confirm that the war is just a nasty imperialist conflict, and that the people of France have nothing to gain by a victory over the Nazis. The "philosemitism" of *L'Humanité* (circulated underground since the end of 1939) undergoes a prolonged eclipse. Between September 1939 and June 1940, not one article refers or makes allusion to the Jewish question. "From June 1940 to May 1941," writes Annie Kriegel, "*L'Humanité* breaks the silence, but without venturing beyond abstractions. It says nothing about the German ordinance of September 27, 1940, concerning the statute for Jews in the occupied zone, nothing about the government text of Vichy of October 3, 1940, promulgating for the two zones a statute even more restrictive than the one demanded by the Germans."[41]

In 1940, the antiracist Duclos is immersed in new endeavors. It is he who drafts the famous letter in which the Communist party demands from the German authorities, who have in the meantime arrived in Paris, legal authorization for the reissuance of the party paper. Under the title "Franco-German Fraternity," the underground *L'Humanité* of July 13, 1940 carries a soothing message in very

21

troubled times. "The friendly conversations between Parisian workers and German soldiers are multiplying. We are very pleased. Let's get to know each other."[42] Everything will change in June 1941 with the breach of the German-Soviet Pact.

★

And the Church? "Remember the countenance, troubled and troubling, of Monseigneur Marty, almost the only one who retained the level of spirituality that was so much needed. With a radiant gentleness that yet betrayed his grief, he prayed 'I ask forgiveness of the Lord.' Although he had nothing to reproach himself for, he still took upon himself the burden of all that was done. . . ."[43]

This ecstatic testimony, which we owe to Jean Daniel in *Le Nouvel Observateur* after Copernic in 1980, is easily interpreted. This time (in 1980), the Catholics are with the Jews against the antisemites.

Only now? Weren't they also with them 50 years ago? In 1933, the announcement of the first Hitlerian persecutions provokes indignation from the highest authorities in the Church of France.[44] The Archbishop of Paris, Monseigneur Verdier, asks the clergy and congregation of the diocese to "pray for the end of the evil suffered now by the Jews, in the name of Christian charity and of the solidarity which unites all children of the same Father." Cardinal Morin, Archbishop of Lyon, offers to the chief Rabbi of the city his fullest expression of sympathy. The Marseille section of the National Catholic Federation rises up "against persecution whose victims are German Jews." Monseigneur Rémond, Bishop of Nice, also denounces "the oppression whose victims are the Israelites of Germany." Abbé Bordron, in a meeting at Lille, proclaims that "treating one's citizens the way Germany treats her Jews is not to be countenanced."

The benevolent attitude of the Church fully emerges in the course of the thirties. "The Church reproves racism and anti-Semitism" explains *Le Droit de Vivre* after Monseigneur Bourgarel's speech at a meeting in Marseille in 1938.[45] "All racism is anti-Christian," states Monseigneur Closa at a meeting in Toulon.[46] "Racism condemned by Cardinal Verdier" we learn from a headline of the same year.[47] "Pius XI has spoken," is the title of the LICA paper that details a series of pontifical declarations condemning anti-Semitism.[48]

After the outspokenness of the thirties, speechlessness marks the beginning of the forties. This time, it is the French government that adopts a discriminatory statute, and it is the French Jews to whom it will apply. "Faced with the law of October 3, 1940, what is the

Catholic hierarchy's reaction? Incontestably, it is silence," writes Jean-Marie Mayeur. Danielle Delmaire, who analyzes the attitude of Cardinal Lienart of Lille, is astonished by the latter's indifference towards the Jews during the Occupation "since before, and above all, after the war, Monseigneur Lienart is found at the forefront of the struggle against anti-Semitism."[49]

★

The Jewish community can count on "innumerable friends," states the president of the FSJU before the national council of his organization in 1980, called together after the Copernic attack.[50] "For in the French people we have friends, each day more numerous, each day more understanding," notes *Le Droit de Vivre* in 1935.[51] In 1938, it headlines "We are not alone," publishing antiracist position papers from a series of public figures.[52] Moreover, the French Jews are not the only ones who are not alone. Even a brief look at Jewish newspapers, country by country, from between the two World Wars, will reveal that the sentiment of having many friends among non-Jews was prevalent throughout Europe. The oft-repeated affirmation of kinship reinforced the morale of the Jewish communities. "Millions of Germans are fighting with us . . ." states a proclamation of the Central Verein addressed to German Jews in December 1931.[53]

Those who say that "we are not alone" are not astigmatic. At the very moment they express this view, in their differing ways, one may find many non-Jews who condemn anti-Semitism, and who resolutely declare themselves ready to fight it. The circumstances vary from one case to another, but the phenomenon is nothing astonishing. For a long time, the Jews are integrated into the societies they live in. They share in the society's culture, and they participate in its history. Humanism and rationalism are deeply rooted in European conscience. Liberalism and socialism are powerful forces on the political scene. It is thus entirely normal that when anti-Semitism awakens, or when anti-Jewish attacks are committed at home or abroad, numerous non-Jewish citizens become sincerely indignant, and publicly express their solidarity with the Jews. This is true for Weimar Germany and for prewar Poland and France. It is especially true for France today, where mental aversion to anti-Semitism is stronger after the horror aroused by the Hitlerian genocide.

It is also natural that the Jews rejoice over the abundant demonstrations of sympathy that are thrown their way. One might wonder, however, why in 1980 the Jewish community leaders of France did not temper their expressions of gratitude with the recollection of recent historical precedents. They know that one might not be alone

23

at a given moment, but can easily become so at another, until yet another, third moment in which those who survive find themselves among friends once again. They know, above all, the sequence of developments capable of splintering the great block of liberals. Some liberals remain liberals and struggle with courage. Others remain liberals, but take refuge in the hour of peril in a cautious stance that forbids the concrete expression of their deep solidarity with persecuted Jews. Other liberals cease to be liberals. They switch camps and thereby change their attitude toward the Jews. The Germans were not Nazis until they became Nazis. The French were not "Pétainists" until they became so.

This dynamic of anti-Semitism escaped the notice of those demonstrators, who, in the large demonstrations after Copernic, were bent on stressing "Jews, non-Jews, same fight!" Their slogan is emblematic of a hope for unanimity and a sincerely felt communion. Its fault lies in its warped logic. "A" and "non-A" will unite in a common cause. Whom shall they oppose? Who are the anti-Semites whom both Jews and non-Jews, in their common ardor and fury, have decided to confront? The anti-Semites are not Martians. The anti-Semites are German, French, Polish. The anti-Semites are non-Jews. One must then distinguish, (beyond the naive perspective of those demonstrators—Jews, non-Jews, same fight!) between nice non-Jews, who are not anti-Semites, and nasty non-Jews, who are. A is surely A, but non-A is divided into two subgroups, on whose relative proportions everything depends. After the murder of Rathenau, and again after the bomb at Copernic, the balance tilts overwhelmingly to the side of the good. The great majority of Germans in 1922 and French in 1980 disapprove of the crime that has been committed. The numerical ratio between the good and the evil is nonetheless not static. It can improve, it can stabilize, but it can also deteriorate. Anti-Semitism must be analyzed in an evolutionary way, rather than in terms of fixed, timeless categories.

It's not that the Jews of France just neglected to look behind them. They did, but their field of vision was foreshortened by a lack of any reference to historical landmarks prior to the Hitlerian genocide. All comparisons they made were inadequate, because their visual system did not allow for more than two images, that of the terrible past and that of the reassuring present. We are not in 1933, they often said in 1978 or 1979, at the time of renewed outbreaks of anti-Semitic incidents. "Copernic is not the Night of Broken Glass," says Robert Badinter after the explosion, indicating thereby that it is already 1938, and no longer 1933, that we are not in.[54] Roger Ascot will put the finishing touches to this dramatic progression of accursed dates, in bringing to the attention of readers of *L'Arche* a pertinent fact: "We are not in 1942," he will write in 1983.[55]

Chapter Two

Appealing to the State

Crowds head in one direction, but also, sometimes, in another. The State, however, remains in place. Two characteristics of the State, in particular, recommend it as an ally against anti-Semitism. First, it does not distinguish among its citizens, who are all treated as equals. If one ethnic group happens to be menaced more than others, the protection accorded to it by the State is a natural right and not a special privilege. Second, it has a monopoly on all requisite measures for preserving public order. The State is democratic, and the State is strong. These two qualities assure automatic and effective protection.

★

Questioned in 1979 on the possible recurrence of dangerous anti-Semitism, Bernard-Henri Lévy answers: "For the first time, in this country and in several others, there are *laws*. Antiracist laws. Laws which, to my knowledge, are for the most part properly applied. As long as these laws exist, as long as racism remains an offense, a blaze of racism, or a great anti-Semitic wave, is unthinkable."[1]

The law of July 29, 1881, on the liberty of the press, restricts injurious attacks against individuals (*someone* is such and such). It doesn't provide, however, for defamation carried out against groups or collectives (*Jews* are such and such). This omission is sorely felt with the publication in 1886 of Edouard Drumont's first book. Immediately, *L'Univers Israélite* demands that the law be revised to prohibit the diffusion of anti-Jewish calumny.[2] The appeal is not heard, and the demand becomes less urgent at the beginning of the twentieth century when the Dreyfus Affair comes to an end. The problem presents itself anew with the return of anti-Semitic agitation in the thirties and finds its solution after the anti-Jewish flare-up of autumn 1938.

The Marchandeau decrees of April 1939 modify articles 32, 33 and 60 of the law of 1881. They prohibit slander against a "group of people who belong, by their origin, to a given race or religion." The promulgation of the law is greeted with fervor. "Racism gagged. The laws are finally signed, French unity is guaranteed," headlines the LICA paper, which also explains to its readers that the "decree against racism is a fundamental event in the history of anti-Semitism in France, and is perhaps even the abolition of this anti-Semitism."[3] Marcel Bloch states, "you can finally defend yourself against racism."[4] In June, 1939, the antisemite Darquier de Pellepoix is indicted.[5]

After 1945, legislative action resumes, not without delay, and finally results in the law of July 1972, which improves upon the Marchandeau decrees. The new law challenges discrimination, hatred, and violence when they affect "a person or group of people by reason of their origin or of their belonging or not belonging to a particular ethnic group, nation, race or religion." It deals also with racism in the administration, racism in public places, and refusal to sell, to rent, or to employ. It orders the dissolution of any organizations or groups that advocate or practice racism. It grants to antiracist organizations, like the MRAP and LICRA, the right to initiate judicial action. Hence, the French social body is ready to deal effectively with the renewed anti-Semitic wave which rises in the country after 1974. This time, society is not caught off-guard, since the adoption of the law precedes the advent of the phenomenon it is meant to liquidate.

And yet, an early assessment made during a juridical conference of the LICA in 1978 is particularly disappointing.[6] Certainly, there has been some success. A new edition of *Mein Kampf* appears in France, but with a preface "explaining the purely documentary character of the publication." An anti-Semitic pamphlet is seized, but this measure affects only 251 copies out of 40,000 distributed to 3,000 sales outlets. There are also formal and technical obstacles to prosecution and other insufficiencies in the law.

The true failure is quantitative. Of the multitude of racist and anti-Semitic incidents that afflict the country, very few actually find their way to court. Very few are the subject of a complaint, an inquiry, or a trial. "There are considerable judicial means, but little judicial activity," laments Robert Badinter. Are the antiracist organizations not doing their job? In order to explain the gap between "the law and the practice of the law," Robert Badinter draws a distinction between overt racism, which is rare due to self-censure, and the daily, common, unavowed racism, which is less spectacular but more widespread. The first form of racism can provide material for a few impressive trials. The second is intangible and does not fit well into the categories arranged by the law.

This conclusion does not apply only to the law of July 1972. It bears equally upon every repressive system that seeks to confront social phenomena with the sole weapons of the laws and the courts. The antiracist law is therefore only very partially punitive. It is not certain that it is even dissuasive. The self-censuring of formal anti-Semitism disseminated in writings or speeches, is not necessarily generated out of fear of juridical complications, but is tied to the memory of the massacre of the Jews, and will endure just as long as that memory endures.

Moreover, it is not enough to abolish an organization in order to suppress a movement, nor to arrest an agitator in order to bring an end to agitation, nor to close down a journal in order to quash its propaganda. Temporarily, administrative measures or an indictment may constrain the group's expansion, but it will not stop it. These measures even benefit them in some cases. The arrested leader becomes a martyr figure, while the struggle for his liberation mobilizes support. The accused benefits from all the protections of the legal defense. He runs no risk, since republican states do not go about throttling Nazis in their cells. The forbidden paper is kept under the counter, or else it changes its title and is promptly reissued. The dissolved organization is reconstituted under another name. The militants may be shaken, but the damage will be short-lived: *Trotz Verbot, nicht tot* ("Forbidden, but not dead"). This was Goebbel's slogan after the interdiction of the Nazi party in Berlin in 1927.

★

Fighting anti-Semitism with the law is not a new idea. In 1944, the British section of the World Jewish Congress publishes a long recapitulation of the antiracist legislation that existed before the war in various countries, such as the United States, Germany, Austria, Czechoslovakia, France, Holland, and so on.[7] Recourse to the courts to combat anti-Jewish defamation began in the last century, but at the time emancipated Judaism was opposed to any kind of specific legislation. They found it too evocative of the medieval statutes, assuring defense, but also perpetuating the segregation of the Jews. It was within the framework of general rights, and not special protective legislation, that legal action ought to proceed. "Our ancestors, as dependent Jews, had to make entreaty. We are citizens of the state and demand our rights," declares a brochure of 1895, calling

29

for German Jews to bring anti-Semitism to justice.[8]

These principles, established at the end of the nineteenth century, led to victory in several trials against antisemites.[9] Strengthened by these experiences, the Central Verein, after the end of the First World War, reactivates and reinforces its methods of intervention.[10] Committees of lawyers all over the country gather individual complaints or anti-Jewish excerpts from the press which might supply material for lawsuits. Conferences of Jewish jurists facilitate the necessary exchange of views and the elaboration of strategies. On June 18 and 19, 1927, 400 people are present, representing 80 towns in the *Juristentagung* organized by the Central Verein in Berlin.[11]

Their actions are based on articles 109 (equality of citizens before the law), 128 (equality in public office) and 135 (freedom of religion and thought) in the Constitution. Practically speaking, they depend on three articles of law which punish insults and defamation, incitement of violence by one segment of the population against another, and denigration of a religious community.[12]

"Lasst euch nicht beschimpfen!" ("Do not let yourself be insulted!") writes the *C.V. Zeitung* in June 1927, reporting on incidents in which antisemites were convicted. Likewise in Koenigsberg, three individuals, having cursed and taunted a group of young Jews, are sentenced: two months and one week of prison for one, one month of prison and a fine for another, and a fine for the third.[13] In the same year, Nazis who attack some Jews in Berlin are sentenced to punishments of up to seven months imprisonment.[14]

In July 1927, the *C.V. Zeitung* publishes a few examples of retractions which, by the terms of the law, the Nazi journals (like Goebbels' *Angriff*) have been forced to publish.[15] Nazi authors of an anti-Jewish poster are sentenced in September.[16] In October, the Reichsbund jüdischer Frontsoldaten wins its trial against the *Stürmer,* which published insults against veteran Jewish soldiers. Streicher is sentenced to three months in prison, Holz to two.[17]

The more the Nazis grow, the more severe is their treatment at the hands of the law. In August 1929, a Nazi named Ley is sentenced to two months in prison for the accusation of a Jewish ritual' crime he made in the *Westdeutschen Beobachter.*[18] The same penalty is imposed on Durr, in Berlin, for anti-Jewish attacks published in the *Angriff.*[19] In Nuremberg, the long court battle between the Central Verein and the *Stürmer* for the latter's slander against the Talmud gives Holz three and a half months and Streicher two months in prison.[20] *"Goebbels hat seinen Richter gefunden"* ("Goebbels has found his judges") writes the *C.V. Zeitung* in September 1930. He has just been sentenced to six weeks in prison with a 500 marks fine.[21] All records are broken by the anti-Semite Theodore Fritsch, who in 1933 has already been sentenced thirty-three times. During the year 1932, the Central Verein obtains numerous judiciary decisions condemning the local Nazi sections for boycotting Jewish stores.

"Danger in sight?" Julien Lehmann asks in the *Israelitiches Familienblatt* of April 26, 1932. "It is certain: we German Jews are heading into increasing difficulties, and so must follow the most recent political developments with the utmost vigilance. But we also do not want to overestimate the undeniable dangers. On the contrary, we must, with gratitude, be aware of the limits imposed on our enemies by the Constitution and the laws of the Reich, which are well applied and cannot be revoked."[22]

Of course, proceedings and trials do not hinder either the Nazis from pursuing their political foment or the Germans from voting for them increasingly in each election. After the Nazis seize power in 1933, not a single significant statement of outrage is issued from within the judicial apparatus of the country. Only the Jews and the few scarce liberals who remain liberals become excluded. The judges will simply apply new laws and pronounce new condemnations.

"Contrary to what some people might have imagined, the law of 1972 did not reduce the number of racist acts. . . . It also did not succeed in reforming those racists whom it judged and condemned," one reads in 1981 in a LICRA brochure, which takes pains, after this assessment, to point out the more positive aspects of the 1972 law.[23] The law against racism must, however, be evaluated impartially. In times of peace, it is not totally useless, since it helps to resolve periodic problems besetting immigrant workers, such as denial of employment or housing. In times of renewed anti-Semitism, it can score a few points against the adversary. But if hatred mounts, if the shifting political tide brings about the rise of a regime that is hostile towards the Jews, or is simply indifferent, the law of July 1972 will be revoked or will become obsolete.

★

The State is not only the law, it is also the police. For several years now, the police in France have guaranteed the security of Jewish institutions and sites. Francois Caviglioli, in a 1982 article devoted to police activities, describes an ordinary police station in Paris where several boards are pinned up: "The eighteen synagogues, chapels and yeshivas under threat of attack, with the names and the addresses of their rabbis. The dates of major Jewish holidays . . . the

31

principal family celebrations and festivals which are to take place in the district, Bar-Mitzvahs, circumcisions, marriages, the number of participants and the necessary number of guards."[24] The defense of Jews is thus institutionalized; it is included among the normal tasks of the French police.

As a matter of fact, a defensive disposition of guards can hardly ward off a surprise attack, which puts considerable strain on the police who provide protection. This classic problem is touched on by Albert Grzesinski, Chief of the Berlin police force, in an article published in *Vorwärts* in September 1931.[25]

On September 12th, on the eve of the Jewish New Year, 12 Hitlerian assault squads converge, with the greatest stealth, upon the Fasanenstrasse synagogue, one of the most important in Berlin. Joining ranks from nearby streets, they strike the congregation at the moment it leaves after services. The assault is countered at great cost by the Jewish self defense; several dozen Jews are bludgeoned before the police arrive. That event leads to about 60 arrests among the Nazis, of whom 30 are given sentences ranging from three to 21 months in prison. The attack, the first on such a scale ever carried out by the Nazis against German Jews, stirs up considerable commotion. Many critics reproach the police for not being stationed on the spot in sufficient force at the very moment of the aggression.[26]

Grzesinski understands the indignation of those who criticize the police, but his argument to the contrary is entirely logical: it was impossible to predict such an event, and therefore to concentrate, in advance, the needed forces. Those are the objective limits of police protection. Grzesinski, incidentally, is anti-Nazi, his second-in-command Bernhard Weiss is a Jewish militant and activist, responsible for keeping the Nazis in line, and the Berlin police are mostly socialist. For Yom Kippur 1931, the security of the synagogues is reinforced and no further incidents arise.

The experience of the twentieth century allows for the enumeration, on this topic, of several models of relations between the police and the Jews. In the optimal case, as one might suspect, the Jews, as such, do not have to be protected by the police. In the next case, the police adequately protect Jewish institutions, as in today's France. In the third case, the police don't participate in anti-Semitic outrages, but they also don't interfere with them, or else intervene too late, or even lash out against the Jews who are defending themselves instead of the anti-Semites attacking them. A fourth possibility, implying an already active collaboration, is illustrated by a photo which circulated in the world press in 1933 during the first Hitlerian persecutions. A

Jewish lawyer of Munich, Spiegel, is paraded through the streets, shoeless, his pants cut to mid-leg. Around his neck, he wears a large placard: "I will not complain to the police anymore." Attacked by the Nazis, he had sought refuge in a police station, but was immediately given over into the hands of his pursuers. He will, moreover, be assassinated shortly thereafter, in Dachau.[27]

Final model: the police themselves hunt the Jews. They make full use of all logistics necessary to the operation. They leave out nothing. "The agents assigned to the arrest make sure, while all of the occupants of the dwelling are taken away, to shut off the gas, electricity and water meters. The animals are entrusted to the caretaker." The caretaker also receives the keys and becomes responsible for the upkeep of the furnishings and effects left in the apartment. All of these meticulous directions figure in the instructions which the superintendent of the police in Paris, Hennequin, gives out on July 12, 1942, in preparation for the great roundup of Jews on the 16th, which will fill up the Vélodrome d'Hiver.

The detailed plan appears in circular number 173–42, dated July 13, 1942. "Each Israelite, man and woman, to be arrested must be recorded on an index card. The cards must be sorted out by ward and placed in alphabetical order. You will split up into arrest teams. Each team will be composed of a member of the force and a civil officer or intelligence agent . . . the teams assigned to make the arrests will have to proceed with the greatest speed possible, without any unnecessary remarks and without comment." The circular goes on to give the composition of the squads assigned in reserve to each precinct. It also outlines the public transport network that is at the disposal of the police.[28]

But nothing is irreversible. The fortieth anniversary of the roundup (and this is the fifth possible model) was commemorated in Paris in 1982 under the protection of the French Police (the second case mentioned).

★

The State, finally, is its personalities. One step is never absent from any program to fight anti-Semitism: the dispatch of a delegation to meet with public officials. One can distinguish among the delegations by the hierarchical level of the personages they visit—Prefects, Ministers, Prime Minister, President of the Republic. One can also grade them according to subject matter. Sometimes the delegation is concerned with anti-Semitism in other lands (nowadays: Russia, Syria) or with French policy in the Near East as it affects Israel. Thus, the leaders of the Jewish community show their effective solidarity with other Jews.

Sometimes, the preoccupation of the delegation is with the situation of the Jews of France themselves. In that case, the delegates come to plead for their own cause, which is more delicate. Happily, all the forms of etiquette are maintained since the visited official is quite benevolent and well versed in all the subtleties of republican language. The circumlocutory dialogue touches upon the grave dangers posed to society by "destabilizing elements," and ends with the assurance that the official powers will do all that is possible to protect France against the enemies of democracy. In other words, the leaders of the Jewish community have come to solicit, and have obtained, reinforced police protection of synagogues and Jewish landmarks. The militants get the same results through raising their voices and trembling with rage. "Le Renouveau juif calls for: the genuine, effective and permanent protection of the Jews of France and their institutions," says a tract of 1980 which allies a commanding tone with traditional content.[29]

But asking for public protection, whether the request be conciliatory or vehement, lays no claim to originality. The large street demonstration is thought to be the first of its kind. The antiracist law is thought innovative. But the view of the delegation is more modest. It dimly perceives that others, in fact numerous others, have preceded it during the two millennia of Jewish Exile. Local Chieftains, Princes, Popes, Sultans, Emperors and Ministers have all granted audience to Jewish delegations come to beseech protection and intervention, or come to demand the revocation of an anti-Jewish decision. Many were routine, while others marked dramatic turning points in the history of the Diaspora.

Here is one which had positive results. Alerted by a letter from Orléans describing the false accusation and torment of Jews in the town of Blois, the leaders of the Jewish community of Paris ask to be received by the King. The interview takes place in Falaise, in the spring of 1171. The delegates would like to see Louis VII in private, but, already informed of their motives for the encounter, he insists that it be public and convenes his entire court. He firmly condemns the crime of Blois, whereby thirty Jews have been burned alive. He denounces the false accusations and reassures the Jews of Paris. They then spread a detailed account of the interview to other Jewish communities.[30]

"With the immense talent he possesses, and in the distinctive tone which the French expect of the president of the Republic, Mr. Giscard d'Estaing said all that could be said to reassure the Jews of France, to comfort them and ease their liaisons with French society," affirms Guy de Rothschild after a declaration by the Chief of State resolutely condemning the Copernic attack. The declaration was made at the close of a Council of Ministers in the autumn of 1980.[31]

What difference, then, between the twelfth and the twentieth century? Some would say, perhaps, that in the Middle Ages protection was a granted privilege, one that could just as well be withdrawn, according to the taste and caprice of the monarch; whereas now, it is an inalienable right inscribed in the legal texts and linked to the very principles of democracy. What was once a transient favor has become immutable law.

This allegation will disappoint those of us who are less certain that dissimilarity of form automatically implies dissimilarity of content. The distinction does not enable us, in any case, to classify all events. In May, 1938, the LICA is received by Georges Mandel, Minister of the Colonies, and by Jules Julien, Minister of the PTT. Audiences are given by Camille Chautemps, Vice-President of the Council, Riccart, Minister of Public Health, and Daladier, Council President.[32] These audiences occur 149 years after the French Revolution, two years before the adoption of the special statute for Jews by the French State and four years before the hunt for Jews by the French police.

The significant date seems to be 1948 rather than 1789. With the creation of the State of Israel, there now exists a country where the Jews can see to their own security. The leaders of the Jewish community in France know, therefore, that they have a concrete alternative. If they follow in the footsteps of their predecessors of the Middle Ages, it is by their own will. The Jews before 1948 were dependents, a state that was unavoidable for them. Those of today are wards of the state by their own free consent.

Chapter Three

Education

What can be done about hatred? "The answer lies in the domain of education," Guy de Rothschild declared soon after Copernic.[1] This theme was repeated, amplified and developed by numerous activists in the Jewish community.

The educators who would like to educate others have not taken the time, however, to educate themselves. The anti-Semites don't know the Jews at all, they say, quoting Péguy. The statement applies just as well to they themselves, although a mild doubt does occasionally ruffle their confidence. If it is so obvious, if it is just so simple, then how could it be that so many generations have allowed themselves to be persecuted without resorting to the "miracle solution" to the Jewish problem, that is, the education of non-Jews? If anti-Semitism is nothing but an enormous misunderstanding, why have we waited so long to dispel it? But such questions are quickly forgotten. Exciting tasks await these educators, latecomers in a great historical trend they hardly know anything about.

In the arsenal of the fight against anti-Semitism, judicial activity and police protection perform the function of an armored breastplate, which blunts the devastating effect of anti-Jewish activism. Education is the sword of combat. It is used to cleave through the arguments of the adversary, demolish the prejudices that nourish his hatred, and expose what really moves him. It deals, or so it believes, with the very roots of hatred.

Besides classical apologetics, whose arguments have grown and developed over centuries, there is also modern apologetics, born in the last third of the nineteenth century. At that time, the emancipated Jews of Western Europe are for the first time forced to confront a wave of racist anti-Semitism, in 1870 in Germany and Austria, and about 15 years later in France. In tandem with anti-Jewish agitation, which temporarily subsides at the turn of the century, Jewish apologetics pass through a dormant phase which ends after the first World War. They enjoy a Golden Age in Germany until 1933, and to a lesser degree in the remainder of Europe and in the United States up until 1939. The "educators" of today thus constitute the third generation of modern apologeticists, linked to the anti-Semitic resurgence of the seventies and eighties.

To whom does education address itself? Less naive than it might appear, it does not seek to convince the anti-Semites themselves. Its explanations aim at public opinion and the undecided masses, who are not anti-Semites, but could become so if the cancer is allowed to flourish without treatment. The form of public education implements the strategy of "curtain fire," aimed at halting the enemy's progress. It also seeks to sway anyone who has been momentarily seduced by the anti-Jewish propagandists.

This program of education makes a sustained appeal for pity. In describing the anti-Jewish atrocities of the past, it endeavors to awaken the public's conscience. In the nineteenth century, it harkened back to the Inquisition. In the twenties, not only referred to the Middle Ages, but also to the extermination of Jews in the Ukraine by Petlioura in 1919–20. "This book which has just appeared ought to be translated into all languages. It ought to be spoken of in all schools, and not solely in Jewish circles," writes the *C. V. Zeitung* in 1927, citing a work concerned with the Ukrainian pogroms that was published in Paris. The article insists on the importance of having non-Jews know of the recent massacres in the Ukraine so that they not be forgotten.[2] In the same year, Bernard Lecache publishes notes and testimonies concerning these same pogroms that he gathered in 1926 in the course of a three month stay in the Soviet Union.[3] In the thirties, the first of Hitler's measures rouses up the indignation of the civilized world and of all liberals, who are likewise incensed at the announcement of anti-Jewish policies instituted in Rumania, Hungary, Italy and Poland. After 1945, the apologetic of compassion is considerably enhanced with the disappearance of an entire third of the Jewish people. It ceases to relate itself to earlier persecutions and instead focuses all its efforts on the Nazi genocide.

Education also makes an appeal to reason. It systematically refutes all anti-Jewish slander. The ancient slanders—ritual crime, deicide, usury—are once again refuted, as are the newer ones—Jewish conspiracy, Jewish treachery, and dual allegiance. Apologetics present incontestable facts: so many great thinkers, so many Jewish scholars—here is the Jewish contribution to progress. So many workers: here is the Jewish proletariat, combative and exploited. The apologetics magnificently demonstrate the inanity of racist "theories." In a word, it establishes once and for all that the Jews are human beings. The evidence is too vast to be recounted. A single example should suffice.

European Jews participated en masse in the first World War, each for his own side. The apologetics of the postwar period develop this theme, in order to demonstrate the falsity of two accusations in one stroke: absence of patriotism and lack of courage. The Jews of Germany set up precise statistics on Jewish soldiers and officers who are shot, injured, and decorated; they publish innumerable accounts of the war, and erect commemorative monuments in every community. The 12,000 German Jews killed on the front lines become an important force in the war against anti-Semitic propaganda. The Jews in France publish similar statistics. In particular, the edifying death of Rabbi Abraham Bloch, saluted by Barrès, will inspire the military apologetics in France. On August 29, 1914, at Taintrux, near Saint-Dié, a Catholic soldier about to die requests the final sacrament. Bloch advances towards him, carrying a crucifix, and falls under enemy fire. The story of the Rabbi who dies as a priest is not without ambiguity. Nonetheless, it is an emblem for the entire postwar generation, and the Chief Rabbi of France will still refer to it after the burning of the synagogue of Drancy in 1978.[4]

Modern education, by appealing to the charitable sentiments or the logic of non-Jews, cannot but reproduce, with some new elements, the methods of classical apologetics. However, since the end of the last century, it has innovated on one essential point.

To the end of mobilizing non-Jews against anti-Semitism, it shows them that the danger is not directed solely against Jews, but also at non-Jews. Fighting against anti-Jewish hatred is therefore not solely a moral or philanthropic duty, it is a political act preserving common interests. Two effects are supposed to proceed. One concerns the Jewish community's dignity: when they fight anti-Semitism, non-Jews are not so much defending Jews as protecting themselves. The other effect is practical: the more the non-Jews feel directly threatened, the more they will organize themselves to fight—and that alone will guarantee victory.

The theme of anti-Semitism which threatens everyone (and not only the Jews) proceeds in two principal directions, at times divergent, but often intersecting. One sees in anti-Jewish hatred the product or instrument of a foreign influence directed against the country. The other makes of it a political medium, employed by a particular social force or class towards the goal of attaining, or maintaining, power within the country itself.

★

Anti-Semitism, the "flower from across the Rhine," has no roots
in France. "It came to us from Russia, from Austria and Germany,
and so there is something comical about this movement that takes
for its motto 'France for the French'—it is exclusively a foreign
import," Charles Gide comments ironically in 1899.[5] In 1898,
Maurice Vernes denounces "this campaign, of origin as foreign as
the name of anti-Semitism."[6]

This diversionary ploy was insufficient. With too much insistence
on the fact that the problem came from abroad, the apologetic ran
the risk of losing its credibility. It had to admit that French anti-
Semitism had its source in France. In that case, so the modified
argument ran, the bulwark of the country must meet the assaults of a
single faction, filled with malicious intent, which presses anti-
Semitism into service as a weapon of ideological warfare. But who,
and against whom? In the beginning, that is to say at the end of the
nineteenth century with the advent of modern anti-Semitism, a great
confusion reigned in the identification of the culprits and the analysis
of their dark motives.

"He basely flatters the anarchists and excites them against the
defenders of the capital," writes Léonce Reynaud, putting the bourgeoisie on its guard against Drumont.[7] "An alliance with the anti-
Semites would gain nothing for the proletariat: it could cost them
dearly," writes a group of revolutionary students in 1900, alerting
the working class to the dangers that would arise from an alliance
with the forces of anti-Jewish hatred.[8] "One begins with the Jew,
and ends with the Jesuit," explains Anatole Leroy Beaulieu before
the Catholic Institute of Paris on February 27, 1897.[9] The Christians
therefore ought to be in opposition to anti-Semitism. Jacques Prolo,
in the publications of the Anticlerical League of France says exactly
the opposite: "Today, the Gesu uses its new catapult: anti-
Semitism."[10] All free thinkers ought therefore to fight anti-Semitism.

At the close of the Dreyfus Affair, after the late, yet meritorious
rally of the majority of Socialists to the camp of the Dreyfusards, the
dividing line becomes more visible. On one side, democratic and
liberal France, and on the other, the clerical and nationalistic reaction.
Very roughly speaking, the Left and the Right.

★

The problem reappears in the thirties. This time anti-Semitism is
not just condemned as being of German inspiration, but also as being

the direct result of a Nazi conspiracy. "We must say that those who create racism seek to weaken France, and so we urge all men to our cause," proposes Jean Goldenberg, militant of the LICA, at a Congress in 1939.[11] "Denounce with us this foreign racism," proclaims a LICA poster in 1938. "Anti-Semitism is not French," affirms *Le Droit de Vivre,* which launches an entire campaign on this theme.[12] The true French are thus put on their guard: if there is xenophobia in the land, it is as a result of an odious foreign plot. . . .

The mechanics of this plot are exposed in 1939 by the *Bulletin* of the Center for Documentation and Vigilance, an organization created in 1936 by French Jews to wage battle against anti-Semitism. Some of its editorials explain, first of all, that anti-Semitism is the "instrument" used by the German Reich to disintegrate a country. The Jewish question is therefore "entirely created by Hitler's propaganda service." Once its principles are set down, the argument of the bulletin shifts to the case of France, and notes, alluding to the anti-Semitic incidents of the autumn of 1938: "German propaganda, under the cover of anti-Semitism, strives to disintegrate France." Fortunately, the government has understood the menace and has adopted the decrees of 1939, which curb propaganda and racial hatred. But "it is wrong to pretend that these decrees are intended to protect only the Jews. The French Israelites integrated into the community would stand no more in need of protection than any other category of citizens, if Germany had not sought to instigate anti-Semitic blood lust in the hope of weakening national unity. It is therefore France that the government hoped to protect by its decrees. . . ."[13]

Along with its "Israelite" version, the plot also appears in a militant left version directed at immigrant Jews. Anti-Semitism is "newly arrived in France," explains a text of the Union of Jewish Societies of France. There were some incidents in Paris, and especially in Alsace-Lorraine, "where the anti-Semitic propaganda bore, at the same time, an anti-French character in the service of Hitlerism." As well, "these systematic anti-Jewish excitations have as their objective the division and discord of the French population." But, "the people of France will not allow themselves to be taken in by such boorish tactics." The French popular organizations condemn the provocations, posters against anti-Semitism are pasted up, and "in many districts, the French workers themselves chase after the troublemakers."[14] The role of the "good French" is taken here by the working class, and not by the government.

The identification of anti-Semitism with what is foreign makes it possible to totally discredit the anti-Semites. They are allies of the ancient hereditary (German) and new ideological (Nazi) enemy. They transmit its ideas, they serve its interests, and are, directly or indirectly, consciously or not, its agents. But the country does not tumble into the trap. "France does not believe in the racial theories from across the Rhine, so contrary to its own nature: it will never follow commanders capable of preaching the extermination or the outlawing of an entire category of the French," writes Alfred Berl in 1936.[15] He only voices a point of view very common at the time. Marcel Déat, who after 1940 will become one of the principal leaders of the collaboration, also states this view at a meeting against anti-Semitism in 1935, when he affirms that racism is a "theory absolutely foreign to French mentality."[16]

This rousing affirmation, repeated so often in the thirties, explains how the Jews arrested by the French police by order of the French Government in 1942 could have such a relatively confident attitude. A German roundup would have aroused more fear, and a larger number of Jews would have tried to flee. By insisting that anti-Semitism was not French, the apologetics of the thirties performed a harmful service to the Jews of France.

★

Anti-Jewish hatred strove to *divide* the French at the end of the last century, and to *disintegrate* France during the thirties. Today, it seeks to *destabilize* the country.

This latest theme is first sketched out in the communiqués of the CRIF. For instance, in April 1979: "The recent past instructs us that aggressions against Jews always forebode a menace to the liberty of all."[17] In September, 1980: "Past experience has taught us that Jews are particularly exposed whenever democracy is endangered by the assaults of despotism and intolerance."[18] The 26th of the same month: "The past teaches us that beyond the Jewish community, it is democracy that is taken aim at."[19]

The same theme bursts forth right after the attack at Copernic. Nothing is known yet about who committed it, but numerous are those who immediately guess at the diabolical intentions of its instigators. A grave danger threatens France. Terrorists conspire to destabilize democracies. Their favorite method? To reactivate anti-Semitism. It is a means, explains the *Tribune Juive,* it is not "a goal in itself." And so, the "decision was taken to make use of the extraordinary resonance created by an anti-Semitic attack, with its thousand implications and its fascist and totalitarian reverberations, in order to intensify the general action of destabilization." Why the Jews? "It is precisely because there exists a large resistance to anti-Semitism that anti-Semitism serves as the favorite instrument in the work of destabilization."[20] The CRIF, also, quickly detected the "machinations of the criminals": "To shatter French society by an escalation of violence: today the Jews . . . tomorrow others . . . until fear penetrates and dissolves the very fiber of the nation."[21]

The theme of destabilization also has more classical formulations. "Beyond the Jewish community, France itself is being targeted," states the great Rabbi Kaplan.[22] "But beyond the Jewish community, it was France in its entirety that was assaulted on that day," says also the great Rabbi Sirat.[23] For the Alliance Israelite Universelle, the attack is a "challenge to the Jewish community, a challenge to the people of France as a whole, a challenge to pluralistic society and to respect for mankind." It is also a "crime against Judaism, against democratic France, and against human dignity."[24]

The idea comes up again in August 1982 after the attack on rue des Rosiers in Paris. "Although not French in origin, a powerful international network of terrorists chose the Jewish community of France as one of its targets in order to instigate a heightened level of violence there, and destabilize French society," writes Jean Daniel.[25] Richard Liscia, at the same moment, warns against anti-Semitism "lying in wait in the democracies, poised as an instrument for an eventful destabilization." Marek Halter considers that "it is not merely by chance that the terrorists chose the Jews as their target; if I were a strategist, to destabilize Europe I would work on the soft underbelly, that is, the Jews."[26]

Jacques Tarnero, in 1983, pursues the same line of thought. "France is the Western European country with the most populous Jewish community. This community, for those who know or observe it, is a crucial stake, an important lever. If the goal of terrorism is to destabilize or to create panic, it must strike where it will do the greatest harm. The place where it would do the greatest harm in France is in its sensitive nerve, the Jewish community. It is obvious that the attacks on rue des Rossiers or on rue Copernic were *explicitly* anti-Semitic, but it is not certain that their ends were *exclusively* anti-Semitic."[27]

Apparently, then, the idea that an anti-Semitic attack might be aimed at the Jews, and not at European democracy, was too superficial to attract the attention of the commentators. As for the hypothesis that one might kill Jews to the end of killing Jews, and not destabilizing France, it is without doubt too anachronistic, in the midst of the twentieth century, to be made the object of careful scrutiny. . . .

This conjecture is not an original one. In 1892, the Zionist Ahad HaAm publishes a remorseless criticism of French Judaism, and beyond that, the whole of emancipated Western Judaism. His text, *Avdut Betoh Herut* (Hebrew for "Slavery in Freedom") has lost none of its acuity of insight, as can be seen in the paragraphs that denounce the tendency to "arouse pity for the Jews by invoking the self-interests of others."[28]

★

Anti-Semitism threatens democracy and the homeland. What is more, it corrupts the souls of non-Jews. "This is perhaps what is most new and most comforting in the midst of this drama," writes Jean Daniel in 1980. "Those who combat racism are not doing so out of generosity towards the victims, but to protect their own souls."[29]

Comforting as this remark may be, it is far from original. It is a classic statement from prewar antiracist literature. "The question goes beyond the Jews: . . . it is above all for us, non-Jews, that anti-Semitism constitutes an offense and an injury," writes Jean Cassou in 1935.[30] "In coming here we come determined to defend the Jews. But we come also to defend the liberties of a people who won them one July day and who have never since bowed their heads," states Marx Dormoy at a mass meeting in November 1938.[31] "Whenever a Jew is struck because he is a Jew, I don't feel pity, but revulsion. Whenever I defend him, it is not for him that I fight, it is for me . . . ," Léo Lagrange remarks in 1939.[32]

The theme has a logical corollary. The non-Jews do not fight to save the Jews, but to save their own souls. The Jews, in that case, do not fight for themselves, but to save France. "And some French Jews will respond as French citizens, participating in the collective responsibility, as much as they will respond as targeted Jews," writes Jean Daniel in 1980.[33] André Wurmser, in 1936, does not allow for halfway measures: "It is not as a Jew that a French Jew should be shocked by anti-Semitism, it is as a Frenchman."[34] Zadoc Kahn, the great Rabbi of France, was in agreement with both back in 1890. "As a Jew, I am afflicted with it, as a Frenchman, I am ashamed," he says of anti-Semitism.[35]

The image of the soul appears frequently in the antiracist repertoire. "The wielder of the bomb aims at the body of the Jew and the soul of the European," asserts André Glucksmann in 1981.[36] "Anti-Semitism is an assault upon the soul," confirms Irene Harand in 1936.[37] "It remains to be known whether, as a civilization, Europe has anything left to defend; whether it is prepared to surrender its soul . . . ," Glucksmann continues. No, proclaims Edouard Herriot in 1939. "As free people, let us not surrender our souls."[38]

★

Might anti-Semitism somehow relate to the Jews? One might doubt it, so impressive is the list of persons and items that are supposed to be its primary targets, from the working class it seeks to divert from its struggle, and the democracy it wishes to destabilize, to the nation it wishes to deliver over to the enemy.

It is quite understandable that the theme of anti-Semitism as a menace to all has reappeared in a different form during each anti-Semitic crisis since the last century. Modern anti-Semitism arises in a period when the Jews are politically and socially integrated into their societies. The walls of the medieval ghetto have long since tumbled down. This history of foregone integration has played a fundamental role in the formation of the apologetic. The evolution of ways of thinking, the advance of science, and the transformations of politics and economics have all contributed to the emancipation of European Jews. If voices of hatred are ever unexpectedly heard, it seems natural, in order to silence them, to resort to explanation and education. The triumph of Reason has cleared the way to emancipation. The weapons of Reason are supposed to guarantee its irrevocability.

This integration also influences the forms that explanation takes. In democratic societies, the Jews, like all citizens, enjoy total freedom of expression. In addition, large numbers of non-Jews are sincerely offended by accusations directed at the Jews, and are inclined to take the Jewish side. And so, in every era, the refutation of anti-Semitism, like every other popular cause, makes use of all available communications media: in the last century, the press, brochures, books, lectures, and conferences; between the world wars, all these plus radio, films and street protests; and in our own day, all these and television as well.

But, most importantly, this integration influences the very themes of the apologetics. The claim that the true target of anti-Semitism is not the Jews, but society as a whole, is a polemical argument intended to discredit the enemy and sensitize the ally. Above all, its implementation reflects an attempt to explain the emergence, or more exactly, the resurgence, of the detested phenomenon. Emancipated Jews (in 1886, 1936, or 1980) who share the mores of their compatriots and participate in all aspects of the life of the country, are reluctant to admit that a movement could strike out at them, and them in particular. The idea appears regressive and archaic.

45

It could, besides, lead some Jews to reconsider the validity of total integration as a solution to the Jewish problem. The idea of anti-Semitism of foreign extraction or caused by subversive faction tends, then, to reassure the Jewish community and stifle the progress of Jewish nationalism in general and Zionism in particular. The idea that anti-Semitism menaces everyone reinserts the Jews into the national collective. . . .

From the liberal's viewpoint, the aristocracy and the Church are secretly consulting in a medieval castle at the top of a precipitous cliff slashed by the wind. They are looking for a scapegoat against whom to direct the anger of honest souls. From the Marxist-Leninist viewpoint, the representatives of the bourgeoisie and the capitalists are deliberating in a fabulous mansion. Champagne flows and the air reeks of cigars. They are deciding to relaunch anti-Semitism as a diversionary tactic, so as to block the march of the international proletariat. In both cases, anti-Semitism is associated with a social force that is decadent and historically condemned. Its disappearance is thus inevitable, but in the meantime education performs the task of enlightening the good citizens (in the first case) or the popular masses (in the second case) about the trap that has been set for them.

In France in 1980, the setting has changed yet again. The meeting happens in an underground lair, stocked with electronic equipment. After a long debate, the terrorists who seek to destabilize France perfect a new strategy. They are going to commit anti-Jewish crimes.

The obsession of the conspirators is, however, not well understood. Why don't they seek to channel the discontent of the masses towards the Champenois, or the Picards, and not the Jews? Why don't the "destabilizers" use hairstylists or cyclists as their fulcrum, and not the Jews? It might be the case, one must admit, that anti-Semitism actually predates the infernal machinations that are said to have fabricated it. It might be that anti-Semitism is an historical phenomenon with its own laws, and periodic manifestations. It might be that anti-Semitism has a real social base, evolving from one situation to another but embracing all strata of society, simultaneously or sequentially.

It is true that anti-Semites are not only anti-Semites. The currents, historical forces, and institutions that carry the movement on have other parallel aims and designs that are more universal. This has, moreover, always been the case. The Crusaders did not join ranks with the goal of massacring the Jews. They had other plans, but they also massacred Jews. Phillipe le Bel did not like Jews, but he didn't like the Templars either. The riot of the Pastoureaux was not originally anti-Jewish. The Inquisition concerned itself with all kinds of heretics, not exclusively the Jews. The Cossack Insurrections of the seventeenth century were directed against the Polish nobility. Nazism was anti-Marxist and anti-liberal, and also anti-Semitic. Stalinism was a total system in which the Jewish question played only an auxiliary role.

And yet, the Jews who are affected should not console themselves with the fact that their enemies are also someone else's enemies. Sometimes they find allies, temporary or lasting, weak or strong, among these other targeted groups. Nevertheless, anti-Semitism is a distinct and specific reality, and the Jewish question demands a specific solution.

Carried to an extreme, modern education has a perverse outcome. It assumes that anti-Semitism is dangerous since, after all, its very mission is to eradicate it. But the notion of foreign hatred aimed at all alike obscures the danger for its true victims. The noisy publicity given to the statements of sympathy issued by non-Jews aims at strengthening the Jews in the conviction that they are not alone, which is true, and that they never will be, which is less certain. In the same way, the excessive "globalization" of the issue weakens Jewish reflection on the real character of anti-Semitism. Education is therefore dangerous. Its stirring message always convinces the Jews. Its success reflects their profound integration into circumambient society and strengthens their feeling that this integration is final and decisive. Some non-Jews, on the other hand, remain stubbornly resistant to this enlightened argument.

Chapter Four
The Combat Front of the German Jews

Is the problem just one of publicity? The apologetic message has value only when it reaches the non-Jews who are susceptible to the propaganda of the other side. It is not sufficient to publish books, journals and brochures; it is also necessary to distribute them in large quantities. Also, if the modern apologetic movements all resemble one another thematically, they still differ considerably, from one country to another, in the kinds of measures they employ. The effort they invest depends on two factors, one external and one internal: the imminence of the danger, and the degree of cohesion and organization among the Jews of a given country.

These two conditions are optimal in Germany in the twenties and early thirties. The danger is most apparent. The Jewish community there is powerful and energetic. In fact, political life is very intense in general. Journals, posters, tracts, street demonstrations, and marches signal the advent of the era of the masses. From the extreme Left to the extreme Right, all of the factions resort to the same means of expression under a regime permitting very great liberty of action. And apologetics, as we have seen, mirror the integration of the Jews into society, both in the themes they develop and in the methods of transmission they employ. Most everyone in Berlin is familiar with the methods of mass communication. Everyone holds meetings. The Jewish organizations are no exception to this rule.

Let us accompany, then, the German Jews from 1928 to 1933. They launch the most powerful, diversified and massive campaign ever conducted by a Jewish community against a rising tide of anti-Semitism.[1]

★

In the beginning of 1928, with the approach of the May Reichstag elections, the Central Verein mobilizes its adherents and sympathizers

49

according to a plan already polished in the course of previous electoral campaigns. It raises funds to finance its antiracist publications.[2]

The *Anti-Anti* (i.e. anti-anti-Semite) is a summary of all there is to be known on the Jewish question, and is supplied to journalists, politicians, professors and all anti-Nazis. It is a series of documentary memoranda, printed in tight characters, but handy to use and regather in a miniature case, in the style of a pocketbook. An index enables the user to find the pertinent data in a moment. Bismarck and the Jews? Card 5. Anti-Semitic lies? Card 15. Desecration of cemeteries and synagogues? Card 20. Goethe and the Jews? Card 22. The number of Jews in Germany and in the entire world? Card 27. The Jews during the war? Card 30. Politics, parties, and Jews? Card 49. Racism and science? Card 52. Ritual murder? Card 62. Jews and socialism? Card 66. The elders of Zion? Card 76 ... all possible and any imaginable themes are covered, accompanied by precise citations and detailed statistics. Up until 1933, the *Anti-Anti* will be updated numerous times and circulated in tens of thousands of copies.[3]

Ordinarily, the *C.V. Zeitung* sends out a monthly edition of about 50,000 copies, addressed to a multitude of non-Jewish personalities in the political arena, in the trade unions and in literary circles. For the elections of 1928, the number mounts to 250,000 copies distributed all over the country. As a vehicle for its propaganda, the Central Verein issues the journal *Deutsche Blätter* and prints several runs of anti-Nazi tracts and posters, such as *"Hitler der Retter"* (Hitler the saviour) in an ironical mode, and *"Tod oder Brot"* (death or bread), in a more dramatic style. Against a frightful background of flaming carnage, a swastika'd skeleton brandishes a murderous grenade; facing him, on the second half of the poster, a young happy family is seated on a lawn, with a little cottage and a bustling factory in the background. *Tod oder Brot?* The choice is clear: vote for the Liberal parties.[4]

Bread wins. The Nationalist camp, as a whole, suffers a crushing defeat, both for its moderate core (the DNVP) and for its fanatical fringe (Nazis and other sub-groups). All together and each separately, the parties of the extreme Right lose votes from the elections of December 1924. The Hitlerians fall from three percent of the vote in 1924 to 2.6 percent in 1928, which makes them the smallest formation represented in the Reichstag, with 12 deputies. On the whole, the anti-Semites are in disarray and the liberal parties are considerably strengthened. The Socialists, who obtain close to 30 percent of the vote, are called upon to form the government. Hermann Müller becomes Chancellor of a Republic henceforth solid and uncontested.

Otto Landsberg, deputy in the Reichstag and retired Minister, expresses his satisfaction to a Jewish activist. There is no cause for concern about a "splinter-group" of 12 parliamentarians. "No! It would be a mistake to take those fellows seriously," he concludes.[5]

However, the Jewish organizations are far from appeased. Detailed analyses of the electoral results, published in the *C.V. Zeitung,* throw a curious phenomenon into relief. In many places, the Nazis collapsed and virtually disappeared from the political landscape. In some others, conversely, they made gains. At times, this was at the expense of other nationalistic elements, as in their bastion of Franconia, where they improved their position slightly. But in other regions—and this is what attracts the attention of the commentators— their gains were superior to the total number of votes lost by other factions on the extreme Right. This was the case in the Rhineland and Palatinate, where the Nazis gained new ground. Their breakthrough was very slight, certainly, but it was also significant, since it reflected the singular vitality of the movement and its aptitude for implanting itself in new territory and enlisting a formerly hostile public to its cause. And that at the time of a general debacle for anti-Liberal forces.[6]

"Nach dem 20. Mai:" the editorial of the *C.V. Zeitung,* in addition, underscores the youthful character of the Nazi electorate and calls for preparation to begin immediately for the next elections.[7] *"Nach der Schlacht:"* the editorial in *Der Schild* (journal of the Association of Jewish War Veterans), after reviewing the electoral results of the Nazis, arrives at a sobering conclusion. "It turns out, despite what has been taking place for close to a decade, that the most trying fights still lie ahead of us. May no one be deluded by the apparent calm. More than ever, in the near future, the RjF must be on guard. So it shall be!"[8]

"Our tasks for the new year." For the Jewish New Year, the *C.V. Zeitung,* on September 14, 1928, publishes a series of statements by well-known people on Jewish identity and the fight against anti-Semitism. "Self-knowledge," writes Leopold Jessner, "is the strongest and surest defense against all attack!" Ludwig Haas, deputy in the Reichstag, reminds readers that "our fight is the fight for our rights. It is also the fight for internal peace in Germany" and it must found itself upon "pride in our past as German Jews."[9] The end of 1928 is marked by a series of conferences, meetings and regional congresses of the Central Verein.[10]

The renewal of Nazi activity begins to manifest in September.

The Jewish press gives detailed accounts of the post-electoral meetings of the NSDAP and reports several cases of Jews being molested in the streets. In Berlin, the Nazis organize a mass assembly on September 30th.[11] The Central Verein continues to keep close watch on them in all regions.[12] Information and on-the-spot analyses are forwarded by its branch operations and centralized in Berlin.

"Nationalsozialistischer Vormarsch!" ("National Socialist Progress!") The *C.V. Zeitung* publishes a complete new report on Nazi meetings to take place in the country. "German Judaism knows what to expect from a stronger Hitlerian party. May it be ever vigilant, and potently assist those who, for love of the German fatherland and of Judaism, take to the ramparts, ready to do battle."[13] *"Der Verführte Mittelstand"* ("The middle class seduced"): Richard Roth describes and analyzes the disturbing advance of anti-Semitism within the ranks of the "petite bourgeoisie" of Germany.[14] *"Front gegen den Nationalsozialismus!"* ("Front against National-Socialism!") headlines the *C.V. Zeitung* in April 1929, publishing an article by a leader of the Catholic Central Party.[15] The journal issues warnings against meetings organized by the Nazis for elementary and high school students.[16]

In the regional elections of Saxony, in May 1929, in those of Baden in October, and in the municipal elections of Prussia in November, the Nazis gain ground. Their greatest success of the year is registered in December: in the parliament of Thuringia, they receive 11 percent of the vote, as opposed to four percent in 1927.

★

The alarm is sounded. The Central Verein decides to redouble its efforts. It creates a political apparatus which it completely, but secretly, finances and directs. Its goal is to combat Nazi anti-Semitism while promoting the idea that the fight is being led by non-Jews who are primarily concerned with the welfare of Germany, and not the good of the Jews. The organization, known as *Wilhelmstrasse Büro,* is designated by its abbreviation, *WB.* The implementation of *WB* is not intended to replace other efforts that are openly and explicitly Jewish. It is meant to reinforce them, and plays an important role in anti-Nazi combat until 1933.

A non-Jew, Max Brunzlow, directs the *WB,* whose chores are twofold. The collection and analysis of information on the Nazis is assigned to Walter Gyssling, another non-Jew, who gathers press clippings and reports that eventually form an enormous system of archives, constantly updated as the misdeeds and progress of the enemy continue. The data bank so created serves the entire camp.

External propaganda is handled by a predominantly Jewish team of journalists, including Arthur Schweriner. It concentrates on the publication of anti-Nazi tracts and posters which it distributes to all liberal parties and organizations. Of all the materials published, we will take specific notice of the *Anti-Nazi*. In its format, it is, like the *Anti-Anti,* composed of a series of documentary cards, but at heart it is exclusively dedicated to an attack on National Socialist ideology. Its argumentation is anti-Fascist in general, and intentionally makes little reference to the Jewish question. The *Anti-Anti* and the *Anti-Nazi* are thus complementary, as are the direct activity and the clandestine work of the Central Verein.

The *Wilhelmstrasse Büro* is not considered innovative solely by virtue of its formation. It also introduces a new *modus operendi* to anti-Nazi action. The liberal organizations, using their customary ponderous and defensive style of rhetoric, could not keep pace with Hitler's carefully planned and executed propaganda campaigns, full of aggressive displays and irrational messages. To the calls of instinct they sought to oppose the arguments of logic. Some militants were disturbed by this discrepancy, which, in a Germany rocked by crisis since 1929, could only benefit the Nazis. Serge Tshakhotine thus took it upon himself to try to convince socialist leaders to harden the tone and modify the methods of Liberal propaganda. His advice was only partially followed by the social-democratic apparatus, but was totally put into practice by the *WB*.[17]

Alarm: at first fortnightly, and then weekly, the journal of the *WB* is sent out in tens of thousands of copies in an attempt to turn the tide of propaganda. It adopts an extremist lexicon, hoping to put the brakes on the progress of Nazi hysteria. Some titles and slogans taken from the *Alarm* of July 28, 1932, on the eve of the elections to the Reichstag, illustrate this intent: Free Germany from the swastika! Ahead to victory! Raise the flags! We will triumph! Youth to the fight; Raise a fist! . . .[18] The journal, which also publishes a multitude of anti-Hitlerian caricatures, calls upon people to vote for political parties that combat Nazism. More particularly, it works very closely with the Eiserne Front (Iron Front), which, with the Socialist party and its paramilitary organizations, forms the Reichsbanner, a large alliance of Liberal forces. The divisions of the Iron Front ensure the widespread diffusion of the *Alarm.*

★

But the end of 1929 is approaching. "More concrete labor! No fancy words!": Alfred Wiener gives precise details on the informational activities of the Central Verein. The written *Aufklärung,* first of all. He cites the non-Jewish edition of the *C.V. Zeitung,* distributed to over 50,000 readers each month. He mentions a series of brochures, like the one that is distributed in 40,000 copies in Franconia and its environs to combat an upsurge of false accusations of ritual murder. He refers also to the basic works on Judaism published by the printing house of the Central Verein, the *Philo-Verlag.* Wiener, in addition, deals with the spoken *Aufklärung.* Conferences and meetings are important to their participants. But their import is enhanced by the coverage they receive in local and regional papers, where they reach a much larger number of non-Jews. It is therefore essential that local chapters of the Jewish organizations accord to journalistic coverage of their activities the attention that it deserves.[19]

In this connection, the brochure *Schafft Aufklärung,* widely distributed to Jewish activists from the end of 1929 on, is a perfect manual for meeting organizers. It explains the prime importance of public speaking, which creates a personal link between the orator and his audience in an epoch when cinema and radio have jointly contributed to the devaluation of writing. It designates targets, categories of the population aimed for in an information campaign. Best of all, it reviews the rules essential to the success of a good public meeting, omitting not a single detail. It covers the choice of speaker, choice of date, and choice of hall (it is better to have a hall that is too small, but full, than one that is too large and so appears empty); invitations to local personalities, publicity in local newspapers, and poster campaigns; security, since Nazis occasionally try to disturb Jewish meetings; press coverage; counters at the entrance where publications of the *Philo-Verlag* can be displayed and distributed; guards on the premises on the chance that adversaries are present . . . it is all there. The Central Verein places speakers at the disposal of all of its local chapters.[20]

These chapters, moreover, are fashioned for this task. They were busily engaged in holding meetings during the first years of the Weimar Republic, and subsequently during each electoral campaign. After 1930, meetings occur with ever greater frequency, peaking in number in 1932. There are two distinct categories of meetings: protest assemblies, designed to denounce anti-Semitic acts committed by the Nazis and to mobilize the Jewish community; and informational meetings, directed towards an essentially non-Jewish public, and rehearsing the themes of antiracism and anti-Hitlerism. In early 1930, assemblies of this kind take place in Mecklemburg, Dortmund, Duisburg, Bochum and Essen in the Ruhr, and at Gorbach, Heppenheim and Offenbach in Hesse. More than a thousand participants attend an April 7 meeting in Frankfurt-on-the-Main.[21]

The *C.V. Zeitung* continues to describe the Hitlerian agitation. It also points out a renewed outbreak of desecrations of Jewish landmarks, whose facades have been vandalized and marked with hostile inscriptions. *"Juda verrecke!"* is scrawled on the walls of a synagogue in Berlin in February.[22] A Jewish merchant is fired upon.[23] The most grave affair is a political one. The Nazis enter the coalition of the State of Thuringia, and their representative, Frick, is named Minister of the Interior for the region, thereby becoming the first Nazi to ascend to a position of such great import.[24] A notorious anti-Semite, he publicly demonstrates his racism in a decision he makes regarding civic instruction in the schools.[25]

The Central Verein launches a national campaign of protest. A meeting in Eisenach on June 15th denounces the violation of equal rights for German Jews and the unconstitutional nature of Frick's policy. In Berlin on the 17th, several concurrent meetings are staged to denounce Nazism and the danger that it poses, not only for the Jews of Germany, but for the country in its entirety. The major Liberal parties send speakers to the assemblies.[26]

In the meantime, on the national level, the economic crisis begins to affect the functioning of political institutions. The Socialist Chancellor, Müller, resigns in March following a debate over unemployment insurance. Brüning, the parliamentary leader of the Catholic Center, replaces him. But he is not successful at selling his financial program to the deputies. In July 1930, he obtains from President Hindenburg the dissolution of the Reichstag. New elections are set for the 14th of September.

The reaction of the Central Verein is instantaneous. *"An die deutschen Juden!* The Reichstag is dissolved. We anticipate a brutal election campaign. National-Socialism hopes to come away with great triumphs. Your duty is to counter, by any method, its hatred for the Jews. We call upon all our friends, we call upon all Jews! Fight against their incitement of pogroms! Fight against the boycott! Fight against every malevolent attack on Jews and on Judaism!"[27]

In early August, a new appeal to the German Jews exhorts them to rise up against the threat and to contribute heavily to the *Kampffonds 1930* (1930 Combat Fund).[28] Jewish youths, in particular, are urged to remember their "responsibility for the honor and the life of our Jewish community."[29] "German Jews, do you want a Hitlerian Germany?" a poster from the Central Verein inquires.[30]

"Stand up and fight against National-Socialism!" writes Marie

Juchacz, a member of the Reichstag, in the *C.V. Zeitung*.[31] An appeal to Jewish women is signed by Margarete Edelheim. She asks them to take active part in the election campaign.[32] The Jews are urged to vote for whichever Liberal party they prefer, so long as they vote against the forces of anti-Semitism, and above all, against the Nazis.[33] A coordinated effort is established between the Central Verein and the other major Jewish organizations of the country. These are: the Community of Berlin, the Zionist Federation, the Reichsbund jüdischer Frontsoldaten and the B'nai B'rith.[34] The work is carried out solely by the Central Verein and its proxy, the *Wilhelmstrasse Büro*.

In addition to the traditional publications of the Central Verein, the local chapters are issued the following: posters with six different texts; stickers and leaflets featuring 16 different slogans in a choice of three colors; a series of ten anti-Nazi postcards; the election journal *Deutschland erwache!*; several series of small brochures and tracts, and a gramophone record of speeches by Jewish leaders.[35]

What are the totals? For the election campaign of 1924, the Central Verein prints a total of eight million tracts and one million journals. During the campaign of 1930, these figures are easily surpassed. These are the quantities of supplies the regional directorate of the Central Verein in the Rhineland sends its division in Neuwied, whose Jewish community numbers, at the most, a few hundred people. Two thousand copies of the *Alarm*. One hundred red stickers, with six different texts. Six hundred tags with ten different texts. Posters. One such shipment is sent on September 1, 1930. A new delivery is prepared for September 7th.[36]

★

The results of the vote far outstrip the most optimistic forecasts of the Hitlerians. They jump from 2.6 percent of the vote and 12 elected in May 1928, to 18.3 percent and 107 elected in September 1930. They were the smallest faction in the Reichstag, and now they are the second most powerful political formation in the country. The splinter-group has put on some weight.

From one election to the next, they move from 810,000 votes to 6,410,000. They take a very large slice from the electorate of the Nationalist far-Right. They smoothly cut into the bourgeois electorate, liberal and conservative, which they will entirely appropriate in the 1932 elections. They take not a single vote from the Catholic Center, nor from the two principal parties of the Left. Conversely, they bring large numbers of abstentionists from 1928 over to their side. Even more significantly, the youths who vote for the first time vote largely for them.

Analyses of the election bring out the profile of the typical Nazi voter. He is rural rather than urban, Protestant rather than Catholic, and a peasant or member of the middle-class (self-employed or salaried, in both the public administration and the private sector) rather than a member of the working class. The proletariat affected by unemployment radicalizes itself, but votes for the Communists, who continue to gain strength from election to election. The middle classes, disquieted by the economic crisis, have begun their process of Nazification. German youth heads towards the Nazis.

★

Never in the history of modern Germany, even at the end of the nineteenth century, did a violently anti-Semitic party ever benefit from such an impressive representation in Parliament. The German correspondent for the Jewish Telegraphic Agency interviews several notable figures from the Jewish community on the meaning they descry in the latest turn of events.[37]

Albert Einstein remembers the anti-Semitism of the Dreyfus Affair, which fortunately was dispelled, and he expects German anti-Semitism to likewise dissolve. The President of the Jewish Community in Berlin offers similar observations. For Klee, vice-President of the Jews of Berlin, what is possible for the fascists in Rumania and Hungary is impossible in Germany. Bernard Kahn, European Director of Joint, expresses his uneasiness but does not think that a lasting political oppression of the Jews in Germany is possible. Ludwig Holländer, Director of the Central Verein, calls for united action by Jews and non-Jews against the danger.

"Clarity, labor, courage!" headlines the *C.V. Zeitung* after the elections. Alfred Wiener emphasizes the lesson learned on September 14th. He comments on the balloting, then poses the question: "Did we do all that was within our power to prevent these results?" He salutes the work and self-sacrifice of the Jewish militants, and mentions the schoolchildren who burst their piggy banks to contribute to the action of the Central Verein. Naturally, improvements are necessary. But, in the last analysis, it is mandatory that the major political parties take the fight against Nazism into their own hands.[38] *"Wer hat Angst?"* ("Who is afraid?"), asks *Der Schild* on October 9th. It vehemently assails Goebbels, who scoffed at the fears of the "Cohn family" on the night of the election returns in September.[39] Attacks against Goebbels are the watchword in the newspapers and journals of Jewish organizations.[40]

To celebrate their success, bands of young Hitlerians shatter Jewish shop-windows in Berlin on October 13th, the day the new Reichstag is first convened. Although the attack is immediately and severely reprimanded by legal authorities, it stirs up feelings of exasperation within the Jewish community. "Our friends must keep their sangfroid and not answer back to this provocation," the *C. V. Zeitung* writes. "We have confidence in the government and the police . . . who know to protect the property and well-being of Jewish citizens as effectively as they protect that of other citizens."[41]

The Jewish mobilization publicly recommences in January 1931. *"Hinein in die Kampffront der deutschen Juden!"* ("Join the combat front of the German Jews!"): the great Jewish organization addresses itself one more time to the Jews of Germany. "The Central Verein is vigilant. It combats the enemies of Judaism, it opens the door to understanding and brotherhood in Germany's internal life, and it fights for every inch of terrain that it can preserve from the forces of destruction, and for the liberty of German Jews. . . . We call upon the living spirit of German Judaism, we call upon its youth . . . *Hinein in die Kampffront der deutschen Juden!"*[42]

"Hinein in den C. V.!" A reader's letter to the *C. V. Zeitung,* published in February 1931, voices the sentiment of rank and file militants. Hans Feilchenfeld recounts how a hoodlum threw an egg at his head to publicly ridicule him. Entering a tramway, he was insulted by the passengers. "We, German Jews, have we now no more rights?" He concludes his letter by remarking on the necessity of fighting anti-Semitism and strengthening the ranks of the Central Verein.[43]

The same issue of the *C. V. Zeitung* announces the formation of an educational institute on anti-Semitism for Jewish high school students. There Jewish youth can learn to confront the adversary. During the entire period, the question of anti-Semitism in the schools and universities continually preoccupies the Central Verein. It implements programs to approach the problem from three angles. It works with Jewish schoolchildren and students, distributing didactic material to enable them to respond to the questions of their comrades. It works with teachers: within the framework of week-ends dedicated to the Jewish question (to which are invited representatives from diverse professional groups), the Central Verein stresses the responsibility of educators in resisting the onslaught of racism. Finally, the Jewish community also works directly with non-Jewish youth. It organizes school visits to synagogues and an assortment of educational conferences. Their efforts are bolstered by the women's chapters of the Central Verein, which concentrate on two key sectors in the fight against anti-Semitism: the schools and schoolchildren, on one side, and the women's and mothers' associations of Germany on the other.[44]

All of these specific activities are of lesser importance, however, than the alliance that is formed between the Central Verein and the Liberal political parties. The disproportion between their respective forces had become such that, after September, the Jewish community could not hope to fight Nazism without solid external support. A permanent accord among the liberal movements is organized by Abegg, Secretary of State for the Interior in the Prussian government. It groups the Socialists, the Catholic Zentrum, the Deutsch Demokratische Partei, the unions, and the Reichsbanner, the Social-Democratic militia. The Central Verein is represented by Hans Reichmann.

The bonds between the Jewish community and the anti-Nazi organizations continue to solidify until 1933. They facilitate exchanges of information on the progress of the enemy. They make widespread circulation of propaganda material furnished by the Central Verein feasible. Non-Jewish orators are delegated to meetings held in protest of anti-Semitism, and Jewish orators speak at anti-Nazi assemblies. The Central Verein finances some of the activities of the Reichsbanner, which thereby benefits from a portion of the funds raised by German Jews. The Jewish vote is decidedly cast for the anti-Nazi parties, with a growing preference for the Socialists.[45]

★

The Central Verein launches an appeal to the Jews of Germany in early 1932. "This is the decisive year. We, and millions of Germans with us, are ready for the decisive combat."[46] "No chants of hatred by the Hitlerian gangs will be able to shake the loyalty of German Jews for their fatherland," states Bruno Weil, who presides over one of three major mass meetings organized simultaneously in Berlin by the Central Verein on January 16, 1932. The resolution adopted by the thousands of participants at the three gatherings proclaims that they are committed to opposing "every infringement upon their rights as citizens."[47]

The Central Verein enters into the most dramatic campaign in its history. The Nazis are tough and menacing. But the constitutional cadres are steadfast, and the liberal parties remain powerful, so nothing is lost, yet. The Iron Front of the Socialists, created at the end of 1931, mobilizes hundreds of thousands of demonstrators. The Communists are numerous and organized. Hitler is still far from power. German Judaism launches itself into an intensive campaign founded on the distribution of written material in unequalled quantities and on the staging of a series of assemblies across the country. The Reichsbund jüdischer Frontsoldaten, alone, organizes 70 gatherings. The Verein zur Abwehr des Anti-Semitismus multiplies its activities. The Central Verein itself organizes several hundred meetings. All the groups redouble their efforts. The decisive year is 1932, for Germany in general, and for the German Jews in particular.

Wir deutschen Juden ("We, German Jews"): of all the didactic material distributed by the Jewish organizations in 1932, let us linger on a particular brochure of the Central Verein. Directed towards the general public, it presents a panorama of the scientific, literary and patriotic contributions made by Jews to German society. It summarizes the history of 1600 years of German Judaism, and tears apart, one by one, all of the anti-Semites' lies. The text is accompanied by numerous illustrations. On one page, a grimacing dragon spewing forth anti-Jewish slogans—ritual murder, international Jewry, etc.—is met by a forthright blade clenched in a steely fist.[48]

The presidential election campaign is in full swing. Hindenburg runs, supported by the coalition of liberal parties. Facing him is Hitler. The Nazis, to discredit the old Marshal, make ample reference to the support the Central Verein furnishes him. *"Die CV-Juden für Hindenburg"* headlines the *Völkischer Beobachter* of February 21st and 22nd.[49] On March 13th, the outgoing President just slightly misses the absolute majority needed for his immediate reelection. He totals 49.6 percent of the vote, against 30.1 percent for Hitler, 13.2 percent for the Communist Thaelmann and 6.8 percent for another candidate of the Right, Duersterberg. "We must continue to fight indefatigably," Brodnitz writes. He calls for the Jews of Germany to contribute substantially to the *Kampffonds 1932* (1932 Combat Fund) which collects funds that are needed for the anti-Nazi campaign of the Central Verein.[50] For *Der Schild*, the results of the voting demonstrate that the danger is very great, certainly, but that it can be faced.[51] "Our Jewish honor, our German will, call us to action," writes the *C. V. Zeitung* on the eve of the second round of presidential balloting.[52]

On April 10th, Hindenburg garners 19.4 million votes against 13.4 million for Hitler and 3.7 million for Thaelman. "The great majority of the German nation rejects National-Socialism...," the *C. V. Zeitung* writes, concluding that in light of the persistent danger, the anti-Nazi work must be amplified.[53] "The front holds," affirms *Der Schild*. "Nearly 20 million German men and women stood up against the horde of brown-shirts."[54]

After new elections in several regional parliaments, including the parliament of Prussia, events begin to unwind. Chancellor Brüning, a loyal Liberal, is dismissed. He is replaced by Von Papen who, on June 4th, decrees the dissolution of the Reichstag and sets elections for the 31st of July. On June 15th, Von Papen lifts the two-month old interdiction of the SA. The brownshirt tide seems to envelop the country and the number of anti-Jewish aggressions rises precipitously.[55]

On June 17th, the assembly of the Jewish community of Berlin reconvenes. Its two primary constituents, the liberals and the Zionists, put an end to a dispute that began several years before. The orientation of all is towards unity. "We believe in the Jewish future," says Stern, President of the Federation of liberal Judaism of Germany. A Zionist leader expresses less optimism, but reiterates his faith in the immortality of Judaism, and in Eretz Israel. Attendance in synagogues increases from 15 to 20 percent over the figures for 1931. This return to Judaism is viewed as a sign and a consequence of difficult times.[56]

"Kampf auf der ganzen Linie" ("Combat all along the line"): the headline of the *C.V. Zeitung* on July 1st concerns the approach of the elections and reflects the rising tension associated with them. "We, German Jews, are not afraid. Our nerves are steady. With jaws set we will protect every acre of our soil, and with courage will defend every article of our rights."[57] Jewish demonstrations multiply further in July. "We raise a solemn protest against the disgraceful anti-Jewish tumults in our native towns," state the Jews of Nuremberg in a mass meeting organized on the 4th.[58] In the space of three days, ten assemblies are convened in Berlin.[59] For the Central Verein alone, there are 18 meetings in Bavaria, seven in Brandenburg, 19 in Rhine-Westphalia, and as many in Pomerania. . . . Another call is sent out to the German people. "Fellow-citizens! Do not heed the calumnies and lies that you are told about Judaism. The German Jews are neither better nor worse than you are. Fight along with us for civil peace. . . ."[60]

At the end of July, the Central Verein organizes a protest meeting in Berlin. The crowd is so large that the organizers must open two adjoining halls and have the speakers circulate among the three. Bernhard Weiss is the recipient, in each of the halls, of a long ovation. His popularity among the Jews of the capital is the result of his having become the symbol of their fight. An officer in the Great War, and a high functionary in the Prussian government, it was he who gave chase in 1922 to Rathenau's assassins. Now vice-president of the powerful Berlin police force, he protects the streets, holding the Nazis at bay.

In 1927, Goebbels fired concentrated volleys of propaganda at Weiss. Someone had brought to his attention that Weiss was an unassailable patriot and therefore a poor target. Goebbels replied, "I have no interest whatsoever in the man. But let's talk about him again three months from now. You'll be astounded to see what I will have made of Weiss." The *Angriff*, the journal created by Goebbels in 1927, unleashed a barrage of calumnies and insults on the official.[61]

Weiss, of course, withstood this abuse well over the years. But in 1932, after a police action against the Nazis under his personal command, certain members of the Jewish community regret the fact that he took charge of the operation. Was he not risking the accusation of utilizing the police to protect the Jews? "More dignity," he replies in June 1932, expressing the sentiment of the great majority of German Jews.[62] Emancipation entails full equality of rights and duties. Jews, like non-Jews, can perform all public duties. Every voluntary abstention from these duties is a renunciation of emancipation itself. At the July meeting, he returns to this theme in front of the crowd, which applauds loudly. "We have too much pride to be continually boasting about the services that we have rendered to our German National collectivity," states the resolution adopted at the end of the meeting.[63]

"Es hat doch Zweck!" ("It is not useless!") writes the *C.V. Zeitung* on July 15th, denouncing the "pessimism and resignation" of those who consider the match to be already over.[64] *"Köpfe Hoch!"* ("Heads high!") is its title on the 22nd, as Jews are confronted with an escalation in acts of intimidation and Hitlerian terror.[65] On July 29th, Brodnitz sends out a final proclamation: "We reply loudly to our enemies: hands off our honor, hands off our equality of rights!"[66]

★

On July 31, 1932, the Nazis obtain 37.3 percent of the vote and become, from out of nowhere, the most important party in the Parliament. Their score is double that of September 1930, and is almost 15 times that of May 1928. This time the Communists come in at 14.3 percent, the Socialists collect 21.6 percent, and the Catholic Zentrum and the Bayerische Volkspartei between them total 15.7 percent of the vote. The Nazis, even allied with the Nationalists and other small parties, do not have a majority in the Reichstag and are not able to form a government. To force the hand of Hindenburg, called upon to confer the Chancellorship upon Hitler, the SA mobilize all over the country. But the venerable Marshal is obstinate, and rejects the Nazis' claims. The audience that he accords Hitler on August 13th results in a setback for the latter. Von Papen is maintained in his post. The Republic does not give in.

Be that as it may, the Reichstag is ungovernable, and new elections are called for November 6, 1932. The election campaign begins on a false note, issued by the Nazis. A telegram allegedly issued by the Central Verein recommends that Jewish voters support the Nationalists of the DNVP. The maneuver is obvious. The Nazis seek to deliver a lethal blow to the DNVP and so drain off all of its voters. The best tactic they can employ in times of such rampant anti-Semitism is to have people believe that the DNVP is no longer an anti-Jewish party, so much so that even Jews are now voting for it. "The Central Verein eyes the forthcoming elections trembling down to its very bones," sneers a Nazi orator in Berlin, before revealing the contents of the (fake) secret telegram. In its reply, the *C.V. Zeitung* adopts a biting tone: "The Central Verein looks ahead to the coming elections, as it did to all the elections before this, with great calm. It seems to us, rather, that it is the National-Socialists whose bones are trembling."[67]

★

Hope did in fact change sides. Made wary by the unwavering attitude of Hindenburg in August, shocked by the excesses of Hitlerian terror and repelled by the internal quarrels of the NSDAP, two million voters abandon the Nazis, who collect no more than 33.1 percent of the vote, as opposed to 37.3 percent on the 31st of July. The party remains the strongest in the Reichstag, but it is in crisis, stricken with disappointment, and suffering from grave financial difficulties. To many observers, the tide has begun to ebb and can only further withdraw, to the great relief of liberals in Germany and throughout the world.

The militant Jews do not solely attribute the reversal to their *Aufklärung,* but they do deduce from this turning of the tide that the wave that washed over Germany can be effectively contained and driven back, and so are encouraged to carry on. Meetings and instructional conferences, already numerous in September and October, are further planned for November and December. Acts of terror have abated everywhere, and the Nazis are in retreat. The Jewish organizations use the time profitably to close ranks. The divisions of the Central Verein convene in local and regional congresses.[68]

The editorial of the *C.V. Zeitung* on December 23, 1932, is dedicated to Hanukkah. It recalls the ancient heroism of the Jewish people and the revolt of the Maccabees. It salutes the silent heroism of the Jews of the Ghetto who maintained their faith in a hostile world. And today? The fight continues for the rights of Jews and for the continuation of Judaism, but also for mankind as a whole.[69] The editorial of *Der Schild* on December 22nd draws up the balance sheet for the year 1932. The Nazis did not seize power, but the danger has not yet been dispelled. The year was a long and hard one. "We part company with it, conscious of not having lost courage or renounced hope, even in the most difficult moments."[70]

In January, the *Aufklärung* resumes on a greater scale. "We talk to our Christian fellow-citizens everywhere," the *C.V. Zeitung* writes in large print, giving a detailed account of a series of propaganda meetings held during the month.[71] "Again and always, *Aufklärung*," is the title of *Der Schild* on January 26, 1933, which describes the gatherings and conferences organized by the RjF since the beginning of the year.[72]

★

For the night of January 30, 1933, a Zionist assembly is planned in the capital to celebrate the 60th birthday of the great Jewish national poet, Chaim Nachman Bialik. After the pogrom in Kishinev, 30 years earlier, he wrote *The City of the Massacre,* which had a profound impact upon the Jewish youth of Russia and the entire world. In 1932, Bialik himself arrived from Tel-Aviv, where he had been living for a number of years, to lead a seminar in Berlin. There he discussed, in particular, the illusion of the emancipation of Western Judaism. . . .[73] On January 30th, the police contact the organizers and advise them to cancel the demonstration.[74] They fear that the many thousands of SA who are to parade the same night before the Chancellory of the Reich might be tempted to attack the gathering.

Why this march? That morning, the dismal rumor that had been traveling through political circles for several days received confirmation. Impressed with the results of regional elections in the miniscule state of Lippe, on January 15th, President Hindenburg finally conferred the directorship of the government upon the leader of the largest political party in the country and charged him to compose a coalition cabinet in which the members of his own party form only a minority. The transference of power was performed in conformity with the rules of the constitution and according to parliamentary and democratic procedures. Adolf Hitler is now Chancellor of the Reich.

The meetings of the *Aufklärung* are continued. One of the last organized by the RjF takes place in Heidelberg, one night after the formation of the new government. Sixty local notables who are invited back out, and a correspondent for *Der Schild* mocks this unex-

64

pected "epidemic of the flu." The meeting takes place in any case with 600 participants.[75] All scheduled meetings continue until the new Reichstag elections of March 5th. There the Nazis receive 43.9 percent of the vote. That is sufficient for them, after allying themselves with the Zentrum and eliminating the Communist members of Parliament, to obtain the two-thirds majority required for the conferment of full powers upon the Chancellor, which occurs on the 23rd of March. For: 441. Against: 84.

"On January 30, 1933, began the heroic epoch of the fight for the emancipation of German Judaism," writes *Der Schild* on February 9th.[76] The great Rabbi Leo Baeck will express a more accurate view, when he says that "the history of German Judaism approaches its end."[77]

Nazi terror assails the Jews even before the elections, and sharply escalates afterwards. The press agencies and correspondents from major international papers report numerous instances of Jews being beaten, arrested, tortured and shot. They mention suicides. The first wave of refugees crosses the frontiers. April 1st is declared a national day for boycotting German Jews. The SA are stationed before stores and shops marked with a six-pointed star and the inscription *"Jude."*

"Tragt ihn mit Stolz, den gelben Fleck!" ("Wear it with pride, the yellow star!") In these days of sadness and humiliation, the Zionist journal, the *Jüdische Rundschau,* issues an appeal to the Jews of Germany: "Judaism committed a gross error in not listening to the appeal of Theodore Herzl, and in even mocking it. The Jews did not want to admit that there was a Jewish problem." It then discusses the long and venerable history of the Jewish people. "Jews, raise again the shield of David, and carry it with honor . . . they remind us that we are Jews. We say yes, and of this we are proud." (*"Wir sagen Ja, und tragen es mit Stolz."*)[78]

65

Chapter Five
Demonstrations and Meetings

Although momentarily dumbfounded by the extent of the disaster, the Jewish communities of the world quickly regain their voices. The torch of anti-Nazi meetings is passed from German Judaism to the Jewish people as a whole.

On March 19, 1933, 1200 delegates representing 600 Jewish organizations in the United States meet in an extraordinary conference and decide upon a plan of protest against anti-Semitism in Germany. On the 23rd, thousands of Jewish veterans march in New York. On the 27th, 250,000 Jews demonstrate in New York and more than a million do so in the country as a whole. A day of mourning is proclaimed in all Jewish congregations.[1]

That very day, the three million Jews of Poland are called to action. Jewish stores and offices close. The Rabbinical authorities order a day of fasting and prayer, and the synagogues are packed. Mass meetings and demonstrations are held in all the cities of the land— Lemberg, Lodz, Cracow, Lublin. . . . In Kielce, twenty thousand Jews, virtually the entire community, march with banners and flags. The day before, the National Committee of protest against the anti-Jewish persecutions in Germany, which brought together the Zionist movements, the whole of religious Jewry and various other national Jewish organizations, launched a solemn appeal: "To the Jewish people in Poland . . . the clouds have moved across the heavens. Our Jewish people are reliving one of the most difficult epochs in the martyrdom of its Exile. . . ."

The largest meeting in Warsaw takes place in Nowosci Hall. The thousands who find no room within carry the demonstration outside. The Jews no longer protest the way they used to, with mere requests, the first speaker explains. Today, they react "like a nation that is reborn." It is necessary, then, to "strike the enemy who wants to destroy us." Hitler is mistaken, Gotlieb (one of the leading figures of the National Committee) declares, if he believes that the Jews are dejected. They are not bemoaning their plight, they are not afraid. Hitler and his gang would like to rid themselves of 600,000 German Jews, but it is 16 million Jews they will be forced to confront, he concludes, to the prolonged applause of the public. The resolution adopted at the close of the assembly asserts that "Brute force will not be able to destroy the eternal People, bruise its stubborn and inflexible hold on liberty and equality of rights, or halt its fight for national liberation and the renewal of the Jewish national home in Eretz-Israel."

Jewish youth and students march on the German embassy to the cry of "Down with Hitler!" and "Long live the Jewish people!" Several groups get past the police blockade and reach the edifice itself before being arrested. All day long, Jewish demonstrators attempt the crossing. At the central station in Warsaw, several thousand Jews accompanying a group of Zionists en route to Eretz-Israel transform the event into an anti-Hitler demonstration. They sing the Hatikvah, the Jewish national anthem.[2]

Jews protest in Canada, Argentina, France, England, Australia, Bulgaria, Syria, Iraq, Czechoslovakia, Austria, Greece, Lithuania. . . . Meetings are held in Tel-Aviv and Haifa. The British police increase the guard at the German consulates in Jerusalem and Jaffa. In early April, a mass meeting draws several thousand Jews in Casablanca, Morocco. Several thousand demonstrate in Brussels and at Antwerp before the German consulate. Indignation spreads to the most isolated Jewish communities, like that of Bombay, India. Another wave of meetings and demonstrations throughout the world protests the burning of Jewish books in Germany on May 10, 1933.[3]

★

The watchword of boycott is universally adopted. Jewish merchants in every country refuse to buy German products so long as the persecution of Jews continues. Special committees are formed to this end in the different Jewish communities. The method is ancient. In May 1556, twenty-four Jews of Anconia stated their preference for fire (at the stake) over water (of baptism) and were burned alive. In reprisal, the city was boycotted by the Jewish tradesmen of Turkey and Salonica. In 1900, a threat to boycott the World's Fair in Paris was issued in the United States as a statement of opposition to the Dreyfus Affair. But in 1933, the movement is worldwide. It complements protest, in the form of meetings and street marches, with this immediately applicable and seemingly effective instrument of battle. "Jews of all the world, unite. Boycott all German goods," say billboards posted up in London.[4]

In this period, in 1933, the Jewish organizations have no difficulty gathering statements of indignation from the political, ecclesiastical, and scholarly arenas. The unanimity is such that strange voices unite in protest. The Jewish community in Italy envisages an international conference against anti-Semitism to be underwritten by the government. On April 24, Mussolini receives the head Rabbi of Rome, who has come to discuss the situation of the Jews in Germany. Mussolini offers him his sympathy.[5]

Some minor false notes, however, are audible in the concert of voices of solidarity. Indeed, when the first Jewish refugees must be relocated, rare are the countries, with the notable exception of France, that are ready to make a serious effort in the matter and welcome them. Great Britain itself is hesitant about increasing the number of immigration certificates for Palestine. Its position is that the Jews of Germany ought to be included within the existing quota. In 1933, the question is not crucial and the false notes are forgotten.

In fact, the Nazis are not at all indifferent toward the protest campaign. First, they fear its economic repercussions. Caught up in their own delirium, they overestimate the power of Jewish money and commerce, and fear a collapse of their exports, already affected by the ongoing economic crisis. The Nazis are anxious, too, about the image of the new regime in the eyes of the world, which is kept well informed by press agencies and foreign correspondents for major international papers about the anti-Jewish measures and acts of terror. They are worried about how the diplomatic fallout might affect a Germany that is still weak and in need of several calm years in which to rearm and restore its power.

For all these reasons, they decide to counterattack. With directly repressive measures and threats of collective reprisals, they forcibly wrest declarations condemning the "propaganda of atrocities" from the leaders of the Jewish community.[6] They also make some effort to bring individual acts of terror in Germany to an end and to stabilize the situation of the Jewish community, provided that the demonstrations cease. German Jewish officialdom bends to necessity and thus sets the standard for the Jewish councils that the Germans will later create in all of occupied Europe. Sharp differences emerge among the Jewish organizations of the world on the choice of a course to follow, but for the most part, the campaign of public protest will be maintained to the very end.

★

During this period, the records for highest numbers of demonstrations belong, of course, to the two most populous Jewish communities in the world, those of the United States and Poland. France comes in far behind, but nonetheless deserves honorable mention.

"The people of Paris rise up against racist barbarism," *Le Droit de Vivre*, mouthpiece of the LICA, headlines victoriously.[7] The good news does not date, contrary to appearances, from October 1980, nor either, alas, from July 1942. It goes back to June 1939. The mass meeting organized by the LICA in the Cirque d'Hiver in Paris was a complete success, with 12,000 participants, not counting the thousands unable to find room inside. That meeting was the last in a long sequence of antiracist assemblies that preceded the massacre of a hundred thousand French Jews.

Until the war, in fact, the LICA held hundreds of gatherings, large and small, in all parts of France and in Algeria. It didn't have a monopoly. Numerous others were organized by Jewish war veterans, organizations of Jewish immigrants, various protest committees, the Zionist movements and Jewish workers' parties. Any total reckoning is impossible, so let us proceed by mentioning specific cases.[8]

Six young Jews shot in Sorocca, Rumania; 5,000 people in Paris, in February 1932. Meetings in Lyon, Lille, Nice, Montpelier, Grenoble and Tours. Hitler takes power: meetings and demonstrations in Paris and the provinces throughout the year 1933. Against French anti-Semitism: meeting in Salle Wagram in April 1934. After the pogrom of Constantina: meeting in August 1934. . . . Against anti-Semitism in France: meeting on March 23, 1936. In support of the Jews of Poland: meeting on March 30th. Protest assemblies in Strasburg, Metz, Nancy, Mulhouse, etc. To commemorate Kalifa and Zaoui, shot in Algeria, and Stephen Lux, who immolated himself at the League of Nations to protest anti-Semitism: meeting in Paris on July 16, 1936. Anti-Semitism in Algeria: meeting on the December 4th. Anti-Semitism in Poland: meeting in Paris on December 17th. Frankfurter, a young Swiss Jew, sentenced to 18 years in prison for having killed Gustloff, the Nazi agitator: huge meeting on December 21, 1936. . . . And so on, until 1939.

The meetings, to be sure, do not slow the advance of anti-Semitism. But they reflect it, like an ultra-sensitive instrument designed to chart the progress of a phenomenon. A pogrom in Poland, a foul act by Hitler, an anti-Jewish demonstration in France? Thousands of people come together, proclaim their anger and reaffirm their will to fight. For an organization, a meeting mobilizes adherents to distribute po-

70

litical tracts, hang posters and sell journals. A meeting is also the tribune from which the most vigorous appeals to public officials are dispatched. Directed towards public opinion and the press, a meeting spreads grand apologetic messages and themes of protest. For the antisemitic enemy, a meeting is a demonstration of force.

Who speaks on the panels? Mostly non-Jews, so as to authenticate the idea that the fight against anti-Semitism is everyone's concern, and not only that of the Jews. Who applauds? In the hall, an overwhelming majority of Jews. . . . At the close, a motion is generally voted upon. The people of Paris, joined together on the at, express their profound indignation and give solemn warning. The style changes at times, depending on whether the purpose is to denounce anti-Semitism in the homes of others or anti-Semitism in one's own home, and on whether the host organization is an activist or moderate one. The end result hardly varies.

The predictable rituals of anti-antisemitic demonstrations are revived in France in the seventies and eighties. Turns of phrase are adapted to suit the changing times, but structurally the discourse of protestation does not change. Some meetings took place in the very same locations, while others occupied more innovative grounds. In January 1938, the great Salle Japy in Paris was needed so that all could gather and state, with Jacob Kaplan, that "by fighting anti-Semitism, the world protects itself."[9] In Autumn 1979, Bernard-Henri Lévy reveals that "the fight that we are conducting goes far beyond the Jews."[10] He addresses his remarks to the crowd assembled in the vast crypt of the Memorial of the Jewish Martyr. Dedicated to the remembrance of six million Jews who were assassinated by non-Jews, the edifice did not exist before the war.

Chapter Six

Self-defense

One weapon remains in the arsenal. Sharp-edged and trenchant, it shines with a strange luster. One might imagine that it has never yet been used.

Self-defense answers a real need. Every human collectivity whose honor and security are threatened has the right and the obligation to defend itself by any available means, and to organize itself to that end. The Jewish community is no exception to this rule, and even has a dual hurdle to overcome. First, indignity: it is humiliating to be in dire need of the protection of others. Second, inefficiency: these days, specifically Jewish security structures are a crucial supplement to police protection. The defensive approach is sometimes complemented, on the part of certain militants, by an offensive thrust advocating violent action against anti-Semitic groups or persons. These actions are meant to serve two functions: to punish anti-Jewish acts already committed and to decrease the likelihood of others being perpetrated. They want to directly confront the propagandists of hatred, compel them to curb their activities, reduce their ranks by engendering a fear of reprisal, and so perhaps eliminate anti-Semitism. In any case, whether the emphasis is placed on protection or attack, the project is sincere and the will to act is undeniable.

Self-defense is sometimes subject to outside criticism. An editorialist for *Le Monde,* in August 1982, reprimands the Israeli head of government, who called upon the young Jews of France to become organized after the attack at rue des Rosiers.[1] His admonition also takes indirect aim at those Jews in France who were inclined to respond positively to this plea. The weekly paper of the extreme Right, *Minute,* launches an alarmist campaign: thousands of young Jews are in secret training somewhere in the heart of Paris.[2]

Self-defense is, at times, also contested from within the Jewish community. Some claim that defending oneself is contrary to Jewish tradition. In April 1981, Pierre Vidal-Naquet is upset: "Last February, on the 6th, four persons destroyed several hundred texts of the revisionist sect. . . ." The revisionist sect in question is a leftist group that denies the veracity of the gas chambers and the Nazi genocide, employing terminology adapted to the tastes of a Marxist or Libertarian intellectual public. Pierre Vidal-Naquet advances a two-pronged argument. One: the use of violence is unreasonable, since it can turn the adversary into a martyr. Two: violence is contrary to Jewish ethics. Jews must always be "on the side of the persecuted."[3]

But the value of self-defense is generally recognized by the Jews of France. Few leaders of organizations restrict their defense effort to the deployment of electronic surveillance systems, such as were installed on all Jewish premises several years ago. The investment in such equipment is perceived as a necessary, but not sufficient, measure.

And in fact, there is no reason why Jewish self-defense in France, after an inevitable period of groping, should not succeed in surmounting its crises of growth. It responds to both an objective need and a subjective desire to act. It will, therefore, discover its optimal arrangement, unified or diversified, and its most effective methods, defensive or offensive.

The real problem is not organizational. It is conceptual, and is located in the image that Jewish self-defense has of itself, and its self-prescribed long term goals. Young Jews who participate in a meeting against anti-Semitism are usually under the impression that they are the very first ones to do so. They feel this even more strongly when the issue is self-defense. "This time, we will fight," the militants and their sympathizers think. The force of the slogan explains the ephemeral but massive prestige which the *Organisation Juive de Défense (OJD)* enjoyed (although it was in reality quite weak, and rapidly disbanding) after the explosion at Copernic in 1980. Its very existence allowed the leaders of the community, even as they cautioned Jewish youth against the "hazard" of violence, to increase pressure on public officials: "intervene quickly against anti-Semitism, for if you do not, we will not be able to keep the situation under control much longer." Although its true stature was, on the whole, overblown by the media, the organization symbolized the will to fight of the Jews of France.

But ignorance of history deprives the militants of a rich reservoir of experience that might prove indispensable to their elaboration of a coherent strategy, and extremely pertinent to issues such as internal organization, recruitment, training, methodology, and task delineation. Ignorance of history above all obscures for the young Jews of France every criterion by which they might measure their own efforts. A Parisian group amasses two hundred iron bars and twenty revolvers: are these many or few? Three hundred young Jews train themselves in Karate; a combat squad attacks the leader of an anti-Jewish group: are there any precedents? Not only does neglect for the past squander an invaluable supply of information about different modes of combat, but it also forbids any reflection on their overall effectiveness and probable results.

★

When attacked, the Jews have always attempted to defend themselves.[4] From among many historical cases, we will describe the little known anti-Semitic pogroms of Alsace in 1848. Semantically speaking, the expression is inadequate. The word "pogrom" does not enter the everyday vocabulary until several dozen years later. The word "anti-Semite," for its part, dates from the last third of the nineteenth century. It is therefore the anti-Jewish riots (and not the anti-Semitic pogroms) of Alsace that we now recall. . . . The trouble breaks out on the morrow of the revolution of February 1848 which drives out Louis-Philippe and instates the Republic. It lasts from the end of February until May and affects many small Jewish communities.

On February 26th, gangs of youths march and chant in the streets of Saverne. On Sunday the 27th, Jewish homes are attacked. The same day, in Altkirch, "not a single Israelite home is left that has not been devastated, a single household that has not been pillaged, a single establishment that has not been plundered," the *Archives Israélites* writes. "The synagogue of Altkirch offers the most horrid sight. Everything there was demolished . . . the sacred scrolls of the Torah (there had been twenty) were shredded, trampled underfoot, and converted into drum skins. Everywhere the ground was strewn with debris; one would think it a place taken by storm! One walks upon the rubbish; one slides over traces of blood, and the silence of death hovers above the desolate ruins. . . ." Among the testimonies: "In broad daylight, under the eyes of the authorities, they destroyed, they smashed everything; they were chasing the Israelites with pistols, with knives . . . mothers who had only recently given birth were fleeing with their infants, risking their lives, preferring to die by the Hand of God than to fall into the hands of those madmen. . . . Our hearts bleed at the recitation of their cruelties; and we are in France! and in the nineteenth century!"

Many times, groups of Jews try to find refuge in Switzerland. The departmental or local authorities generally react with firmness, and bring in the troops or the national guard. The priest of Durmenach demonstrates rare "admirable" conduct when he hides a hunted Jew, the octogenarian Felix Kahn.

And self-defense? The word did not exist but the practice did. The Rabbi of Hegenheim, Nordmann, organized a force of eighty Jews "determined to dearly defend their lives. . . . He divided his little troop into four squads, stationed them in the areas that were most vulnerable to attack, set up regular patrols and reconnaissance missions, and finally took his troop to the offensive. With a generous group of reinforcements supplied by the national guard and the garrison of Huningue, he seized a large number of bandits and brought them to the prisons of Hagenthal."[5]

★

In the twentieth century, collective self-defense has been practiced along with individual action. The Bundist Hirsh Lekert fires at the governor of Vilna, who had ordered Jewish demonstrators whipped. In 1903, the Zionist Socialist Pinhas Dashevsky wounds the instigator of the Kishinev pogrom, the anti-Semite Krutshevan. In 1926, Shalom Schwarzbard executes the Ukrainian anti-Semite, Petlioura, in Paris. In 1936, the young Frankfurter kills a Nazi agitator in Switzerland. In 1938, Herschl Grynspan shoots the diplomat von Rath at the German embassy in Paris.

A prototype for collective self-defense emerges in the fight against pogroms. Two possibilities become delineated. If the pogromists are soldiers or paramilitary groups, as in the Ukraine in 1920, Jewish defense tries to organize itself, but the balance of forces is highly unfavorable. Conversely, if it is the populace of a town or locality that attacks the Jews living there, an organized resistance is more feasible. The Russo-Polish case at the turn of the century, and cases in numerous other communities all over demonstrate this. Of course, even when the assailants are repulsed, the balance-sheet for the confrontation is always asymmetrical. There are losses on both sides—but if houses are burned, they are Jewish houses, if women are raped, they are Jewish women, and if children are killed, they, too, are Jewish children. A pogrom held in check is still a pogrom, whatever the value and effectiveness of the defense may be.

The capacity that the Jews have to turn back the adversary depends on several factors. First, on their spotting the early signs of trouble. If an aggression is preceded by unrest, rumors, and hostile gatherings, then there is time to warn Jewish youth to mobilize themselves. Secondly, on the degree of previous preparation by the Jewish population. The Jewish communities of Russia, where both Bundists and Zionists are numerous, are more inclined to fight than communities in which traditionalist elements predominate. A third factor: the layout and the population density of the Jewish community attacked. In July 1931, the pogromists of Salonica charge towards the principal Jewish quarter but are repelled by the Jewish defense. Their second attack is directed against a marginal quarter that is less well protected, the Campbell, where they have an open field before them.[6] Finally, the attitude of the police is decisive. At Rabat, Morocco, in May 1933, word gets around that a Jew has stabbed an Arab in self-defense. A riot breaks out, but the police quickly intervene and protect the Jewish quarter.[7] In numerous cases, the authorities wait several hours or days before intervening.

The riposte to the pogromists rests for a large part upon improvisation. In the period between the two wars, the problem takes a new form. The anti-Semite finds a new milieu in militia-like, mass political movements, which forces the Jewish world to equip itself with combat groups structured for ongoing action. This self-defense is not the resistance movement of the years of war and extermination, and it is not the desperate and heroic insurrection of the ghettos and deportation camps. When it takes up its position in the twenties and thirties, it is with the express mission of assuring Jews of complete security in the countries where they live. It is preventative. In the three examples that we will confine ourselves to—France and Algeria, Poland, and Germany—it does the job well until 1940, 1939, and 1933, respectively.

★

"Whoever does violence or injury to a Jew, because he is a Jew, should know that one day violence and injury will be done to him," the OJD declares in October 1980.[8] "Whoever attacks us will find us ready to answer, and by all means," we read in the journal of the LICA in May 1936.[9]

The Jews of Algeria began experimenting with street combat against anti-Semites at the close of the nineteenth century. Their self-defense reconstitutes itself in the thirties, particularly after the pogrom of Constantina in August 1934. At the source of the massacre was an inebriated Jewish soldier who tried to enter a mosque. The Muslim crowd, encouraged by anti-Jewish French, went on a rampage through the Jewish quarters. Official statistics listed 25 dead, of whom 22 were Jews, women and children among them. Two Jewish families were slaughtered. Non-official sources intimated that the true number of victims was considerably higher. Jewish shops and houses were torched. Multiple confrontations took place between Jewish defenders and their assailants. "Jewish blood has been spilled in France!" *Le Droit de Vivre* headlined, describing the events of "Constantina the red."[10]

During the electoral campaign of April 1936, the anti-Semite Coston, who is a candidate in Alger, decorates the balcony of his headquarters with a large anti-Jewish banderole. A team of Jewish youths forces its way onto the grounds to tear down the banner. A guard fires at them. Ben Kalifa is killed. 20,000 Algerian Jews transform his burial into an enormous demonstration.[11] In May, exchanges of fire in Algers between youths of the LICA and the Camelots du Roy are reported.[12] In June, Zaoui, a Jew from Oran, is assassinated by members of a fascist group. Some 30,000 people attend his funeral cortege.[13] On the whole, the Jewish self-defense of Algeria, like that of the Mother country, is organized by the LICA, which under the guidance of Bernard Lecache takes powerful root in North Africa.

All through the thirties, until the adoption of anti-Jewish measures by the Vichy government and the rescindment of French nationality from the Jews of Algeria, the country witnesses sporadic encounters between Jews and fascists.

In France proper, the militants of the LICA fight their first battles in February 1931 against the Camelots du Roy, who are demonstrating against a theater production on the Dreyfus Affair. The defense group, Lecache writes, "has made seditious persons who would seek to revive anti-Semitism in Paris and in France listen to reason."[14] The doctrine of self-defense is established during a hearing of the central committee of the organization that same year.[15] Battles occasionally erupt over the years: an attack against vendors of *Le Droit de Vivre* at the end of 1933 is successfully countered. "The rejoinder was not slow to arrive. The young bludgeoners soon fled the confrontation, leaving six of their friends behind, lying beaten and demoralized."[16] The scuffles continue in 1934.[17] In September 1935, 200 members of a fascist group called "French Solidarity" launch a raid against the Jewish quarter of the fourth Ward of Paris, but are stopped at rue Vieille-du-Temple by the LICA.[18] In 1936 further attacks are attempted and repulsed in the same manner. In December, Pierre Cot pays homage to the defense teams of the LICA "who, by their defensive but decisive action, have arrested the spread of anti-Semitism in France."[19]

An issue of *Le Droit de Vivre* features photographs of two squads of its defense group above the caption "Those who defend you."[20] The paper often gushes with exaltation. "We must concentrate our courage and our devotion around our self-defense, so that we may avoid the bitterness of defeat and the shame of not having resisted. On guard, stand up, be ready! Comrades, to us!" we read in the LICA news in 1934.[21] Or, using a less emphatic style: "Ever ready, and despite its critics, the self-defense of the LICA improves, its discipline increases. And it is for that reason, and only for that reason, that anti-Semitism in France does not increase." The same issue of the journal contains general instructions for the Defense Groups: "Group A: remain in a state of 'alert' throughout the month . . . Groups B and C: only valid are those orders issuing from the Executive . . . no telephone communication is permitted. Weekly reunions at the usual times and places."[22]

The congratulations cease as of late Autumn, 1938. Already, at the end of April, a meeting of the LICA was attacked in Nice in a joint maneuver by the members of the PPF (French Popular Party of Doriot) and the Action Française. There were wounded on both sides, but the advantage was with the assailants, who were far more numerous.[23] The situation rapidly deteriorates during the Munich crisis and the mobilization of troops that it entails. A relatively grave anti-Semitic crisis suddenly threatens the Jews of France.

It manifests in three arenas. The first one is political. The Jews are accused of outright bellicosity in their desire for vengeance against Germany. This is utilized in a more or less discreet fashion by pacifists within each party of the political spectrum, with the exception of the Communists, who are all opposed to Munich. The second arena is popular. The Jews are reproached for being "shirkers," for wanting war but not wanting to take part. It's a classical insult. The third is addressed to the true extremists and anti-Jewish hysterics, and is frequently heard in the streets. The Jews are accused of working for Germany and of engaging in espionage for the Nazis.

In Strasburg, Jewish stores are pillaged, and passersby are bludgeoned by groups of fascists.[24] At Saint-Quentin, "women were molested by anti-Semites," writes *Le Droit de Vivre*. At Lille, a Jew attacked by an anti-Semite in a restaurant fires at his aggressor to defend himself.[25] At Nancy, on September 26th, a gang accuses the merchant Silberstein of having in the cellar of his store a direct hotline to Hitler. The store is demolished.[26] In Paris, numerous brawls break out; *Le Droit de Vivre* counts 20 in a period of 15 days. Often, the police arrest the Jews who are defending themselves. "And it is in such manner that Sam Rudetsky and his sons, our comrade Belili and still others were dragged to the police station in the Saint-Louis hospital district, where constables 9719 and 1431 distinguished themselves by their abusiveness and brutality: Get down on your knees, Yids. . . ." Another example: "Wednesday in Belleville, two Israelites were arrested, beaten unmercifully and indicted. Their names are Benhini and Glickstein. One is a French citizen and a native of Algeria, the other a Polish national. Both are accused of having cried out: Long live Hitler! Long live Germany!"[27]

"They are resorting to bombs," the journal of the LICA exclaims. An explosive device was tossed at Silberstein's store in Nancy.[28] Other bombs will explode in that city, one in an assembly of the LICA, and two at other Jewish sites, before the year is out.[29] In Metz, repeated attacks occur: shops are ravaged and people injured.[30] At Constantina, the extreme Right starts a boycott against the Jews.[31] The most serious incident occurs in Dijon, where an excited crowd of about 500 people goes on a rampage against the store of the Lerner family on October 1st.[32] Throughout the country, the tension continues until the end of the year. The events of autumn, 1938, are reminiscent of those of winter, 1898—the anti-Jewish demonstrations that accompanied the trial of Zola. Although they are negligible when measured against the German pogroms of November 1938, called the Night of Broken Glass, they enable us to better understand the behavior of the French towards the Jews of France a few years later.

A few hundred committed Jews were sufficient, before 1938, to contain fascist raids into the Jewish districts of the capital, but because of the sudden rise in the level of anti-Jewish violence, they are now totally swept aside. Anti-Semitism is already far too strong to be effectively contained by the LICA, whose defense groups, as courageous and organized as they are, nonetheless stand by, overwhelmed and powerless, as events unfold. They have reached their breaking point. Before, self-defense was still feasible. Now, the Jewish defensive front is helplessly driven back.

★

In 1982, Jean Daniel expounds on the fighting spirit of the Jews of France. "Anti-Semitic violence will no longer be written off as simple harassment, but will now lead to a veritable war."[33] In 1936, the leader of the Bund, Zygelboim, describes the Jewish working class of Poland: "With them it will be war, and never pogroms that go unpunished."[34]

The *Ordener-Grup* of the Bund is formed in independent Poland after the First World War.[35] Originally conceived to protect the activities of the party, it rapidly becomes one of the principal forces of self-defense for the Jewish community of the country. Composed of a permanent nucleus that is enlarged by reserves when need arises, it stations 2,000 militants in Warsaw for the protection of Jewish demonstrations, which are often attacked by fascists. The *Ordener-Grup* is made up of teams of ten fighters, armed with metal bars. The team leaders are generally equipped with firearms. When demonstrations are held, in addition to the units that directly accompany the marchers, the *Ordener-Grup* deploys a motorized force and a group of scouts. An information team is assigned to spy on the opposing camp and to determine its intentions.

In the daily fight against anti-Semitism, many different tactics are practiced: rapid intervention, when the aggression takes place in a precise area; ongoing presence, as a deterrent in places where Polish ruffians are accustomed to molesting Jews; demonstrations of force, to show support for Jewish students facing anti-Semitism in the universities; dispatch of reinforcements from one city to another, as needed. The *Ordener-Grup* also goes further and attacks directly. In retaliation for an attack on the Bund headquarters in 1937, it sacks the premises of an anti-Semitic organization, the Nara. A commando approaches the enemy house and cuts the electric and telephone wires. Quickly, the place is taken and destroyed, its defenders severely beaten.

The *Ordener-Grup* is often strengthened by militia from the Jewish trade unions. Most often it acts in partnership with the youth of the Bund, the *Tsukunft* (Future). In the early thirties this group established a paramilitary wing, the *Tsukunft-Shturem,* organized on the model of the defense organizations of Austrian Socialism. Ten militants form a group, commanded by a *"grupn-firer";* five or six such groups form a section. In their case too, the equipment is standard, and only group leaders have revolvers. As was customary in those days within formations of its kind, the members of the *Tsukunft-Shturem,* whose activities are divided between street marches and self-defense work, are bedizened in uniforms. Furthermore, the Bund is in close collaboration with the Polish socialists of the PPS. The two parties tightly coordinate their fight against fascism and anti-Semitism.

Jewish self-defense is not limited to the Bund. It also includes the Zionists, for ideological reasons obviously opposed to those of the Bund, since the Zionists see no future, in the long run, for the Jews in Poland, and promote departure for Eretz-Israel as a practical solution to the Jewish problem.[36] It also has a popular base, not organized into movements and parties, but always ready to act. It enjoys the greatest alignment of forces that a Jewish defense has ever known. In fact, the three million Jews who live in Poland form more than ten percent of the entire population of the country. In the large cities, the percentage of Jews rises to 30 or 40 percent. The feeling of strength this gives them explains the militant tone of speeches and editorials, like that of the Bund paper on March 18, 1936. "The Jewish worker will not allow himself to be butchered. He will confront his enemies, who threaten his life and honor, and who wish to transform him into a defenseless sheep whom anyone may attack, assassinate, or slaughter."[37]

In practice, although many anti-Semites are hit, wounded, or even killed, anti-Semitism never stops growing. Self-defense succeeds in securing a relative degree of protection for the Jewish districts of the large cities. It often stands up for Jewish students in the fight they wage against the founding of "ghetto benches," separate seating that their anti-Semitic fellow students wish to impose upon them. But it is powerless against the boycott of Jewish shops and the exclusion of Jews from many sectors of Polish economic life. Above all, it is futile, given the countless acts of endemic anti-Jewish violence that characterize the thirties and become more and more pronounced until 1938, easing off slightly at the start of 1939. The "permanent pogrom" is actually a multitude of incidents, some provoked by the extreme Right and some spontaneous. For the year 1936, and just for the region of Byalistock, a report by the Prime Minister before the Polish Parliament offers an account of 348 attacks against the Jews, including 20 were pogroms, 99 beatings, and 161 cases of smashed window fronts.[38] The sociologist Yakov Lestshinsky tries to evaluate the number of Jews harmed by these anti-Semitic aggressions. He estimates at several thousand the figure for those injured between May 1935 and August 1936. Of course, he specifies, these figures are infinitely small compared to the total of three million Polish Jews who led their lives, for the most part, without ever being personally affected by the phenomenon.[39] As for the occasional pogroms, they hardly compare with those of the turn of the century, and especially not with the Ukrainian massacres of 1919 and 1920. The number of victims is very limited. But they contribute to the general climate of insecurity that hangs over the Jewish community.

★

"If it is going to be a fight between the Nazis and the Jews alone, we will have to conduct it with equanimity and resolution," says Alain Geismar after Copernic, not without first introducing himself:

Frenchman and Jew.[40] "Arise, Jewish soldiers of the front, rejoin us in the fight for our honor and our rights as Germans and as Jews!" the inaugural address of the *Reichsbund jüdischer Frontsoldaten (RjF)* proclaims in January 1919.[41]

In Germany, self-defense springs up in the immediate aftermath of the War, when Jewish soldiers and officers of the old Imperial army take up, as their new principal task, the struggle against anti-Semitic uprisings, which are intensifying as a result of political troubles and economic uncertainty. In 1920, an initial coordination is established between the RjF and diverse Jewish youth and student organizations. The RjF implements a defense division, the *Abwehrleitung,* which passes the test of fire with success. In early November, 1923, at the moment when Hitler makes his piteous attempt at a *coup d'etat* in Munich, violent riots break out in Berlin. The rioters descend upon a district where many Jewish immigrants from central Europe live. The situation worsens under the adverse influence of nationalistic elements. Stores are plundered, and Jews beaten. The Jewish veterans, organized into groups of twenty-five and armed with clubs and revolvers, converge on the endangered area, take up the fight and clean the place out. An anti-Semite is killed.

The police seize a cache of clubs, firearms and munitions and arrest five Jewish defenders. Among them are Löwenstein, the founder of the RjF, and Toller, the *Abwehrleitung* commander. They are all tried and acquitted in May 1924. The tribunal decides that their actions were in legitimate self-defense.[42]

In Berlin, the *Abwehrleitung* is organized into districts *(Bezirk),* and those further subdivided into several guard centers *(Wachlokal).* The groups exist where the divisions of the RjF are located, that is, in most of the Jewish communities of the country. They are entrusted with the defense of Jewish synagogues, sites and meetings. At times reinforced with squads brought in from neighboring towns, they interfere with nationalistic and anti-Semitic meetings. The *Abwehrleitung* of Silesia consists of: 620 men in Breslau, 15 in Waldenburg, over 40 in Gorlitz, and 85 in Gleiwitz. In Munich, police reports estimate a Jewish force of 150 men.[43] "During this period," Ruth Pierson writes, "the numbers of the *Reichsbund jüdischer Frontsoldaten* could compare favorably with those of any single anti-Semitic freebooter or paramilitary group."[44]

At the end of 1926, Goebbels comes to Berlin, assigned by Hitler to reorganize the Nazi party, which is in its sorriest state in the capital. It consists in toto of about 1000 adherents, of whom several hundred are less than fully committed. One of the first decisions the young propagandist makes is to exclude them. In the elections of December 1924, 1.6 percent of the electoral ballots cast in the largest city in the country went to the Nazis, against 19.1 percent that went to the Communists and 32.5 percent to the Socialists. In an effort to assert himself, Goebbels provokes the Communists with a small but vociferous march and a meeting. The squabble gets rough, the police intervene, the Berlin press talks at length about the incident, and so the result is attained. Two thousand six hundred new adherents enter the Nazi party and a few hundred are ready to enlist in the SA. The fight for Berlin *(Kampf um Berlin),* whose sinister saga Goebbels will later recount, has just begun.[45]

In a bind, the Nazis attack the Jews. At this early stage their efforts are not all that serious, to be sure, but nevertheless people chosen at random are assailed by young Hitlerians in the streets of Berlin. The scenario is oft repeated. A gang marches down a street or springs out by surprise somewhere. It pounces on the first "Jewish-looking" passerby it runs across, hurriedly beats him up, leaving him bloodied on the ground, and then runs off before the police arrive.[46] For the 170,000 Jews of the city, these few cases are hardly noticeable. The wave of violence, slight as it is, has no influence at all upon the Jewish physicians and lawyers, officials and journalists, students and teachers, and artisans and merchants who are immersed in their usual routines. The Jewish organizations nevertheless dramatize each event and give each aggression intensive press coverage. Two meetings are convened by the Reichsbund jüdischer Frontsoldaten on April 7, 1927. In one of the gatherings, 1600 participants are counted, and in the other, 1000, for a total of 2600.[47]

The similarity of figures is fortuitous, but worthy of some reflection. With 2600 people, the Jewish organizations are still far from having realized their maximum potential for militant mobilization, but this potential is limited. With 2600 new adherents, the Nazis still occupy the weakest position on the chessboard of Berlin politics, but the large numerical jump they make in the space of a few months of activism bears triple witness: they possess a considerable potential for growth, they are aware of it, and they know how to act so as to make the most effective use of it. The balance of 1927 (2600 Jews assembled in Berlin as opposed to 2600 new adherents to the NSDAP) is therefore a misleading equilibrium that conceals, for a while, the more fundamental disproportion. The Jews form four percent of the population of Berlin. The non-Jews, to whom the Hitlerians address themselves without initial success, but later with increasing reward, constitute the remaining 96 percent. For the whole of Germany, the ratio is even more flagrant. One Jew for every one hundred non-Jews.

For now, *Der Schild* can take a hard stance towards a hostile journal that has sarcastically proposed recreating a ghetto in order to facilitate the task of the police who are to protect the Jews. The Jewish paper reminds them of the precedent set in November 1923 and concludes with a warning. "We at the RjF have, as one might have noticed, very simple methods for successfully dealing with the 'heroic' acts of the National-Socialists. . . ."[48]

A new Jewish defense organization comes into being at that time: the *Jüdischer Abwehr Dienst,* known under the initials JAD, (which is translated into English as the Jewish Defense Service, not to be confused with Jewish Defense Organization, the OJD, created a little over 50 years later in Paris). The *Jüdischer Abwehr Dienst* is composed of Jewish veterans from the Great War, to whom are added members of the Bar Kochba and Maccabee sporting groups, and other youths not belonging to any particular group. Its recruitment policy is very selective and has a self-imposed limit, which for Berlin is only a few hundred members. The training includes, within the framework of a thorough paramilitary education, practice in combat sports and preparation for street warfare. The Jewish sporting associations are also involved and serve to fortify the system, for which the *jiu-jitsu* group of the RjF acts as an official cover. The team is well known in the country, since it often comes out on top in intra-German competitions. The territorial structure of the JAD is identical to that of the *Abwehrleitung* of the early 1920's.

But calm is quickly restored. In May 1927 the Nazis are outlawed in Berlin, and in the country at large very few physical attacks against Jews are recorded in 1928 and 1929. The Republican police are fully able to maintain order and the Jewish self-defense infrastructure has little reason to intervene. In October 1928, after several new attacks against Jews in a few different cities, Löwenstein reiterates his warning. "A brief reminder," he writes: in Autumn 1923, the RjF knew how to hold the anti-Jewish unrest in check.[49]

But everything changes in 1930. The Nazis collect 6,410,000 votes in the September poll. The Nazi electorate, which roughly speaking makes up the base for recruitment into the SA, constitutes more than ten times the Jewish population as a whole. Hitler, still a minority figure but no longer marginal, now has at his disposal an army of several tens of thousands of disciplined and unscrupulous men, whose ranks never cease to grow. The Jewish self-defense increases its ranks by adding many young Jews who are sobered by the

85

progress of the enemy, but its effort scarcely measures up. It is already on the verge of being wiped out. In other words, a return to the conditions of November 1923 is from then on out of the question.

In a Germany that the enormous push of the Nazis will drive to the brink of civil war, the JAD and other Jewish groups can do little but dig their way into a strictly defensive position. In coordination with the police, they protect Jewish synagogues and property and assume responsibility for security at Jewish meetings and assemblies. The information service (*Nachrichtendienst*) set up by the veterans' association keeps an eye out for any coming aggressions, but the massive attack on the *Fasanenstrasse* in September 1931 takes both the Jewish self-defense and the police force by surprise. After the aggression the Reichsbund jüdischer Frontsoldaten launches a public appeal to the Jews of Germany. The young, in particular, are invited to enlist in "the sporting organizations" so as to be able, in case of physical attack, to "give the assailant the appropriate response."[50]

At heart, the Jewish organizations are fully aware of their extreme numerical inferiority. The Reichsbanner, the mass paramilitary organization of the Socialist party, is the only national force, with the exception of the communist militia, that is capable of facing up to the Nazis. Many individual Jews belong to it at every echelon of its hierarchy and in every one of its divisions. On the whole, the Jewish self-defense effort cooperates with the general antifascist force, while retaining its independence with regard to recruitment and operation in its own domain, which is the protection of the Jewish community. In August 1932, after the Nazi electoral victory of July 31, the Liberal camp fears a Nazi putsch. The RjF and the other Jewish defense groups ready themselves by the side of the Reichsbanner to ward off the danger. But Hitler stays within legal bounds and the expected confrontation never develops.

On January 26, 1933, the *C.V. Zeitung* reports on a case of individual self-defense. In a small town near Cologne, a Jewish family, the Metzgers, were prey to an ongoing harassment campaign on the part of local Nazis. One night, the anti-Semites attacked their home. The Metzger son overpowered and beat the chief assailant. He was acquitted by the tribunal, which recognized that he acted in legitimate self-defense.[51] After January 30th, the date of Hitler's accession to the Chancellory of the Reich, the Jewish self-defense teams suffer the same fate as all anti-Nazi combat units. Many of its members nonetheless succeed in leaving Germany and making their way to Palestine, where they later contribute to the edification and defense of the future Jewish State.

In 1924, *Der Schild*, the journal of the Reichsbund jüdischer Frontsoldaten, published a drawing that illustrated their fight. An anti-Semite serpent marked with a swastika spits out its venom, but a helmeted Jewish soldier, armed with a heavy sword, is poised to slice off its head. The two figures are of the same stature.[52] In 1933, it seems that the proportions have changed and that the serpent has grown much larger.

★

"We have decided not to remain passive . . . eye for eye, tooth for tooth, we will not hesitate to apply the law of retaliation if a single one of ours is touched," Jean Pierre Bloch, president of the LICRA, declares in 1980 during a meeting in Marseille.[53] Before 15,000 participants at an anti-Hitlerian rally in Paris in 1933, Bernard Lecache reminds his listeners of the Nazis' threats against Einstein: " . . . if they ever dare to touch Albert Einstein, we have already selected the hostages to be taken in Paris *(very animated applause).* . . ."[54]

On the topic of anti-Semitism, such oratorical excesses are able to dodge the hard realities, but not to transform them.

Jews in every country seek only to live in peace. The initiative in a confrontation thus belongs entirely to the opposing side. This is not an ethnic conflict between two peoples coveting the same territory, nor is it a civil war between two parts of the same nation. The targeted group is only a minority of men, women and children who form only a minute fraction of the total population. It is divided up within the country and blended in with the non-Jewish majority, even if it often aggregates in certain cities and districts. The Jewish population is civil, small, and dispersed—the target is both weak and scattered.

Does Jewish self-defense try to be protective? It can guard Jewish environs, patrol areas with a highly dense Jewish population, and control the streets. Even so, its protection is limited since it cannot cope with the problems posed by bombs and mass attacks. In addition, Jews who are isolated—schoolchildren, shopkeepers, and sales clerks—remain on the outside of the protected domain. Attacks are unpredictable and can strike anyone, anytime, and anywhere. Their timing, their form and their intensity remain entirely at the discretion of the attackers.

Does Jewish self-defense then try to fight? When informed early enough, Jewish defense forces show up at the scene of the hostilities. Sometimes they repel the assailants, inflicting losses upon them. Everything depends, at that point, on the attitude of the police and other authorities. If they are supportive, they intervene quickly (as in

Weimar Germany and present-day France). If not, the tussle is prolonged and numerical superiority becomes the decisive factor. In cases of desecrations, or detonation of explosives, Jewish self-defense obviously cannot arrive until after the damage is done, and then only to assess the damage and issue a stern warning.

Does Jewish self-defense want to retaliate, once the violence is done? Reprisals are really unthinkable when popular anti-Semitism or terrorist activity by unknown parties is to blame. The asymmetry is obvious. The anti-Semites attack a civilian population, but the Jewish defenders can hardly counterattack the non-Jewish population. It would be absurd, since the hatred only flows in one direction, and suicidal, for reasons that are evident. In the case of an act that is "signed" or where the guilty parties belong to a specific organization, a reply is at least theoretically possible. But in practice, this is not as evident. The anti-Semites, even if a minority, know how to protect themselves. And so, attacking a Nazi establishment in response to the aggression perpetrated against the synagogue on Fasanenstrasse is just out of the question. The Communist combat regiments or the units of the Socialist Reichsbanner, although incomparably stronger than the Jewish self-defense force in Germany, would not themselves risk it. But in any case, if the Jewish reprisals are followed by counter-reprisals by the anti-Semites, these latter will once again direct themselves at "civilian" targets and toward the unarmed Jewish population at large.

The layout of the terrain is unfavorable. The rules of the game are unjust. The real disproportion clearly lies in the number of combatants that the Jews on the one side, and anti-Semites on the other are able to recruit. The former group represents only a tiny segment of the population of the country. Even allowing for the optimum case in which all Jews who are of fighting age receive the proper training, the number of Jewish combatants would quickly reach its peak, as dictated by the total number of Jews living in the country. The anti-Semites have a much larger recruitment base. At the outset they are in the extreme minority. If the Jews are organized, the two camps are of comparable stature, and the blows are both given and received. The Jewish defense functions only under ideal conditions: when it has the assistance of the police and the judicial system, and the support of the vast majority of the public. At those times, a climate of euphoria settles over the Jewish militants as they savor their early successes: such and such anti-Semite beaten, such and such fascist meeting sabotaged. This time, they say, we are fighting. But the balance is unstable. When anti-Jewish activism, whether organized or popular, gains a little more ground, the fragile balance is lost. Then, for each Jew who is mobilized, there are suddenly two, three, five and then ten non-Jews who have become hostile. It isn't Auschwitz, and it isn't the Night of Broken Glass, but it is already the breaking point.

The "war" is thus lost before it is begun. Is it therefore necessary to take to the offensive and crush the monster in its egg? This conclusion seems logical enough, but to arrive at it one must already have admitted that anti-Semitism, although insignificant at a given moment, could quickly become threatening at another. The profusion of systems of self-reassurance that accompanied the first demonstrations of renewed anti-Semitism in France several years ago showed that this vision of things is far from universally accepted. What is small, people think, will remain small.

But even when this psychological obstacle is overcome, the problem remains. Dynamiting some place or cudgeling some ringleader is not enough to liquidate an organization. Liquidating an organization is not enough to destroy the inspiration that brings it to life. Beating up on the anti-Semites is certainly satisfying, for they deserve it, but does not annihilate anti-Semitism. One can frighten off one or several individuals, but one doesn't thereby frighten away a social phenomenon. And what's more, the road from speech to action is long and not easily traversed. "Antisemites, tremble!" It has been several years now since this bold slogan first made its appearance on the walls of Paris. It is not known whether the anti-Semites in question have done much trembling.

"So long as we are there, racism will not arise," Bernard Lecache writes in 1936.[55] "It is usually enough for us to be there, for our presence and determination to be noted, for there to be no further act of violence whatsoever," the militants of the Federation of French Jews think in March 1982. Their organization was born of the explosion on rue Copernic and the emotion that it elicited. It attracts "French Jews desirous of retaining their Judaism who are at the same time determined to remain French citizens," an article in the *Tribune Juive* explains. Its goal? "To endow the Jewish community in France with the forces it needs to secure its defense, and to show the anti-Semites on all sides that the French Jews are strong enough." Its methods? "Today it has the use of impressive facilities, a headquarters which resembles a fortified bunker, with television cameras scanning the entrance, reinforced screen doors and chambers in which visitors are scrutinized. . . . The training halls, underground, are equipped with air conditioning. . . ."[56] The Federation of French

Jews is ready for anything, but it has not completely learned the lessons of History.

Chapter Seven

Before and Now

"The age of the cowering Jew is definitely over," the OJD pronounces during a press conference in October 1980.[1] "And so ended the politics of resignation," *Le Droit de Vivre* explains in 1933.[2] The rhetoric of combat is the expression of an ambitious project of global scope and import: the protection of the Jews of every country against any assault on their rights as citizens, their human dignity, or their persons. Thematically speaking, it makes use of a rich display of words and images, the masterpiece of which is the description of the "earlier Jew".

"The Jews of 1980 no longer have the mentality of those of 1940," Jean Pierre Bloch, president of LICRA, announces.[3] His predecessor, Bernard Lecache, used to say the same thing in 1935. "The centuries upon centuries of humiliation, the ongoing sense of resignation, the hunching shoulders, the useless fists—that was the Jew of the past. Today, in May 1935, we are without fear, without resignation, without concessions."[4]

"For History is no longer what it once was, and the Jew of today is not the one of yesterday: he is no longer resigned to submission and suffering; his persecutors would do well to take note of this," André Frossard asserts in October 1980.[5] This was just as true in January 1933 when Charles-Auguste Bontemps felt it necessary to cool the tempers of LICA militants who were proclaiming "that for every Jew who is killed it will be necessary to execute four anti-Semites."[6]

Numerous stories circulate in 1980 to illustrate the will to fight that today vivifies the Jews of France. Here is one reported from rue des Rosiers by *Le Monde.* "They speak of an anti-Semite, during the Occupation, who rolled the hat of a passing Jew into the gutter. The latter waited until the other went off and, in a dignified manner, picked up his bowler, whispering to his young son: 'There is no need to respond, for they will soon see that we are more intelligent than they are! Today, it would be a punch in the jaw,' Samy the furrier comments."[7]

Samy is undoubtedly too young to be familiar with a short paragraph—one among many—that appeared in *Le Droit de Vivre* in 1933. "Again, just recently, on the corner of faubourg Montmartre and rue Geoffrey-Marie, a driver who was spotted sporting a fancy swastika on his windshield was dragged from his car and beaten unmercifully. He sought the protection of three policemen, who had a hard time putting a stop to the beating. . . ."[8]

Often, it is in the rhetorical devices themselves, and not just their subject matter, that the past is repeated. In 1980, Jean-Pierre Pierre Bloch, the deputy of Paris, employs a style of false astonishment to convey the dumb amazement of the anti-Semites. "How could it be? The Jews seem to be organizing themselves and are no longer willing to be the victims of Hitler's admirers. They refuse to allow themselves to be persecuted and abused, or to see their schools and synagogues machine-gunned and burned. Their audacity knows no bounds any more." He continues trenchantly. "What ever happened to those good old Jews of yesteryear? Those good fellows, the customers of the pogroms, who used to shakily accept the blows and even death . . . what a shame! The nice Jews so dear to the anti-Semites don't exist any more. . . ." And he concludes: "As for us, we know how to defend ourselves."[9]

In April 1938, Bernard Lecache resorts to the same tone, both mocking and cutting. "How could it be? These traditional victims are now resisting! But in that case, is everything that has been said and written about the pogroms, about the 'wandering Jews,' about the 'wretched race,' about those strange characters, starving and downtrodden, who have made their way across human civilization, getting their behinds kicked and saying thanks, is it now no longer true?" He then proclaims, before sending off a warning to "anti-Semites of every breed": "I don't take myself for a meek sheep, nor do any of my friends either. Between the sheep and us, there is this simple difference: we do not want to take the road to the slaughter-house."[10]

The diatribes of 1938 and 1980 were drafted under analogous circumstances, in the wake of brawls between young Jews and anti-Semites. In 1938, the fascist Jean-Charles Legrand receives a fist in the jaw. In 1980, the bodyguards of the neo-Nazi Friedriksen are roughed up by members of the OJD. "Hitler is not entirely dead, clearly. But something is quite different now," *L'Arche* notes, giving an account of the most recent confrontation (that of 1980) but ignoring the earlier one (of 1938): that is how it can affirm that something has truly changed.[11]

The stereotype of the fearful and submissive Jew of the thirties is the foil against which the image of the modern, confident French Jew of the eighties is valorized. Half a century ago, it was the stereotypical image of the fearful and submissive Jew of the Middle Ages that used to serve as the counterpoint to the image of the modern, different and confident Jew of the twentieth century. The rhetoric of combat sets its own position off from that of the "earlier Jew" as a polemical device intended to valorize the Jew of today and to reject any possible comparison between the past and the present.

★

The end to Jewish tribulations is proven in several different ways. The main one is to attribute all responsibility for anti-Jewish massacres to Torquemada or Hitler, and to then establish once and for all that they are quite dead and so cannot attack again. Alternatively, anti-Semitism is linked to the plague of the fourteenth century or the economic crisis of 1929, and since the epidemic is long gone and the crisis has been surmounted, the Jews have nothing more to fear. A second form of argumentation is far more subtle than the first. "They have changed!" They, the non-Jews, have finally understood the deleterious nature of anti-Jewish hatred and will never allow it to take hold of them again. For the LICA in the thirties, the date of this turnabout is 1789. For the French Jews of 1980, the date is 1945.

But it is insufficient to simply affirm that others have changed. It is also important to claim that Jews themselves are no longer the same. Affirming that this time they are ready to fight solves two problems at once: that of effectiveness and that of self-concern. From now on, the fate of the Jews depends upon the Jews themselves, and is no longer strictly tied to the evolution of the non-Jewish majority's mood, or to the possible "transformations" of political regimes. The fate of the Jews will be a direct result of the manner in which they react. And so, if they react with vigor, anti-Semitism will no longer take hold.

But to make this threat (towards the anti-Semites) plausible, and this appeal (within the ranks of the Jews) entirely convincing, the failures of the past must be accounted for. There was a time— centuries ago, for the Jews of the thirties, decades ago for the Jews of

1980—when the Jews were heavily persecuted . . . and there is only one explanation that makes the correct link between the sad memory of the past and the combative present. Here is that explanation: Before, the Jews were submissive, they didn't fight.

"The new generations of Jews are not at all satisfied with soothing speeches, anesthetizing attitudes or hollow promises. They no longer accept being the appointed victims, nor do they submit passively to attacks on their persons or on their identity," we read after Copernic in the editorials of the *Bulletin de l'ATJ*.[12] In contradistinction to the new generations so described, the old ones are drawn out of the mists of historical obscurity in strange caricatures.

The "earlier Jews" are sometimes taken for imbeciles who didn't see or understand anything at all. They are also taken for cowards, who perceived the danger, but stayed home and hid in the cellar, quaking with fear. "Whatever happens, we will not fall into the rut of feeling inferior, submissive, and fearful, which was the plight of previous generations," Guy de Rothschild boldly promises after Copernic.[13]

★

The "earlier Jews" are not a historical category but an operational concept, a rhetorical figure used to prove to what degree the Jews have now changed.

In the thirties, belittling the Jew of the past feeds two specific currents of thought. Emancipation, an ideological project for resolving the Jewish question, compares the modern, integrated Jew to the old Jew, shut up within his ghetto. The theme dates back to the nineteenth century but undergoes a revival in the thirties, with the onset of new perils. The anti-religious campaigns of the Bund, the anti-Zionist wing of Jewish socialism, associate the image of the "earlier Jew" with that of the Orthodox Jew, withering away inside his narrow universe. The Jew of the future, who is secular and rational, is open to the non-Jewish world, while retaining his Jewish heritage. He is no longer afraid of pogroms since he knows how to fight, and in addition, has at his disposal the unshakable support of the international proletariat.

But two other currents resist the flow of that channel of thought. Traditional Judaism, without repudiating the benefits of the Emancipation, valorize the age of the ghetto when the Jews were bent upon safeguarding their faith and their identity. Zionism, also, violently criticizes emancipated Judaism, which liquidates the Jewish nation and parcels it out into as many fractions as there are dispersed

Jewish communities, each one supposedly belonging to the country in which it resides. As a counterpoint, it recalls who the "earlier Jews" were in two preceding stages of Jewish history. It invokes the memory of the ancient Jewish people, living free and sovereign on their own land. It recalls the Jew of the ghetto, harassed and beaten, but fortified by courageous loyalty to his own ideals, and by the certitude that the day would come when the Jewish people will return to their homeland.

The more the danger rises, the more the "earlier Jew" becomes a source of inspiration and a reference point. "It is worth fighting for the people whose ancestors went to the stake for their Hear O Israel," a Jewish public figure declares in Berlin in 1933.[14] "My Israelite brothers, you are made of the same metal as your ancestors," Jacob Kaplan says in 1941 to exhort the Jews of France to be courageous.[15] As viewed in Germany in 1933 or in France in 1941, the "earlier Jews" are great figures once again.

★

In France today, the "earlier Jews" are those of before the Hitlerian genocide, and no longer those of before the Emancipation. How are they regarded?

Some have a distorted image of them as a result of vulgar ignorance of facts. An oversimplified Jewish past created of kind sentiments and old folk customs is invented for Poland and the East, and one of assimilation and loss of identity is invented for Western Europe. Over there (in the East), the Jews were all craftsmen and spent all their time singing and searching out husbands for their daughters. Here, in the West, they were all bankers and though of nothing but climbing the social ladder. The former lived fearfully, withdrawn into themselves on the outskirts of the "city." The latter, consumed by their desire to be integrated, forgot their concerns as Jews. When, here or there, the signs of danger appeared, the Jews were either simply unable to detect them, or else pulled their shutters closed in fear and panic.

Others have a distorted image of the Jews of the past that is more elaborate and not just a result of ignorance. The myth of the "earlier Jew" is born from a curious dislocation of historical facts. They don't deny that there were powerful mass movements, a multitude of ideological strands, or virulent polemics within the Jewish communities before the war. They are familiar with the major Jewish journals that circulated through all the countries of Europe and with the extraordinary Jewish literary achievements that were published in Hebrew, Yiddish, and many other languages. They ignore neither the Jewish soldiers of the First World War, nor the Jewish revolutionaries and intellectuals, nor the Zionist pioneers. In all things, they perceive the Jewish world as it truly was—militant, activist, and highly politicized. A modern world.

In all things, that is, save for one. As soon as the question of the attitude of the Jews towards the menace that loomed ever larger in the thirties (and which obviously constituted the principal topic of their collective concern, from Salonica to Anvers and from Riga to Tunis) arises, suddenly there is a black hole. Everything is jumbled and falls apart. The Jewish political parties dissolve, their hundreds of thousands of adherents disappear, the journals close down, the ideologies dwindle, and the youth movements leave the keys under the doormat.

The photos of the long columns that marched to their deaths do not accord with those of the great Jewish demonstrations of Warsaw in the thirties. We think only of the former and ignore the latter. If the Jews were killed, it must be because they didn't protest. It is impossible for them to have acted in the thirties and yet be beaten, humiliated, tortured, raped and burned in the forties. The two series of photos belong to two different universes, which one refuses to recognize as having been temporally successive. The Jews are assumed to have died well before ever having been shot.

The presumption of Jewish passivity before 1939 has an impact on how the Hitlerian genocide is viewed today. The myth suggests, in effect, an indirect responsibility on the part of the victims for the troubles that befell them. They saw nothing, did nothing? They cannot blame their misfortunes, then on anything but their own inactivity. This theme has two resonances. One with the non-Jews, who relieve themselves of the weight of the crime. The Jews did not help themselves, so they can hardly reproach others for remaining indifferent. The other resonance is within and among the Jewish people. Sparks of irritation, and even anger result when today's Jews hear that the incomprehensible Jews of the past lacked the presence of mind, while there was still time, to organize protest meetings against anti-Semitism.

Most certainly, innumerable studies have definitively portrayed the true image of the Jew *during* the War. Those studies depict the insurrections in the ghettos and camps, they describe the massive participation of Jews in resistance movements all over German-occupied Europe, and they enumerate the Jewish troops in both the Soviet and allied armies. The Jewish people suffered more than any other people. They also fought more than any other people.

But there is silence, conversely, concerning the years *preceding* the War. Homage is paid to the Jews of Warsaw who threw incendiary bombs at the Nazis in 1943. One hardly hears about their protests against Nazism in 1933. The courage of the Baum group of German Jews in 1942 is praised. But the militant youth of the Jüdischer Abwehr Dienst in 1927 are ignored. One knows of the French Jews who fought in the Resistance, but one hardly takes notice of them gathered at the Mutualité a few years earlier.

But the born-again rhetoric of combat does not have an easy task. During the thirties, the "earlier Jew" was lost in Medieval darkness and in the imprecision of the centuries. Today, the "before" in question is much too recent. The sources and the eyewitnesses abound. Most important of all, the major currents of thought that animate the Jews of France today were already present in the thirties. Emancipation, in all its permutations, dates back to the early nineteenth century. The Jewish National movement and the Jewish workers' movement, in all their different shapes and interweavings and with all their various antagonisms, attained maturity in the first third of the twentieth century. Sympathies for the construction of a homeland became universal in the Jewish world after the Balfour declaration of 1917. Zionism (in the sense of Jewish nationalism or support for Jewish Palestine) very quickly became the dominant force in countless Jewish communities.

Historical proximity explains many things. There is no new method for combatting anti-Semitism that was not already heavily practiced before the War. There is no new argument that has not already been repeated over and over with full conviction. There is no article and no speech whose double was not written or spoken a half-century ago. The Jews of 1980 are similar to those of 1930, especially in their sincere belief that they are profoundly different from "earlier Jews."

The Jews of the Middle Ages and the Jews of 1930 had parallel situations: dispersion among the nations and minority status within them. The resemblance between the Jews of 1930 and the Jews of 1980 is augmented by a perfect analogy between the social codes governing their relationships with non-Jews. The Jews of France do not wear the yellow star these days, but neither did they wear it before the War. The Jews of France are integrated into French society, but they were just as integrated in the thirties. There are Jewish Ministers in government, but there were then, too.

There is also a striking resemblance between the ideological and organizational structures of the Jewish communities then and now. Emancipation, Jewish Nationalism, Zionism, Socialism and religion are conjoined or juxtaposed within them in identical ways. The proportion and relative weight of each of these tendencies have changed. So have their modes of expression. There have also been certain demographic and sociological shifts. But the two Judaisms (the one of 1930 and the one of 1980) are essentially one.

It is therefore much more difficult in 1980 to demarcate oneself from the "earlier Jews." They are too near. The effort to forget, not the terrible years, but those that preceded them, must be as great as the resemblance that it wants to blur. The resemblance is total. The forgetting must be total. The "earlier Jews" did nothing to stop anti-Semitism? What was an optional trope in the language of combat before 1939 has become an axiomatic certainty in statements proffered today. What was a poor interpretation of Jewish history has become an outright falsification, an indispensable aid to the resurgence of the Jewish rhetoric of combat.

★

The distantiation is usually chronological. The Jews of *today* are different from those of *yesterday*. But sometimes it is lateral, from one country to another in the same period: the Jews *here* are different from the Jews *over there*. The LICA of the thirties sees Nazism triumph first in Germany (1933), then in Austria (1938) and then in Czechoslovakia (1939). It watches racism spread in Poland, Hungary, and Rumania. It must explain this series of victories by the anti-Semites to the militants whom it tries to galvanize into action. But it cannot refer to the deeper causes of defeat—the numerical inferiority and objective vulnerability of the Jewish communities—since these causes are equally present in France. The only way it can sustain the rhetoric of combat is by maintaining that the other Jews did not fight and did not protest—and so anti-Semitism was able to overcome them. And so, the Jewish activists in France begin to attribute to the Jews of neighboring countries the same passive disposition that will be imputed, a few decades later, to the totality of Jewish Europe before 1939.

After 1933 and the initial triumph of Nazism, the LICA becomes very harsh towards German Jews. In May 1933, it remarks that they has become "indifferent."[16] In June, Pierre Paraf, mentioning "experiences in foreign lands," rejects the route "of timidity that leads to capitulation."[17] In 1936, *Le Droit de Vivre* warns the "Nazis of Paris" that the Jews and non-Jews of the LICA are not suffering from any "inferiority complex," unlike the "pusillanimous" German Jews. "We are bred of another school, and we have given ample proof of it."[18] In October 1938, the reproof aims at the Jews of every country in which anti-Semitism is strong. And so: "It has already triumphed in Germany, in Austria, in Hungary, in Rumania, in Poland and in Italy. We are feeling it, more and more strongly, in France. What is there to do? Must we, before the rising peril, hide our convictions, our sentiments and our ideas? The Jews of Germany and all the other countries that we have just listed did so. They bowed their heads before the tempest. They burrowed and hid, in the hope that by keeping silent, by playing dead, they would not be noticed."[19] In February 1939, referring to Germany, Austria and Italy, *Le Droit de Vivre* declares: "They did not have the LICA in those countries."[20]

The myth is born. It does not spring from on ignorance of facts. *Le Droit de Vivre* is very well informed about attempts made by Jews in every country to fight the surge of anti-Semitism. The journal mentions the activities of antiracists in Germany (until 1933) and Austria (until 1938) many times. It comments often on the progress of Jewish self-defense in Poland and on efforts made by Rumanian and Hungarian Jewry to organize and take action. But, when anti-Semitism takes the upper hand or attains a level of outright predominance, the LICA forgets all that it previously knew about the Jews of the afflicted country. It suddenly discovers that they were actually passive. But the sincerity of Lecache and his friends is not the issue. The myth of the passivity of others, which they propagate, is an integral part of the rhetoric of combat they seek to instill in all French Jews. If they were to admit that Jews in Germany organized meetings, or that Austrian Jews published protest pamphlets, they would, in principle, be admitting that those Jews *did* try to take action, and yet were defeated, which would topple the whole ideological platform the French Jewish activists themselves fervently believe in and desperately cling to.

★

The Jews of the past, or the Jews "over there," did nothing. A third form of differentiation often arises in one particular country during a single period. It distinguishes those who are active from those who are passive within each Jewish community, and does so withing the context of the classical, perpetually reenacted debate between the two ways of fighting anti-Semitism.

Sometimes the dispute is along tactical lines. In 1933 the major American Jewish organizations are divided on what their response to the first German persecutions should be. The American Jewish Committee and the B'nai B'rith promote discreet action, governmental intervention, and the sheltering of Jewish refugees. The

99

American Jewish Congress, a more popular movement having the support of the Zionist movement and the Jewish workers' unions is, on the contrary, in favor of mass action. It is they who successfully organize the great demonstrations March 27th and May 10, 1933. In May, the dispute comes out into the open and relations between the two blocs are broken off, each one accusing the other of jeopardizing the common cause.[21]

Sometimes the conflict is more ideological. In Poland, the Bundists routinely denounce the Zionists, who brazenly assert that the solution to the Jewish problem in Europe is the creation of a Jewish State in Palestine. But they also direct their fire against the Jewish bourgeoisie and religious orthodoxy. What do those groups do about anti-Semitism? "The Jewish bourgeoisie has always submitted and lowered its head. . . ," Victor Alter declares at a meeting in 1936. He goes on to extoll the actions of the Bund, consisting of "strikes and combat."[22] H. Erlich mocks "the religious," who lead the "fight," as he ironically puts it, with fasting and prayers. The real fight is the one fought by the Bund, as endorsed by the Polish proletariat.[23]

The French version of this schism pits the LICA to the Israeli Consistory. "The only doctrine against Hitlerism: that of the LICA," an article in *Le Droit de Vivre* argues, criticizing "the politics of working in silence, of intervention through official channels and of neutrality towards all political parties,"[24] as practiced by the majority of major Jewish organizations, which favor "discreet negotiation along with mild pressure on the polemics of the press over noisy meetings and marches in combat formation."[25] "Good and bad methods for fighting racism," Georges Zerapha writes in 1938. In opposition to the traditional method of the Consistory, he promotes "a hard and visible fight led by responsible Jews against the anti-Semites themselves."[26] In February 1939, *Le Droit de Vivre* offers this assessment of all the committees and organizations in the fight against anti-Semitism. "And if it were not for the old dependable LICA, its 50,000 adherents, its elect, its zealous youths . . . where would we be?"[27]

★

In light of what happened during the War, the polemic of the thirties loses its significance. In the thirties the Consistory and LICA differed in their choice of methods. The first entrusted the welfare of the Jews of France to protection afforded by the State and the institutions of the Republic. The second vouched for their future through the organization of mass demonstrations. But both groups, at heart, were saying precisely the same thing: they both sang of

France and of democracy.

Nuances of style mask unity of content again in France in the eighties, in a polemic that opposes the Renouveau juif to the established community. The two are similar in their sincere pro-Israelism, on the one hand, and in their affirmation of the French Jews as truly French, on the other. Neither the Renouveau juif nor the CRIF are Zionists, since they do not advocate the return of French Jews to their homeland, Israel. The two differ, conversely, in verbal style and in militant practice, the latter emphasized more by the Renouveau.

The Jews of the prewar period are inevitably saddled with a bad reputation. A speaker can always convincingly distance himself from them by insisting that today's Jews are different from those of yesterday, a theme that in every Jewish mass meeting is sure to meet with instant approval. Then, with growing emotion, he will most likely blurt out some of the stock banalities of the thirties, presenting them, and indeed experiencing them, as something truly novel. The permanent virginity of the rhetoric of combat deprives those who speak, as it does those who listen, of all their critical faculties.

"We are no longer the French of the Mosaic faith' but French Jews," the great Rabbi René Sirat says in an interview in *L'Arche* in 1983. He also states that "it is therefore the duty of the authorities in our country to make sure that terrorism is banished from our streets, since one of the avowed goals of anti-Semitic terrorism is precisely to separate the Jews from the rest of the nation."[28] But not a single spiritual leader of the Jewish community in the nineteenth century would have disavowed either the substance or the tone of his concern.

★

"We certify that there will not be any anti-Semitism in France. We certify and we guarantee it, as we shall not hesitate to react," the journal of the LICA writes in 1935.[29] Such grandiosity is essential to the system. In Europe in the thirties, however, proclamations are accompanied by real preparations. The Central Verein is not satisfied with affirming that the Germans must be convinced of the injuriousness of anti-Semitism. It circulates its views in millions of political tracts and posters. The Polish Bund does not rest satisfied with the solidarity it has achieved with the non-Jewish proletariat. It organizes strikes, days of action and protest demonstrations. On a smaller scale, the French LICA, like similar organizations fighting anti-Semitism in every country, increases its defensive efforts.

In the France of the eighties, concern for concrete measures is relegated to the rear. The conviction shared by many activists that they were the first to suggest that the Jews ought to defend themselves, satisfies them. They spare themselves the effort of aligning their practical deeds with their theoretical positions.[30] "We will resist. But the fascists will not attack, since they know there would be a defense and so do not dare to approach," the president of a Jewish community in the Parisian suburbs declares in June 1980.[31] This is undoubtedly true of the fascists of 1980, of whom the most that need be said is that there is nothing especially dreadful about them. But if raised to a universal principal, the optimism of his declaration is certainly excessive.

But again, in 1980, French anti-Semitism is weak. It is potent enough to keep Jewish defense prepared, but it is of course incapable of overcoming it. For the Jewish militants, as for the leaders of the community, A mythic view of the past justifies all the erroneous inferences that follow. Many feel they have warded off the evil by just being prepared; exactly what the "earlier Jews," who remained passive, did not understand how to do. The harsh reality of violent, pitiless, and murderous hatred is banished, courtesy of a myth that is at once mobilizing (see what will happen to you if you do nothing!), explanatory (here is why it happened!) and reassuring (if you uphold your dignity then nothing will happen to you). The error in appraising the "earlier Jews" leads to an underestimation of the danger.

★

"We are here and we are not afraid. We belong to a generation of Jews for whom anti-Semitism is not a faceless demon, but the object of a fight," Rabbi Williams declares on the steps of his synagogue on rue Copernic, after the explosion of 1980.[32]

Might he be acquainted with *Jüdische Front,* the journal of the Jewish war veterans in Austria? On May 15, 1936, under the title *Judentum im Kampf* ("Judaism to the fight"), one reads: "We, Jews of the war generation . . . we have learned how to fight and, when it is necessary, to die. But not without defense, burned by our persecutors at the stake. Rather, as we learned how to do as old soldiers in the fight for our honor . . . in the fight for our children and our women, man against man, right until the final breath."[33]

The first Jewish defense force in the Austrian capital assembles in the period following the Great War, as Manés Sperber recounts. "The majority of our elders in the Schomrim, the Jewish youth organization, Haschomer Hatzair, had been front-line soldiers, cadets or officers. They directed the defensive maneuvers we participated in, all of us youths of thirteen and fourteen years. We were equipped with brass-knuckles and mountaineers' staffs. The oldest had pistols and blades, which they were not to use except in the case of extreme peril."[34]

102

The fighting resumes in the early thirties against the Austrian Nazis, who had grown in proportion with their German counterparts. In June 1932, the president of the Union of Austrian Jews sends out an appeal for unity within the Jewish community and for the mobilization of all, young and old alike, for the fight against anti-Semitism.[35] On June 25th, a Nazi attack on a Jewish quarter of Vienna is driven back by the militants of the Jewish sports organization, Hakoach (in Hebrew: the strength). Casualties are reported on both sides.[36]

The Bund Jüdischer Frontsoldaten Oesterreichs, the Austrian equivalent of the German Reichsbund jüdischer Frontsoldaten, takes final form by the end of 1932. "The way is difficult, the hostile prejudices are potent. Jews, I call on you all, come to us and add to our ranks!" writes Emil Sommer, retired General of the Imperial army. "We are on the Jewish front and the decisive battle has begun. Everyone's gaze is upon us. The Bund Jüdischer Frontsoldaten marches courageously into combat for the existence and honor of the Jewish people," Oskar Grünbaum writes.[37]

In 1933, Austrian Nazis are inspired by the victory of Hitler in Germany and multiply their hostile attacks. The tension reaches its zenith. The March 18th *Bulletin* of the Jewish Telegraphic Agency proffers two news items about the attitude of the Jews in Austria. The first concerns a self-defense group operating in the country. It bears the name Haganah (in Hebrew: defense), the name also used by the Jewish armed organization in Palestine since 1920. Second item. On March 17th a violent confrontation between Nazi and Jewish students takes place at the University. There are wounded on both sides.[38]

The Jewish community prepares a demonstration of strength for June 18, 1933. The Hakoach and Maccabee sporting organizations and the groups of the Haganah mobilize their adherents for a mass assembly, which is dominated by the members of the Bund Jüdischer Frontsoldaten, all in uniform. Representatives from the army and civil authorities also attend the demonstration. "June 18, 1933, has made its mark on the history of Austrian Jews," *Jüdische Front* writes.[39]

One might observe that Austrian Judaism is, for the most part, resolutely pro-Zionist and lends active support to the establishment of Eretz-Israel. In June 1935, close to thirty thousand Jews gather before the tomb of Theodore Herzl. The chief Rabbi of Vienna is at the head of the procession.[40]

The BJF Oesterreichs has its uniformed contingents, its hymns and its slogans. It forms youth associations whose members receive paramilitary training.[41] In April 1936, *Jüdische Front* again requests that parents send Jewish youths to the BJF so that they can receive an education in self-defense and group discipline. In the same issue of that journal one reads the following incident, characteristic of the journey of the Yiddish writer Shalom Ash in Palestine. At Kibbutz Givat Brenner, he sees young Jews newly arrived from Germany cutting the straps off their backpacks. "Why?" Shalom Ash asks. A chalutz (pioneer) answers: "This is the last stop for the Jewish people. From here we will never again depart."[42]

In February 1937, *Jüdische Front* tells of the activities of the Jungbund youth organization, which goes by the motto *"Zum jüdischen Geist, die judische Faust"* ("The Jewish fist in service of the Jewish spirit").[43] In May 1937, the journal writes that defense is crucial and describes the situation as grave. "As it was in the past, the Bund Jüdischer Frontsoldaten is stationed at the leading edge of the fight against anti-Jewish attack."[44] In July, *Jüdische Front* recalls the heroism of the Jews in the war against the Romans. It also publishes several Zionist poems.[45] Jewish sporting competitions are staged in Vienna on February 13, 1938 to celebrate the 40th anniversary of the Maccabee organization.[46] Founded at the end of the nineteenth century, it not only develops athletic prowess but instills feelings of Jewish pride in Jewish communities all over the world.

★

In March 1938, the Chancellor Schussnigg, who had planned to organize a plebiscite to confirm the independence of his country, capitulates under pressure from Hitler. The Nazis take power. It is the Anschluss. The calamity falls upon 200,000 Jews. Their synagogues are defiled, desecrated or destroyed. Jewish stores are ransacked by rioters. Arrests, followed by torture and deportation, or liquidation, number in the thousands.[47]

Terror reigns in the streets. To the utmost delight of the bystanders, work squads of Jews are forced to wash the walls of Vienna and to erase all of the patriotic Austrian and anti-Nazi slogans that cover them. The conscripted spend long hours scrubbing, sometimes with their bare hands. "For the first few weeks, the behavior of the Vienna Nazis was worse than anything I had seen in Germany," William L. Shirer writes. "There was an orgy of sadism. Day after day, large numbers of Jewish men and women could be seen scrubbing Schussnigg signs off the sidewalk and cleaning the gutters. While they worked on their hands and knees with jeering storm troopers standing over them, crowds gathered to taunt them. Hundreds of Jews, men and women, were picked off the streets and put to work cleaning the public latrines and the toilets of the barracks where the SA and the SS were quartered. Tens of thousands more were jailed."[48]

The Jews are picked up in the avenues and exposed to public ridicule. Young Jews are stripped of their clothing and paraded through the town. On April 24th, 400 Jewish men, women, elderly folk and children are assembled in Prater's gardens. There they are forced to walk on all fours, eat the grass, and clamber up into the trees.[49] Anny Letour recounts this one scene, one among many of its kind: "I saw a Jewish doctor, the head of the clinic, licking up filthy ammoniated water poured out onto the pavement by the Viennese Nazis, their jackboots on the nape of the gentleman's neck. In the very heart of Vienna. 'That's enough for today; tomorrow you will return at the same time, with your wife.' Tomorrow? Tomorrow they will be found hanged, he and his wife. They opted for death."[50]

Under this pall of humiliation, suicides multiply. They mount to several dozen each day during March and April of 1938. Long lines of despondent Jews wait outside the foreign consulates, in quest of hypothetical immigration visas. The obstacles to acquiring a visa are very difficult to surmount. No nation, near or far, is prepared to receive a significant number of Jewish refugees. The doors are closed. In Palestine, Great Britain, still concerned about the Arab unrest of 1936, restricts the number of immigration certificates granted to the Jewish people.

The Jews of Austria discover a doubly cruel reality. On one side is an enemy whose force is so overwhelming that the fortune of the Jews is left to the goodwill of non-Jews. On the other is an indifferent world whose offers of salvation are extremely scarce. The iron jaws that will soon pulverize six million Jews have tightened another notch. The fight against anti-Semitism has been to no avail.

Part Two

Can Anti-Semitism be Foreseen?

Chapter Eight

Apprehensions

"Grab your raincoats!" Cassandra cries to a small group of pedestrians strolling under a cloudless sky. For the briefest moment, she beheld a torrential downpour bursting out of an apocalyptic sky. "Grab your raincoats!" she wails, but her voice rings false in the warm and clear air.

Before the storm comes, there is no storm. Before the crisis descends, there is no crisis. Before the war breaks out, there is no war. Cassandra inevitably looks ludicrous. She announces distant tragedies that are contradicted by tangible evidence—beautiful weather, prosperity, peace. . . .

Her tirades sometimes irritate people, because they disrupt the peaceful rhythm of the day, but they more often draw ridicule. Their interest piqued, some sensible folk press her for more details. They badger her to reveal the precise moment at which the catastrophe will take place and what exact form it will take. Cassandra stammers. They persist, demanding to know why the dark prediction must be fulfilled. Cassandra falters. Her interlocutors generously offer Cassandra a final chance to redeem herself, but their offer conceals a final trap. They ask her for proofs, theoretical or logical, of the future event. Cassandra collapses, to the great amusement of the onlookers. Sometimes, the exchange is more heated. Sensible people accuse of her hoping that the catastrophe will occur just so she can experience the pleasure of being proven right, or of instigating its occurrence by demoralizing people. Storms, crisis, and wars always happen in the past and never in the future, always to others and never to oneself.

Rejected when all goes well, Cassandra is the victim of ingratitude when all goes poorly, that is, when the disaster strikes. It was unforeseeable, totally unforeseeable, the survivors say. Oh! If only we had been warned, they add, firmly vowing to never again relax their vigilance. Not understood before, Cassandra is now forgotten. Before there was no one who would believe her, and now there is no one to thank her.

Solitude is an inherent risk for those in the prophetic calling. This is true whether they predict individual calamities (a fall on slippery ground), familial ones (the burglary of a poorly secured apartment), socio-economic ones (rising unemployment), political ones (the accession of an authoritarian regime), national ones (the closing of all Chinese restaurants), or global ones (a nuclear war). This applies to catastrophes that occur suddenly as well as to situations that deteriorate gradually, to catastrophes whose effects are irremediable as well as to those that can be recovered from. It applies, finally, to a desperate announcement of an unavoidable event, one that will happen no matter what its future victims do (All is lost! The end of the world approaches!). But it also applies to predictions that mobilize people to find a solution that, if adopted in time, will guarantee their salvation (Grab your raincoats, it's going to rain!)

★

No general theory of the prediction of catastrophes can ignore the Jewish question. One would think that those who fear a renewal of anti-Semitism would have every opportunity to make themselves heard. The evil force that they see approaching is known to be frequent, to be omnipresent in space and time, to take multiple forms and to wield enormous destructive power. With this statistical support, it would seem likely that those who announce a future recurrence of anti-Semitism would have little difficulty convincing their audiences.

This is not the case. Far from engendering a rational approach to the real situation of the Jews, knowledge of past violence produces an emotional myopia that privileges a fervent vision of things as one would like them to be (there is no anti-Semitism) over lucid observation of things as they are (there can be anti-Semitism). No, it can never happen again! The cry is profoundly human, whether it is plainly uttered, or given sophisticated articulation in order to prove, in scholarly and peremptory terms, that the hotbeds of bigotry have finally been extinguished. But the passionate claim that a new upsurge of anti-Semitism is inconceivable is a value judgment without much practical support or application.

Admitting that a phenomenon can be forecast is tantamount to granting that its resurgence is possible. To reject this possibility is therefore to undermine the very notion of prediction. The editorial of *L'Arche,* in March 1979, concerns the Jews of Iran at the time of Khomeini's return. Their situation, stable under the reign of the Shah, has abruptly become uncertain. Adam Loss, alluding to certain Zionists, reprimands the critics who sermonize to the Jews of the Diaspora. "Such lessons, or rather warnings, are derisive to those who live in the midst of terror . . . and ridiculous to those whose situation warrants no comparison with that of the Jews of Iran."[1] When things are going badly, it is thus *derisive* to predict that they could get worse. When things are going well, it is *ridiculous* to think that they could one day go sour. Foresight is simply disallowed.

Adam Loss could make good use of a lesson from the past that is also a rule of elementary logic. Before things go badly, everything's okay. Before the pogrom, there is no pogrom. A Jewish community in danger is a community that, before being so, wasn't. By criticizing all "warnings" as insulting or absurd, he ignores the dynamic element of the Jewish situation, for there are no communities in which all goes badly permanently and none in which everything stays fine forever. Their situations are always undergoing modifications or alterations of one form or another, sometimes slowly and sometimes very quickly.

Their dismissive attitude promotes an image of the Jews as a rather peculiar people. They are willing and able to discuss every conceivable subject in any field. They are keen to explore specifically Jewish questions as well as the major problems of civilization, or indeed the interaction of the former with the latter. Only one topic is proscribed from the field of legitimate investigation. Only one topic is taboo. Only one, and not the least important one, since it concerns their future security. As soon as any debate comes around to the eventuality of an anti-Semitic revival, their thinking regresses to the level of dreamy fantasy.

Distancing oneself from a painful past, immersing oneself in a quite acceptable present, and refusing to envisage a markedly different future constitute three facets of the same approach. What was will never again be. What is, shall be. The Jews of France who refuse to be "warned" are placing themselves outside of the flow of history in general and of Jewish history in particular. They are also removing themselves from political life, understood as the ability of a human collectivity to reflect on its future and to organize itself towards fashioning this future as it sees fit.

★

"Why we do not believe in an explosion of anti-Jewish hatred."[2] This grand title belongs to an editorial in *La Tribune Juive* on April 3, 1936. The text develops one of the many arguments that were tendered in those days (and are still popular today) to establish, in no uncertain terms, that no serious danger exists. This sort of denial is not specific to France and, in fact, the rule of refutation holds in all Jewish communities. "If anyone had told the Jews of Russia of the impending disaster even a month before it came, he would have been mocked as a madman," the Zionist Peretz Smolenskin wrote after the great Russian pogroms of 1881.[3] Incredulity vis á vis anti-Semitism is not directed solely at the prophet who presages a future debacle. It is also directed at the messenger who gives notice of an immediate danger and who, far from offering vague hypotheses, relies upon concrete facts that are well authenticated. Two examples taken from a long history should be proof enough.

In the eleventh century, with the formation of the armed forces of the first Crusade, persecutions befall the Jews of certain towns in France. Messengers are sent to the Jewish communities of the Rhine, the next stopover on the route of the liberators of Saint Sepulchre, their express mission to forewarn the Jews there of the persecutions and thereby put them on their guard. The news elicits the compassion of the Jews of Mainz who engage in fasting, mourning and prayers to show solidarity with their brothers. But, they in their reply, as far as they're concerned, "we don't have as much to fear." Soon after, the Crusaders reach Mainz. Some Jews desperately defend themselves, then commit suicide rather than fall into the hands of the enemy; others manage to conceal themselves in the outlying townships. The community is destroyed.[4]

Another much more recent example: Until 1944, the Jews of Hungary go through the war without ever being massacred, even though they are victims of administrative persecutions and forced labor. Their situation changes with the arrival of the Germans and installation of Eichmann in Budapest. The young Zionists of the *Vaad Hahatzala* (in Hebrew: Salvation Committee) try to impress the gravity of the situation upon the Jewish community and to persuade the Jews to hide themselves wherever they can. They rely on direct testimony brought by Jewish refugees from Poland and on incontestable documentation. They run up against the following argument: "Hungary is not like those other countries. What happened in Poland, in Czechoslovakia, cannot happen to us here."[5] Several hundred thousand Hungarian Jews are deported and exterminated in Auschwitz during the summer of 1944.

★

The debate with Cassandra takes many forms in today's France. One form is a dialogue with a fictitious partner whom one assumes is scared out of his wits and so reassures in a calm, sure voice. "We are not in 1942," Roger Ascot proclaims in *L'Arche* in July of 1983.[6] Yes, we've come a long way. In fact, no matter how closely one reads the newspapers of the past few years, one will be hard-pressed to find anyone—absolutely anyone—who claims that we are in 1942. A new historical precision is nevertheless furnished by the Editor-in-chief of *L'Arche* in July of 1983: "But we may rest easy about it: the accursed time was under the Occupation."[7]

Along the same lines, André Wormser, the president of the political commission of the CRIF, travels to Israel after the Copernic bombing to explain the situation of the French Jews to Israeli officials. "I tried to point out to may interlocutors that there are no pogroms in France . . ." he comments ironically upon his return.[8] In the discourse of reassurance, the incorrigible "panicker" whose fears are so easy to refute has now become an Israeli.

He is an American, from Robert Badinter's viewpoint. "To hear some people speak, France has become, in these last few months, a country ravaged by anti-Semitism. I confess to being totally stupefied by such talk. I see no trace, no perceptible sign, of a wave of anti-Semitism menacing France. . ." he states after a trip to the United States in 1983.[9] This attitude is more rational. It takes for granted that we are not in 1942 and thus feels no need to keep emphasizing that fact. It emphasizes, rather, the absence of any signs that would indicate a future anti-Jewish upheaval and, in so doing, suggests a direction for research: spotting the indicators.

Let us follow in this direction.

Chapter Nine
Description

We are not living in 1942. Why is it that such a curious formulation has been able to thrive? No surge of anti-Semitism is foreseeable. So what has happened in France in the last few years to make it necessary to proclaim this verity so insistently?

Anti-Semitism is measured in two different ways. When it is rampant, one counts the victims. By hundreds, by thousands, by hundreds of thousands, or by millions, according to the cases, eras, and countries involved. When anti-Semitism is limited, one lists the acts and incidents which, without directly resulting in any deaths, still demonstrate a certain degree of violence. Such research is not new. It was practiced in Weimar Germany and in Poland in the twenties, and is being practiced again in certain Jewish communities today. It might be worthwhile, then, to briefly discuss these methods of computation and to apply them to contemporary France.

Exogenous facts should obviously be excluded from the field of investigation. International attacks and Palestinian bombings are anti-Jewish, certainly, but are not of French origin. They pose a problem to which the Jews of France, like those of the entire world, must pay attention. But they are not constitutive of the Jewish question in France itself.

★

From where does the information come? A spiteful swastika engraved in the bark of a tree in the middle of a secluded wood will not be seen by anyone. "Jewish thieves" scrawled on an obscure wall will perhaps be seen by a few passersby, but there is little chance that among them will be a militant antiracist who might be sensitive to the meaning of the words. The desecration of an old cemetery can remain ignored for a long time. The three acts—engraving, inscription and desecration—are extremely benign. They express an anti-Jewish impulse that few will take notice of. Simple as it may be, an anti-Semitic act, to be fully reckoned as such, must be spotted by witnesses or experienced by one or more victims. These might be individual victims, in the case of an insult shouted in the street or a rock tossed through the window of a store; or institutional victims, when, for example, slogans are painted above the door of a local Jewish organization.

The information must, in those cases, be passed along. The initiative belongs to the witness or to the victim, and two obstacles have to be surmounted. One is natural, and that is indifference. The incident is ridiculous, it isn't worth making a big fuss over. The other is voluntary, and that is self-censure. The persons involved might feel reticent about denouncing an act whose authors are known (as in an insult delivered in the course of a dispute) or presumed (as in an anonymous phone call announcing that Hitler is back) to be living in their immediate vicinity. The silence of certain leaders of Jewish communities in the suburbs and in provinces has another origin beyond this desire to not aggravate matters. If it is known for certain that there is no anti-Semitism in France, then the inscription "Death to the Jews" on the wall of a synagogue must be an act of general vandalism and not one of anti-Jewish hatred. It is therefore enough to wipe away the hostile markings and pointless to file a complaint.

Once his decision is made, the victim must know whom to contact. Not everyone is familiar with the local divisions of the MRAP or LICRA. Not everyone is in touch with the CRIF or some other Jewish organization. Few people have contact with the press. Of course, with a little effort everything can be found. But the procedure appears quite complicated for incidents that, when all things are considered, are not really terrible. Those who, at this stage, have not already given up must face two further ordeals. The news must be authenticated by the informed party in order to avoid exaggeration or misrepresentation. And it must, if it is to continue along the tortuous route of public information, be deemed sufficiently important. This condition is always at work in the press, whether it is national, regional or local. Thus the mild but repetitive character of small anti-Jewish acts works in the Jews' disfavor. No one bothers to announce that, for the nth time, three Jewish merchants of a given place have received a threatening letter. It is published one time, the first time, in a note on the bottom of the page: the news, viewed in and of itself, does not merit any greater coverage. The publicity given to incidents is greater when the victim files a complaint for injuries he has sustained. But in any case, only a small portion of the reality of anti-Semitism is able to pass through the sieve.

Information that is not blocked at one stage or another of its peregrination is still not at the end of its difficulties. It arrives through one of many disparate channels, which rarely meet. Each paper has its dossiers, and each organization keeps its own accounts, some more meticulously than others. To apprehend the whole picture, it is necessary to collate all these miscellaneous accounts, and rake through the journals of Paris and the provinces to turn up all the reported incidents. Once this is done, they have to be indexed chronologically, or by category, or both. But accumulation and permanent storage of information is not practiced in a centralized or systematic fashion in France today. Collecting a multitude of scattered elements and processing the information that is gathered is a matter of improvisation. There is no central data bank about tiny anti-Jewish demonstrations comparable to the one that was set up in the early twenties by the Central Verein in Germany.

The most complete compilation pertaining to contemporary France is found in the *Survey on Anti-Semitic Events* published in Israel. Issued bimonthly, it covers all of the incidents recorded in the Jewish communities of the world, basing its coverage essentially on extracts from Jewish and non-Jewish papers. One also finds an abundance of factual documentation in the thesis that Eric Benmergui wrote on the resurgence of anti-Semitism in France during the period from mid-1974 to the beginning of 1981.[1]

By looking over the facts that have appeared in *Le Droit de Vivre, Droit et Liberté* and the *Bulletin quotidien de l'Agence Télégraphique Juive (ATJ),* as well as in the Jewish community press and the major papers of the country, and by relying upon the *Survey on Anti-Semitic Events* and the thesis of Eric Benmergui, one succeeds, after much patient effort, in piecing together the chronicle of small anti-Jewish acts.

★

What does it look like? Physically, it covers dozens of typewritten pages which list, month by month, the facts that have been recorded. Citing them all would be an interminable exercise. To gain a rudimentary understanding, we must only unwind the reel before our eyes (in a highly edited, condensed form), after we select a year at random. Here, 1978.

January 1978: anti-Semitic campaign in Dijon. Attack against the headquarters of the Federation of Jewish Societies of France and CLESS. Attack on the Discount Bank, a member of the Rothschild group. Anti-Jewish articles in *Aspects de la France*. In Marseille, young schoolchildren wear T-shirts saying "Put the Jews in your oven." Inscriptions, threatening letters, and so on. February: Defacement of the walls of the synagogue and community center in Marseille. Smashed shop windows of a kosher butcher shop in Avignon, two months after the desecration of the cemetery of L'isle-sur-la-Sorgue. Anti-Semitic campaign in Montpelier. Publications and threats. March: Campaign in Nice. April: After many protests, a Nazi film is withdrawn from a pro-Palestinian film festival in Valence. Scattered incidents. May: Campaign in Nice. June: Bomb in the Club Méditerranée, claimed by the French National Liberation Front, acting "against the Jewish occupation." Anti-Semitic inscriptions in several locations. July: Destruction of the stained glass windows of the synagogue in Lille. Attack against Mr. Dutourd, "who put his pen into the service of the Jewish press." Anti-Semitic inscriptions in le Raincy. August: Attack against Yves Mourousi, for "his Jewish connections." Various profanations. Fights in Juan-les-Pins. September: Nothing to report.

October: A young Jew is molested in Lyon. The brochure *Rabbi Salomon and the Black Tide* banned through the intervention of the LICA. The MRAP brings complaint against the sect of the "Children of God." Interviewed in *L'Express,* Darquier de Pellepoix asserts that at Auschwitz "only lice were gassed." November: Desecration of the synagogue of Saint-Dié in the Vosges. Brawl in a synagogue in Marseille. Anti-Semitic tracts in Vésinet and Toulouse. Anti-Semitic inscriptions at Vincennes and Gennevilliers. Sale of Nazi paraphernalia in Rennes. Faurisson suspended for 30 days from the University of Lyon after publishing an article denying the existence of the gas chambers. The LICA brings a complaint against François Brigneau for racist statements. The Fabre-Luce Affair intensifies. A protest demonstration before the Memorial draws thousands of people. Several assemblies take place in other cities. December: Attack against the headquarters of the Betar Zionist movement. This act, the CRIF says, "joins the long list of aggressions that have been perpetrated against personalities and institutions of the Jewish community of both Paris and the Province." Desecrations of synagogues in Avignon and Reims. Anti-Semitic inscriptions in Paris, Toulouse, Nice, etc. Diverse instances of sales of Nazi records and objects. Widespread anti-Jewish publications. On the night of the 18th, the synagogue of Drancy is set ablaze. "For the first time since the Second World War, a synagogue has burned in Europe," the *Bulletin de l'ATJ* writes.

A chronological list groups events by the most simple criterion: their date of occurrence. This method is employed by the Central Verein in its published record of anti-Jewish aggressions committed by the Nazis in 1929, 1930 and 1931.[3] It is also employed by the LICA, which offers a serial account of incidents from September 1935 to May 1936.[4]

Such a list only stockpiles information, which must then be processed for analysis. A first step in this direction is to consolidate all the facts. An official French report cited by *Le Canard Enchîné* in October 1980 gives an account of 21 anti-Semitic incidents in 1978 and 92 in 1979.[5] The report on racism and anti-Semitism prepared by the Commission on Assessment (instituted after the election of François Mitterand to the Presidency of the Republic in May 1981) enumerates, for the year 1975: 53 anti-Jewish incidents, of which 17 are particularly serious. For 1976: 68, of which 33 are considered serious. For 1977: 112, and 40. 1978: 126, and 40. 1979: 175, and 61. And in 1980: 235, and 75. In all, 769 aggressions, of which 266 are particularly serious.[6]

"Fabulous and absurd figures," Annie Kriegel writes. "They add together, without prudence, without any critical analysis of the incidents they have indexed, disparate events and incidents that are not uniformly verified, crimes of such incomparable gravity, like graffiti and manslaughter, that presenting them as members of a single series makes practically no sense."[7] She is right, of course, as regards the method. But she is mistaken when, on the basis of this elementary observation, she at the same time casts doubt upon the legitimacy of any enumeration of anti-Jewish acts and on the authenticity of the anti-Jewish acts reported in France. She uses the difficulty we have quantifying the phenomenon as a pretext for repudiating its existence.

Fortunately, by 1982, quantitative analysis of anti-Semitism was already well beyond the stage of rough, indiscriminate compilation, which juxtaposes horses, rabbits, and larks, i.e. admixes serious acts with benign ones, without taking the relative gravity into account. That is why all the summations we know of (in Germany in the twenties, Poland in the thirties, the United States . . .) are listed by type of incident, and are not all mixed together. Undifferentiated totals are, at most, rough indications of the tendency as a whole. Assessed over a prolonged period of time in France, the balance sheet would show a very noticeable drop in the number of incidents in 1981, and then a new rise in 1982, without the "peaks" of 1979 and 1980 ever again being reached.

The Anti-Defamation League (ADL), an American Jewish organization that fights anti-Semitism, uses a more elaborate typology. Its annual report lists, for the period from August 1979 to July 1980, a total of 377 anti-Semitic acts in American territory, of which there are "112 anti-Semitic incidents involving bodily assaults against Jews, or harassments or threats by phone or mail directed at Jewish institutions, their officials or private Jewish citizens." The 377 acts are listed, for the whole country and by state, with the aid of a double-entry system. Listed by type of aggression, the 377 incidents are subdivided into 354 "graffitis," swastikas and acts of vandalism, 10 arsons, two attempted arsons, four fire-bombings, two attempted fire-bombings and five desecrations of Jewish cemeteries. By affected targets, the 377 divide up into 157 directed against Jewish institutions, 160 against private Jewish properties and 60 against public buildings.[8]

An algebraic matrix thus takes shape. In the columns are aligned the types of aggressions committed. Inscriptions, threats, injuries, brawls, acts of vandalism, desecrations of synagogues and cemeteries, bombings, arsons, and shootings. In the lines are displayed the victims. Jewish public figures and antiracist militants. Shops and enterprises belonging to Jews. Jewish schools, youth movements, synagogues, headquarters of Jewish associations. And so, a swastika painted on the door of a synagogue is listed in the intersection of: "abusive inscriptions"—that is the act—and "synagogue"—the objective. A Jew beaten up by a gang of ruffians is registered at the interstices of "aggressions against individuals"—the type of action—and "Jewish persons"—the target. The explosive destruction of the apartment of a Jewish leader is classified at the crossing of the rubric "bombing attacks" and the category "personalities." And so on.

★

Is this the best method? The matrix-like display allows us to see more clearly through the entanglement, but does not address the basic problem. The report of the ADL already cited states precisely that, in fact, "many incidents in which anti-Semitism is a factor go unreported," and concludes that it is "likely that the actual number of anti-Semitic episodes was considerably higher than the 377 cited in the 1980 audit." The many episodes counted in 1980 are not only a marked increase over the preceding year, but a confirmation that a "disturbingly high quotient of anti-Semitic and anti-Jewish hostility exists just beneath the surface of American life." The acts we know of are only the waves rising from shadowy, unseen depths. The problem of defining the "shadow zone" is not new in the social sciences. It is encountered in every statistical analysis of a phenomenon that is diffuse and thereby difficult to perceive.

With regard to anti-Semitic incidents, the shadow zone varies, first of all, by region. An energetic Jewish community will motivate its militant members to keep account of every hostile act. Another, in a nearby city, will leave the decision up to each individual. A third will advise against pursuing the matter at all. A regional journal that is sympathetic will pass information along. Another will be more cautious. All of these variations help shape the topographical map of anti-Jewish incidents. A sudden rise or fall in the number of events reported in a given region is not a compelling indication of a progression or recession in anti-Semitic activity. Such vicissitudes perhaps attest to an improvement in or deterioration of the circuits of transmission themselves. This possibility alone is enough to put us on our guard against the temptation to over-analyze.

The shadow zone also varies over time. It is subject te the tides of current affairs. And so, each time a major anti-Jewish crime is committed, each time the Jewish question again becomes the center of a public controversy, a recrudescence of minor incidents all over is identified. Some blame this on the "resonance effect": talking about the Jews arouses dormant anti-Semitic passions in people. But there is another possible causal relation at work. The frequency with which acts occur has not been modified: they occurred just as often before the notable event as they will after it is over. Rather, the jolt of public attention *reinforces* the motivation of a victim to file a complaint, *heightens* the receptivity of the press to all that concerns the subject of the Jews, and *mobilizes* organizations and communities. The shadow zone has withdrawn considerably, but will soon return to its customary dimensions.

The shadow zone, lastly, is not uniform. It varies among the different categories of acts. The more serious they are, the more it shrinks, and the more benign they are, the more it expands. A bombing, an assassination attempt against a popular figure, and the burning of a synagogue are almost always clearly exhibited. Acts of this severity rarely go unnoticed.

Situated just below them on the scale of importance are profanations of places of worship, which are usually, but not always, reported. By some estimations, the shadow zone covers a full third of all vandalism cases, while according to others, it conceals a good half. Thus, for every ten cases that come to the attention of the Jewish press or institutions, there are actually between fifteen and twenty cases that occur. The discrepancy is even larger for the destruction of tombs. For the two, synagogues and cemeteries, there are equally

119

many reported and unreported cases.

As we scan further down, seeking out incidents of even lesser gravity, we find the shadow zone extending out much further. "On December 27, 1974, towards 1700 hours, Mrs. R.E. was the victim in the corridor of her building ... of abuses of a racist character proffered in public by a certain L.G., an electrician who was at the time carrying out some electrical work. ... She was called "dirty Jew," then violently struck by her aggressor."[9]

This banal news item is known to us because of a subsequent judicial hearing. Since then, numerous incidents of the same kind have become objects of judicial scrutiny, and the guilty party has generally been condemned. All these cases were discussed in the antiracist press. What no one is able to say for sure is how many similar affairs took place without the victim ever having filed a complaint. Two for one, five for one, ten for one? One senses the existence of a large shadow zone, but is incapable of delimiting its exact dimensions. The same goes for the whole plenum of small anti-Semitic acts: fights in the schools, threatening letters to Jewish merchants, bomb alerts in Jewish areas, and various sorts of inscriptions. The extreme case—writing about each swastika that is seen in Paris or Bordeaux—is not sensible. By searching well on any given night, one would be able to find them in Lille, Brest and Marseille or in any other city in France.

Let us suppose that over a given number of months within a given year, two bombing attacks, two synagogue desecrations, two aggressions against individuals in the streets, two threatening letters aimed at Jewish stores and two anti-Semitic inscriptions on walls are reported. Apparently, then, two, two, two, two and two. What reality hides itself behind these figures? For the bombs, the figure of two is exact. For the synagogues, the real figure is perhaps three or four. As for individual insults or aggressions, five or six probably occur. Threatening letters are uncountable. The real figure for graffiti is some whole number between two and infinity. The less serious the act is, the less the "two" events cited in the chronicle are representative of what in fact took place in the country.

The matrix for the year 1980 would show for the target "shops belonging to Jews" a total of 14 aggressions. Five by bombing or burning. Nine by racist inscription on facades or by window-shattering. Taking account of the difference in gravity among these acts, the figure "five" is undoubtedly representative of its category but the figure "nine" reveals only a portion (how much?) of the total number of cases in which injurious inscriptions were scrawled or painted on Jewish stores. Therefore, the figure "fourteen," which is the sum of the two, has no meaning. Another example, also taken from the year 1980. For the target "aggressions against persons," the column "insults" shows six cases. The column "fights and gang attacks" shows eight. But the second, graver than the first, is less uncertain—the shadow zone is smaller. The "eight" cases are rather close to the real number, whereas the "six" cases are quite remote from it. Adding together the two figures is absurd. Representing them side by side in a table presents a distorted image of the phenomenon.

We take exception to such tables, then. Aggregate sums should be reserved for identical acts. The Central Verein adds together desecrations of cemeteries and synagogues without distinguishing between profanation by exterior defilement (e.g. lettering) and profanation by destruction of the edifice or tomb.[10] In 1937, the sociologist Lestshinsky, at the behest of the World Jewish Congress, compiles a list of bombing attacks on Jewish synagogues, shops and centers in Poland. He distinguishes, for each city, between bombs proper, firecrackers set off to frighten people, and stink-bombs.[11]

Equipped with data, but aware of its inherent limitations, our analysis will proceed with an attempt at historical comparison. A first jump will take us twenty-five years back.[12]

In 1958, a series of incidents are reported. During June and July a lot of graffiti is spotted in the metro. In September, anti-Jewish inscriptions turn up in Vitry-le-François, and later in Paris, Nancy and Lunville. At Saint-Quentin, a butcher mistreats a Jewish child. Windows are broken in three Parisian synagogues on Christmas night. The year 1959 is rather calm. A bottle of ink is thrown at the facade of the Memorial of the Unknown Jewish Martyr on the night of May 7th. Other scattered incidents are pointed out, among which are anti-Jewish tracts and graffiti. "Once again, an anti-Semitic incident," *Droit et Liberté* notes. "On the night of September 24th, vandals tore two plaques off of the Federation of Jewish Societies building on rue Saint-Lazare." The paper also laments the anti-Semitic political affair of Senator Auberger in Bellerive-sur-Allier.

Suddenly, there is mobilization. "Antiracist France takes up the challenge of the neo-Nazis," the journal of the MRAP headlines in January 1960. "Answering to the call of the LICA and the antiracists, Paris and France take up the challenge of anti-Semitism," the mouthpiece of the LICA confirms. Several thousand participants throng together at a meeting of the MRAP on January 7th. Five thousand are in the hall of the Mutualité for the meeting of the LICA on January 12th, and several thousand more are turned away at the door. On January 10, 1960, to the call of the CRIF and many other organizations, 30,000 people gather in front of the Memorial. Many meetings are organized in the provinces, and educational campaigns are conducted in the schools.

What could have happened to create such a stir? During the final week of December, gaudy swastikas were painted in more than twenty cities in France. Synagogues were sacrileged in Lille and Bordeau. In February, a monument to the Resistance is dynamited. In Paris, two Jewish properties are pillaged, including that of Hashomer Hatzair, the Socialist Zionist youth movement. An arson is carried out against the headquarters of the Jewish Agency in Marseille. Towards the end of June, the Jewish cemetery in Thann is desecrated. The wave ends and everything returns to normal.

What would later be called "the epidemic of swastikas," aroused considerable feeling at the time. But the crisis quickly dissolved. Its actual dimensions, in terms of anti-Semitic acts or crimes, seem rather meagre in comparison with the figures reported in France in the late seventies.

★

Are we in 1936? Now the historical comparisons we are drawing will look at 1976 over and against 1936. The two years will engage in a dialogue over the span of forty years. For the prewar period, our sources will be *Le Populaire* (the socialist daily) and *Le Droit de Vivre* (the antiracist weekly).[13]

January 1936. Anti-Semitic posters are spotted in Paris. "Sidi-Bel-Abbés can no longer remain in the hands of the anti-Semites," the journal of the LICA writes. In February, Léon Blum is the victim of a fascist aggression. Gigantic protest demonstrations are organized all over the country. In February, anti-Semitic tracts are distributed in Algeria. In March, *Le Droit de Vivre* depicts "the workings of the Nazi lair in France." In March and April the anti-Semite Morinaud continues his provocations in Constantine. Elie Benayoun and Charles Bettan are wounded in brawls in Oran. In April, there is the verdict of Riom: "She is only the daughter of an Algerian Jew," says the judge about a young rape victim. The electoral campaign is marked by confrontations with anti-Semitic candidates like Michel Parrés, who is running for office in the IVth ward of Paris. Ben Kalifa is assassinated in Algeria during his attempt to pull down an anti-Semitic banner. Twenty thousand people attend his funeral.

January 1976. The kidnappers of the industrialist Louis Hazan declare anti-Semitism as their motive. In February: anti-Jewish posters in Neuilly. Anti-Jewish aspersions cast by police officers in Lyon. In March: desecration of the synagogue of Verneuil at the

Jewish cemetery of Bagneux. Outlaw of the sale of Nazi emblems in Paris. Burglaries in Jewish offices. In April: anti-Semitic slogans chanted by demonstrators in Saint-Germain des Prés.

May 1936. "The abominable Morinaud, champion of Algerian anti-Semitism," Serge Moati writes in a May 3rd issue of *Le Populaire* that outlines the anti-Jewish unrest in Algeria. "Has Alsace gone over to Hitler?" *Le Droit de Vivre* asks in May 1936. Anti-Semitic slogans are painted on Jewish stores and the courthouse in Strasburg. A synagogue is desecrated during the night of the 25th. Scuffles are reported in Metz. In Paris, five members of the LICA are attacked by young fascists: the photograph of the wounded Maurice Meinster and Louis Dorfman is printed in *Le Populaire.* many other riots break out, provoked by the Far Right. Darquier de Pellepoix confronts three young Jews in a restaurant. "If I desire it, 10,000 men will pour out into the streets and kill 100,000 Jews," the anti-Semite boasts. Zaoui is shot in Oran on June 30th. The victory of the Popular Front exacerbates the campaign of hatred against Léon Blum. But it also puts the repressive devices of the State apparatus (police, laws) into the hands of the antifascist Left.

May 1976. An attempted burning of a Strasburg synagogue. Desecration of the cemetery of Gerstheim. Burning of the museum commemorating the concentration camp of Struthof. Bombing of a branch of the Rothschild Bank in Paris. Reissuance of a violently anti-Semitic book. In it, the Jewish messiah is portrayed as a "villain of enormous proportions, a depraved monster." In June, a foiled attack against a synagogue in Paris. Publication of the fifth issue of the *Anti Youtre,* devoted to "Israel, the enemy of France." A pro-Palestinian demonstration on a related theme takes place in Paris. Jean-Jacques Pauvent republishes *Les Décombres* of Lucien Rebatet, which was a great literary success under the Occupation.

July 1936. Brawls between the LICA and anti-Semites in Paris. A police officer makes abusive remarks. The racist Eschbach is condemned by a tribunal. Incidents in Metz. At Relizane, in Algeria, swastikas are painted on a synagogue. In October, the Benguigui pharmacy in Oran is covered with anti-Jewish inscriptions. In Paris, a LICA militant, Ben Kalifa, the cousin of the person assassinated in Alger, is caught by a policeman in the act of tearing up a fascist poster. He is struck by the officer. A Jewish shop in Constantine is sullied by a swastika in December.

July 1976. Desecration of the synagogue in Cannes. Bombing of the headquarters of the B'nai B'rith in Paris. For the CRIF, this act "adds itself to the long list of racist aggressions that have been directed against Jewish public figures and institutions." The French division of the World Jewish Congress notices a "recrudescence of violent acts directed primarily at Jewish organizations." A grenade is thrown at a Jewish community center in Marseille. Several days later, a high-powered bomb aimed at a synagogue in the same city is safely defused. A warehouse belonging to a Jew in Marseille comes under attack. In Paris a bomb explodes in the offices of the LICA. There are diverse anti-Jewish publications and incidents. An incendiary bomb strikes the offices of the *Union des Juifs pour la Résistance et l'Entraide*. In August: attack on the headquarters of the League of Human Rights and break-in at the offices of the MRAP. Anti-Semitic inscriptions on the walls of the synagogue in Valence. Before the year is out, further attacks against Jewish institutions in Nice and the Yavneh School in Marseille, as well as inscriptions on Jewish property and synagogues and death threats against Beate Klarsfeld are registered. During an auction of souvenirs of Pétain, in Versailles, a few young Jews who come to protest are thrown out to cries of "Youdis" and "Jews, go to Tel-Aviv" hurled about the hall by the buyers. A television program about the Jews stirs up a flurry of protest. Tens of thousands of copies of two Nazi publications are distributed.

★

Although the choice of the years 1936 and 1976 is arbitrary, the two are in fact representative of their respective periods, and their comparison enables us to grasp certain differences between anti-Semitism yesterday and today.

In 1936, there are many street brawls between Jews and fascists. Anti-Semitism is openly expressed in France, and especially in Algeria. The press of the Far Right spits out its hatred for Blum and the Jews. In 1976, organized or expressed anti-Semitism exists, but it is more restrained. Conversely, the anti-Semites of 1976 perform bombings, arsons, and desecrations on a much larger scale than did their predecessors before the War. For the entire decade of the thirties in France, there are only three cases of anti-Jewish bombings. They occur in Nancy, during and after the crisis of Autumn 1938. Desecrations of synagogues are rare. Attacks against Jewish or antiracist public figures are practically nonexistent. The premises of the LICA are threatened but never touched.

Didn't the anti-Semites have for explosives in the thirties? In Poland, during 1936 alone, eight bombs are set off in Warsaw, five in Lodz, six in Vilna and three in Cracow, excluding firecrackers and other sundry explosives. For its part, French anti-Semitism does not

124

resort to such heinous attacks as night bombing (to destroy an office or a synagogue) or day bombing (to kill people).

It doesn't reach that level of brutality until 1940. All through the War, French extremist groups, sometimes encouraged by the occupying forces but more often acting on their own, organize attacks against Jewish targets, mostly synagogues. They operate on the fringes of the Franco-German policy of anti-Jewish persecution, impatient with the sluggishness of the official program and striving to accelerate it. In August 1940, the monument to the Jews who died in Verdun is profaned. On the night of October 2, 1940, several synagogues in Paris, including one on rue Copernic and one on rue de la Victoire, are damaged by explosives. Further serious aggressions take place in Marseille and Bordeaux in 1941. In Lyon in 1943, bombs are thrown at people attending services.[14]

"It is definitely wrong to identify 1982 with 1942 . . . or even with 1936 or 1938. . . ." Henri Amouroux states in the *Quotidien de Paris* on August 12, 1982, after the attack on rue des Rosiers.[15] His argument turns on the years 1936 and 1938. In those days, racist journals, like *Je suis partout,* published brazen and venomous diatribes against the Jews. "Forty years ago, men used to boldly declare themselves racists and anti-Semites." Fortunately, this is no longer the case today, he declares. However, Amouroux goes on: "What used to be expressed from the heart and under the open sky is now subterranean, covert but probably still alive."

This marvel has a very simple explanation. "The memory of the Holocaust is blurry but still stigmatizes the spirits of men. Even on the most indecent of men it imposes some degree of decency," Amouroux adds. It's true. The memory of the genocide haunts the conscience of the public. Anti-Semitism at the superstructural level is therefore restrained and not easily ascertained. It is maintained at an artificially low level as a result of an external constraint that hinders its development and limits its faculties of expression. In France during the thirties, there was a clear correspondence between proclaimed anti-Semitism and actual anti-Semitism. In France today, there is an imbalance. The hatred that is paraded about is smaller, much smaller, than the hatred that is practiced. The *Rassemblement antijuif de France* no longer holds public meetings. *Je suis partout* is no longer for sale in the kiosks. Anti-Jewish addresses are no longer held in Parliament. What once expressed itself *vocally* now expresses itself on the sly. What once expressed itself in *deeds* still expresses itself in deeds. The weight of the past therefore works something like a defective muzzle. It hinders the bark but leaves room for the bite.

★

Is the wave silent? This is a somewhat extreme supposition, but could lead to progress in our analysis. It might explain the difficulty the Jewish community of France has perceiving the extent of current anti-Semitism.

A reaction of incredulity always greets the enumeration of anti-Jewish acts. Combining various acts in one list, as we saw earlier, is not an adequate way to portray a reality that is multifaceted and informal. Personal experience is also totally incapable of grasping a diffuse sprinkling of events. Series of aggressions, from bombings to insignificant insults, are geographically well-distributed and temporally extended. They affect a community of 600,000 people. Statistically, it is quite likely that only a few Jews have had direct exposure to anti-Semitic incidents over the last few years. Indirect accounts from family members or circles of acquaintances are more frequent—a friend whose child was insulted by bullies at school, a cousin who announces that his synagogue was desecrated, a business colleague who received a threatening letter. The disquiet that is sometimes provoked by such announcements dissipates quickly, their cadence of appearance is very leisurely and the image they present of the problem is extremely partial. The daily lives of the Jews of France has obviously not been affected.

This problem is found in every Jewish community that faces an analogous situation of restrained endemic violence, that is, witnesses sporadic incidents and criminal ventures that are not institutionalized by the State. It is not a matter of pogroms, nor, in most instances, of bloody attacks. It is another thing entirely that needs to be captured. A series of small incidents that, taken one by one, are totally insignificant, but taken all together nevertheless have meaning. Perception of this whole is not automatic. It involves labor and demands research.

How is one to know that a synagogue in Toulouse was desecrated? Aside from living right next to it or being one of its faithful members, the only way to gain access to the information is to read about it in a newspaper. The news must therefore, first of all, clear the many hurdles that separate it from publication, and then, once printed, it must be read. How is one to know how many synagogues were desecrated in France over the last year? An organizational effort to collect and analyze the data is indispensable. If this effort collapses or is ignored, then as if by magic anti-Semitism disappears.

★

Another curious phenomenon further increases the confusion. It is what we must call the miracle of polls.[16]

"Retreat of anti-Semitism in France."[17] This encouraging news, announced by *L'Arche* in 1977, is based upon a poll by Louis Harris France published in *Le Matin.* The French Jewish monthly informs us that 29 percent of the French would reject a Jewish President of the Republic, compared to 50 percent during an earlier poll in 1966, and that 17 percent of the people questioned think the Jews too numerous in France. The same poll also indicates that 24 percent of the French would shun having a Jew for an in-law, against 37 percent in 1966.

The downwards tendency is confirmed in a study conducted for a French weekly in 1978. Five percent of the French declare themselves anti-Semites, whereas there were nine percent who did in 1966. In addition, ten percent of the people interrogated feel sympathy for the Jews (four percent in 1966) and four percent antipathy (ten percent in 1966). Sixteen percent of the French would never vote for a Jewish deputy, against 33 percent in 1966. The slide accelerates in a new poll published by *L'Express* after the Copernic bomb.

Is a Jew as French as any other Frenchman? One version of this question sets up a comparison between Jews and other minorities. In the first IFOP poll in 1946, 37 percent of those interrogated respond positively. Seventy-five percent think the same thing of Corsicans, 65 percent of Alsatians, and 83 percent of Bretons. In the IFOP poll of 1966, 60 percent of the French consider the Jews to be as French as anyone else. The percentages for Corsicans, Alsatians and Bretons rise to 75, 82 and 94, respectively. In 1977, the three provinces collect positive responses on the order of 84, 90 and 94 percent. The Jews get 65 percent.

Corsicans, Alsatians and Bretons improve their positions from one inquiry to another, which speaks of a tendency away from regionalism in the thinking of the majority of the French. The Jews, conversely, make a significant leap from 1946 to 1966, which is undoubtedly due to the wide influence that anti-Semitism still commanded immediately after the War. But from 1966 to 1977 they gain only five points, which tells us that they have in fact stabilized at a level of acceptance clearly inferior to that accorded the other minorities. In point of fact, then, the "retreat of anti-Semitism" happened between 1946 and 1966, and not between 1966 and 1977. The Jews are French like anyone else in the eyes of just two-thirds of the population. After Copernic, 87 percent of the French respond "yes" to the question.

Are there too many Jews in France? A second type of question examines the Jews alongside other victims of racism. Yes, 17 percent of the French respond about the Jews in 1977. But there are 63 percent who think the same thing of North Africans and 61 percent of foreigners in general. These figures (weak for the Jews, strong for the others) support the widely held idea that anti-Semitism is in regression, whereas racism and xenophobia are in progression. "A xenophobic surge, the analysis of the opinion polls reveals, aimed at the Arabs, the Portuguese or the Blacks, is systematically compensating for the drop in anti-Semitism," Jacques Sabbath writes in *L'Arche* in 1979. He calls upon the Jews to become active, consequently, in the fight against racism towards immigrants.[18]

But, in 1980, 12 percent of the French (and not 17 percent) think that there are too many Jews, 49 percent (and not 63 percent) think the same of North Africans and 43 percent (and not 61 percent) think it of foreigners in general. All in all, from 1977 to 1980, it is the whole lot of racist prejudices that diminish considerably, and not just anti-Jewish sentiments. The thesis of a compensation between falling anti-Semitism and rising xenophobia is thus found to be invalid, since the two diminish simultaneously over a span of three years. And in both cases, of course, the reality of anti-Jewish or anti-Arab aggression produces the same percussive denial of the happy tendency indicated by the poll. . . .

In other words, it is evident that a great majority of French people disapprove of anti-Semitism today. One really needs no polls to know this, but these nonetheless furnish interesting material for further reflection, material that is too often overlooked by the heralds of the "retreat of anti-Semitism," who are prone to cursory reading. Here are a few interesting figures. In 1977, 52 percent of the people questioned consider there to be too many Jews in finance, and 69 percent feel that there are too many in commerce. In 1978, 17 percent of the French "would shun" using a Jewish physician. In 1980, although 44 percent think that Valéry Giscard d'Estaing ought to have visited the synagogue on rue Copernic after the attack, 37 percent of the French think that he ought not to have made such an appearance. In the same poll, 13 percent of the people questioned estimate that anti-Semitism is very widespread in France, and 42 percent that it is fairly widespread. If one is to believe the polls, then, anti-Semitism hs fallen back but still holds a firm position.

We must still account for the discrepancy between the revival of anti-Semitic activism after 1974, and the regression of the phe-

128

nomenon (very slight, as we have seen, but noticeable all the same) that is shown in the opinion polls. Is one responsible for the other? French opinion in 1980 is, all in all, antiracist. It will perhaps circle back in the future, but for the time being it is antiracist. When there is a revival of anti-Jewish activity, the reflex linked to the memory of past persecutions plays a decisive role. Some people who are primarily anti-Semitic, and who normally consider there to be too many Jews in France, respond differently to the question when it is posed in the context of anti-Jewish incidents. Polite anti-Semitism is startled by the awakening of violent anti-Semitism. It declines in the polls but does not disappear in reality.

But the debate has lost its sense of urgency. The excitement about the "retreat of anti-Semitism" shown in the polls has subsided. "Anti-Semitism is not on the decline in France and is growing among the younger generations, according to a sociological survey organized by CRIF," reports the *Jewish Chronicle* of London in January 1982.[19] Strangely, the survey in question has never been published and, unless I am mistaken, its contents have never been brought to the attention of the Jews of France. Are we to deduce from this that there are pleasant polls worth publicizing, but also gloomy analyses better off left in the drawer? This question perhaps best summarizes the problem of the official reaction of the Jewish community in France to the renewed anti-Semitism of these past few years.

Chapter Ten

Reactions

Traditionally, reactions to a wave of anti-Semitism washing over a given country are of two types. There are mitigative reactions, which tend to relativize the importance of the phenomenon, and combative reactions, which call for mobilization and action. Both of these types are present in France in the late seventies and early eighties.[1]

★

The year 1979 begins on a bad note for the Jews in France.[2] *January.* The Jewish cemetery of Bagneux is desecrated and the museum of the Struthof concentration camp, already burned once in May 1976, is plundered. Faurisson is heckled in Lyon. *February.* A film by Wajda having obvious anti-Semitic overtones is protested. Antisemitic inscriptions appear on Jewish shops and establishments. Shots are fired at a Jewish store in Bordeaux. The cemetery at Montfermeil is desecrated. Diverse tracts circulate. An insulting article is printed in *Minute* following the screening of the *Holocaust* television series.

March. Anti-Jewish inscriptions are found in many locations. Various expressions of anti-Semitism appear in the press. In a secondary school in Lille, children find a stray cat hanged, bearing the tag: *Jew.* Various cases of telephone threats are reported. A Molotov cocktail is thrown at the cultural center in Vincennes during the screening of a film that criticizes Hitler. Jewish cemeteries in Poissy and Toulouse are desecrated. Synagogues in Toulouse, Reims, Valenciennes and La Courneuve are defiled. An attack is attempted against a synagogue in Paris. An arson is attempted on the synagogue of Fontenay-aux-Roses during services. "This is the first time in France that they have ever tried to destroy a synagogue together with its occupants," the *Bulletin de l'ATJ* writes. A low-powered bomb explodes in the entrance of a store belonging to a Jew near the Opéra in Paris. On March 27, the most serious attack of all takes place. Thirty people are injured by a bomb that strikes a Jewish university restaurant in Paris' quartier latin. "A new echelon in the escalation of anti-Semitic violence has been attained, the blood of young Jews has been spilled in Paris," the CRIF states.

April. An assault is attempted on the Olympic theatre, where an exhibition on Jewish culture is on display. "Easter week was rife with synagogue desecrations," the *Tribune Juive* writes, mentioning Antibes and Sélestat in particular. An assault on the stele of Georges Mandel is taken credit for by the "league of French fighters against the Jewish occupation," which also flings two Molotov cocktails into a home for the Jewish elderly in Paris and sets off a bomb in front of *Le Monde*'s offices because of the collaboration of the press with the "Jewish tyranny. . . ."

As the year passes, a total of fifteen synagogues become the objects of more or less serious aggressions, ranging from simple desecration to incendiary bombing. The wave never reaches cataclysmic proportions, but warrants the grave appeal sent to the government in September 1979 by the Chief Rabbi, Kaplan, in which he reviews the growing number of assaults.

As a preliminary reference point, subject to further and deeper investigation, let us note on a corner of the page the list of anti-Jewish profanations that occurred in Germany in 1929. On the night of January 19th, five Jewish tombs are destroyed in Gladbeck. In September, two overturned graves are discovered in Hermeskeil and swastikas are found on 14 graves in Niederstetten. On the night of October 28th, a few tombs are destroyed in Floss. On the night of November 3rd, the wave of profanation reaches Rodelsee. At the end of December it hits the Jewish cemetery in Gunzenhausen. In all, six cemeteries: one in the Rhineland, one in Wurtemberg, one in Westphalia and three in Bavaria. As for synagogues, only one aggression in Arnsberg is mentioned. In early April, at the end of a National-Socialist gathering, a small group tries to force its way into the synagogue but is turned back. It ravages a classroom situated in the same building instead. "The authorities responded with alacrity," the local correspondent for the *C.V. Zeitung* notes. The five guilty parties are arrested the very next day.[3]

Now let us review the editorials of *L'Arche* from the year 1979. In March, there is considerable fear of "uncertain tomorrows," but in Iran, not France. The April editorial deals with the Israeli-Egyptian peace effort. That of May returns to France to sound off anxiously about a certain mentality affecting the Jewish community in France. In June the readers are invited to meditate on "the effervescence of Islam," and in July on the "second Israel." In August, some "concerns that we believe have been forgotten" are recalled: they revolve around the refugees from Vietnam. In September-October, the editorial treats relations between Israel and the Diaspora. In November, it propounds "a new cultural type." In December, it appeals to society as a whole and to the Jews in particular to respond to the serious "challenge of violence" that threatens our civilization. The anti-Semitic resurgence is mentioned several times in the body of the text, but only a small portion of the total number of events reported during the year are covered. There is an obvious gap between the serene, cosmopolitan perspective of the editorials and a local situation that is degenerating and, at the very least, leaving some very serious questions unanswered.

In September-October, 1979, *L'Arche* issues a special edition devoted to the question of whether or not the French are anti-Semites. The coverage is assigned to Wolinski, who is not known for his Jewish militantism. "Daddy, what is a racist?" a child asks his father, who responds calmly while continuing to water his garden: "Above all, an imbecile." The image is pastoral. An article by Léon Poliakov is meticulous in its reckoning of the number of evil profaners: tens, hundreds, thousands at most. It is bombastic, conversely, when it counts the good, "the millions from whom *Holocaust* drew tears." This dual system of calculation sanctions, on the subject of future anti-Semitism, an optimistic conclusion: "We can therefore safely predict that, barring a major catastrophe in the Middle-East or elsewhere, although the Jews will continue to give us a lot to talk about, they have no particular grounds for feeling apprehensive about the future."[4]

The meaning of anti-Jewish incidents is reduced when emphasis is placed on the small number of anti-Semites who are directly responsible (a few thousand). What also captures the attention of observers is the relatively small number of aggressions themselves. "There are in France, all together, some 200 to 250 synagogues, and at least as many other Jewish institutions," writes Jacques Grunewald in the *Tribune Juive* in early 1979. If there really were a "reawakening" of hatred, as some people believe, then it would have to manifest itself in one form or another. "But, virtually none of the synagogues and institutions mentioned at the beginning of this article, nor other individuals or groups who exhibit their Jewish identity in public, are

133

victims of anti-Semitic acts." From whence the title of the editorial: "When the wolf is not here."[5]

This argument belongs to the same family as "we are not living in. . . ," but proceeds with its own brand of fallacious reasoning. If the better part of all the synagogues of France had already burned, Jacques Grunewald would not have to wonder about a possible "reawakening" of anti-Semitism. Such a preliminary stage would have already been surpassed. Contrasting the large number of Jewish institutions in France to the small number of assaults certainly allows us to conclude that we are not in 1942, but this is already a foregone conclusion. But on the other hand, it does not support the claim that there is no "reawakening" of hatred. To be fair and consistent, the editor of the *Tribune Juive* should have compared the number of assaults against Jewish institutions in France in the seventies to the corresponding number in Germany in the twenties, a period of undeniable anti-Semitic "reawakening."

Where could he find the necessary sources of information? Quite simply, in the back issues of his own journal from half-century ago. On August 24, 1928, the *Tribune Juive* informs us that on the night of August 10th red swastikas were painted on a synagogue in Dusseldorf.[6] The edition of November 30th reports the 66th profanation, having begun counting in 1923.[7] The 68th is announced in the December 7th issue.[8]

By carrying this research further, one can discern the total number and even the exact list of the profanations that occurred in that period. From January 1923 to December 1928, 72 cemeteries were desecrated in Germany. That is, on average, 12 per year. In that same length of time, 20 synagogues were sullied. That is an average of a little more than three per year. In 1928, the number of profanations is double the yearly average: 20 cemeteries and seven synagogues. In 1929, however, as we have already mentioned, the figures are particularly low: six cemeteries and only one synagogue. These figures are not all that high when we consider the impressive fund of some hundreds of Jewish institutions, large and small, old and new, in Weimar Germany.

And this is where the paradox arises. The Jews of the late twenties, like their counterparts of the late seventies, dread anti-Semitism. For the first group, the desecration of a Jewish cemetery constitutes a serious violation that must be fervently condemned. The second, conversely, are haunted by images of trains and gas chambers. To them, a few desecrated synagogues here and there seem lacking in importance. From this angle, and contrary to what is generally felt to be the case, the memory of the Hitlerian genocide has not sharpened the vigilance of the Jews. It has, on the contrary, dulled it, by stripping their judgement of all sense of the import of these milder expressions of anti-Semitism.

★

False composure, downplayed anti-Semitism, and artificial marginalization of the anti-Jewish current. The stage is set for the appearance of the first great "self-reassurance system" of the late seventies.

Roger Ascot calls to our attention, in *Le Monde* on September 21, 1979, that "the French police, in 1979, no longer arrest Jews in the wee hours," which is yet another way of saying that we are no longer living in 1942. Then he throws out a question while speaking about the racism that threatens immigrant laborers: "Who can honestly that racism towards Jews, among the many forms of racism that must be fought today, takes precedence?"[9]

Who can say? Let us listen to Bernard-Henri Lévy at the Memorial of the Jewish Martyr in October 1979. "It is simply not true that we are nowadays experiencing an upsurge of anti-Semitism that is in any way comparable to that which other, infinitely more gloomy, periods knew. I also feel that it would be insulting to those here among us who escaped from death to draw the least parallel between their suffering and the concerns that we have today," he points out. "Better yet, it is incumbent on the Jews of this country to realize and to exclaim that there are other, far more murderous racisms about today that we must also fight. . . ."[10]

Transference of concern is sometimes accompanied by an attempt to weigh off the various sorts of violence. "It is a thousand times worse for a Black, an Arab or a Gypsy in France than it is for a Jew," Jean Daniel writes in September. And, later on: "Why is it that people everywhere feel it their duty to announce to us the next upsurge of a great wave of anti-Semitism? Where are the premonitory signs of this new 'Night of Broken Glass' that would send us back to the Germany of 1938?"[11]

The first two are not in 1942, and the third is not in 1938. For all three, the true enemy is racism. Their assertions rest on facts that are commonly accepted, since France has been experiencing a resurgence of unrest affecting Arabs, Blacks, and immigrant workers in general since 1974. This racism finds expression in both individual and collective acts of violence, ranging from discrimination to murder, as well as in repressive administrative measures and revolting living and working conditions. The temptation is therefore great to introduce the anti-Semitic renewal as just another step in this general racist advance. Is this justifiable?

The hatreds differ, first of all, in their victims. Foreigners in France suffer economic exploitation and social segregation. The Jews of France are fully integrated into the society and the nation. Immigrant laborers are concentrated in vocational sectors the native French do not want to work in. The Jews of France likewise occupy a specific socio-economic station, whose historical origins are well known, but theirs is not in any way comparable to that of the immigrant laborers. Racism is the welling up of feelings of resentment towards strangers on the lowest rungs of the social ladder. Anti-Semitism exposes feelings of hatred towards a group whose social success is indisputable. The stranger is perceived as different. The Jew is perceived as the same, and at the same time as mysteriously other.

The hatreds also differ thematically. Anti-Semitism draws together lucubrations on religion (the killing of Christ), satanism (ritual crimes, poisonings, sexual depravities), economics (usury, wealth, parasitism), and politics (world domination, treachery, Judeo-Bolshevism, Judeo-Plutocracy, Judeo-Imperialism). Anti-Semites, as we well know, did not wait until the publication of Gobineau's first book to begin persecuting and massacring the Jews. There was a time, too, when Jews were killed because they refused to convert to the dominant religion, Christian or Islamic. Understood against the background of the long martyrology of Israel in Exile, racism is only a very recent apparition. It is only one element in an enormous arsenal of hatred forged over the ages and covers only one, late chapter in the history of anti-Jewish persecution. For the Jews, racism is just one variety of anti-Semitism among many.

The hatreds differ in compass. Immigrant workers are faced with violence in the form of insults, blows, expulsions and occasional assassinations. The purview demonstrated by anti-Semitism is larger, and that in two ways. In the first case, an indiscreet remark innocently spoken in the course of an elegant Parisian dinner puts the Jew on the spot, forcing him to choose between unpleasant alternatives: pretending not to have heard anything and quickly guiding the conversation on, or else responding, and in that case choosing between two ripostes: the moderate counterthrust or the scandalous exposure. In the second case, at the other extreme, trains depart for Poland laden with human cargo. The Jews—men, women and children—that they transport were arrested, then herded together, and then guarded by police officers and French officials, all according to a well-organized plan. . . . In France, racism oppresses, but anti-Semitism ex-

136

terminates. Not today, of course. But a situation is not appraised only in terms of the immediate present, as if all archives have been burned. It is judged in terms of an ongoing history and in anticipation of its potential developments.

The hatreds differ, most of all, in their degree of permanence. Before the War, France had between two and three million foreigners on her soil, among whom were Italians, Poles and Spaniards numbering in the hundreds of thousands, and Germans, Russians, Czechoslovakians, Hungarians, and Yugoslavs numbering in the tens of thousands. Immigrant Jews represented but an infinitesimal fraction of this group of foreigners.[12] Xenophobia lashed out, without distinction, at all the "aliens" and "macaronis," as well as the "yids." There was, moreover, racism aimed at Arabs and Blacks both in France and the colonies. And there was, lastly, anti-Semitism. The rest is history. In 1942, only the Jewish children were penned up in the *Velodrome d'Hiver*—no Italians, Arabs or Yugoslavs. The xenophobia towards aliens unloaded itself on the Jews, and the Jews alone. Even today there exists a current of French anti-Semitism that loathes well-established French Jews as much as it does immigrant Jews and their offspring. There is no longer any Italian problem, any Russian problem, or any Czechoslovakian problem in France. In the space of one generation, those who were "aliens" before the war have become totally integrated into the life of the country.

Racism and anti-Semitism occasionally display common symptoms, but there the similarity ends. "In view of the real tendency to trivialize the Holocaust, we must be cautious," Wladimir Jankelevitch pronounced in front of the Memorial to the Jewish Martyr, "Anti-Semitism is not a simple variety of racism, a single case of a universal moral infirmity . . . anti-Semitism is not commensurate and not comparable."[13] It's simple, true, and not all that difficult to understand.

But the stance of the MRAP should not take anyone by surprise. Its reductionist attitude is a response to a tactical concern. The MRAP is concerned with reaching a new audience of young people, who are less sensitized to anti-Semitism, and immigrant laborers, many of whom know of no clear distinction between anti-Semitism and anti-Zionism. The MRAP therefore changes its title in 1977. The Movement against Racism, Anti-Semitism and for Peace becomes the Movement against Racism and for Amity between Peoples. This sleight-of-hand performed on Anti-Semitism' also expresses the organization's basic ideological view concerning the nature of the Jewish problem.

One must also keep in mind, in this context, the constant anxiety that drives the leaders of the MRAP on. After each anti-Jewish assault, they fear a renewal of anti-Arab racism. "By an anti-Jewish crime, they wanted to generate anti-Arab racism," Albert Lévy remarks after the assault on Medicis in 1979.[14] The idea returns to him after the Copernic attack. He dreads "the creation of a current of anti-Arab racism from an act of anti-Jewish racism."[15] François Gremy, the president of the movement, is equally perturbed in August 1982. "After the killings on rue des Rosiers, we reject any attempts to stir up hatred towards the Arab community."[16]

Antiracism also plays an internal role in the Jewish community. It calms Jewish apprehensions. Anti-Semitism dwindles, while racism grows: it is therefore racism that must be fought. The reassuring effect of this transference of concern works in three ways. First, the origins of the sickness are understood to be general, and not specifically anti-Jewish. Second, the focus of concern is shifted away from the Jews: others are more adversely affected, so we Jews do not have the most to complain about. Third, it suggests a plan for action: the collective solution of a collective (and not specifically Jewish) problem.

The edifice appears solid but conceals a defect of construction. Interrogated on the question of whether "the Jews of France are French," the leaders of the community respond with a resounding "yes!" This is the logical outcome of their system of identification. But, when one asks them whether there is anti-Semitism in France in 1979, many assert "No. There is racism that affects immigrants." This is the logical consequence of their system of self-reassurance. But the two propositions are antinomical. To liken the desecration of a synagogue in Alsace or in Comtat Venaissin to an attack against a rooming house of immigrant Turks is appropriate from a moral standpoint. But it is strange from a political point of view, since it is commonly maintained that the Jews are French. By incessantly stating that the xenophobes are attacking both Jews and foreigners alike, one eventually accredits the idea that the Jews, who are victims of xenophobia, are foreigners in France. That was not the anticipated result, but that is the natural consequence of an attitude that eschews any specific reality to anti-Jewish hatred.

★

This conflation of anti-Semitism and racism seems suddenly dangerous. Thus a second form of extensive generalization begins to be practiced alongside it, constituting the second major system of self-reassurance of the times.

A wave of violence inundates French society. Assaults of all kinds are reported everywhere. Quite naturally, they also affect the Jews, but do not aim at them directly. Let us read what the editorialist of the *Tribune Juive* writes in an article in which he rejoices over the relatively small number of anti-Jewish incidents that take place in 1978, producing a list (and a very partial one, at that) to substantiate his claim. "Each one of these initiatives, some of which could only have been the work of a single individual, is scandalous in itself. But they don't give us the impression, even if we take into account the most recent incidents, the ones that have occurred over the last ten days in Reims, Avignon, La Varenne and Nice, that Judaism is the prime target, since these days bombs are being set off in the BHV, are demolishing the chateau of Versailles and perpetually threatening one church or another. . . ."[17] This approach to anti-Semitism in France also has a much broader version, tailored to the terrible conflagrations rocking the globe as a whole.[18]

France in the thirties was a somewhat peaceable place, and at the end of the last century, bucolic. Weimar Germany was a tranquil paradise. In those bygone days, there were anti-Semites who took aim at Jews precisely because they were Jews. But during the seventies, violence made its appearance in History. It is indiscriminate, striking at everyone. Today, when synagogues are profaned or Jewish offices dynamited, these events should not be placed side by side with anti-Jewish aggressions committed in other times and other places. It is no longer anti-Semitism, but now violence, very modern and very regrettable violence, that is the culprit. . . .

Violence and anti-Semitism are of course affiliated. The correlation is far from absolute, since there can be violence in society that is not anti-Semitic, and there can likewise be anti-Semitism in periods of peace and prosperity. But the correlation is strong. Europe, in the fourteenth century, had general insecurity along *with* massacres of Jews. The Ukraine, in the seventeenth century, joined merciless combat *with* massacres of Jews. Russia, in 1905, hosted counter-revolution along *with* massacres of Jews. The recent past has seen world war *with* massacres of Jews. This correlation can be found again and again, on a less catastrophic level, during critical phases in the internal evolution of regimes and societies. In capitalist countries, there is often antirepublican strife along *with* anti-Semitism or unemployment along *with* anti-Semitism. In socialist countries, one often finds Stalinist crackdowns accompanied by anti-Semitism, followed by anti-Stalinist reactions that are joined *with* anti-Semitism. In all these instances, the concomitant political issue takes nothing away from the particular nature of anti-Jewish hatred nor from its distinctly aggressive character.

Let us therefore suppose that a "rising tide of violence" is declared from atop the ramparts. It is necessary, then, and without delay, to set off the alarm and call for vigilance. This general violence might in fact be accompanied by a new outburst of anti-Semitism. Not automatically, not necessarily, but most probably, since it often has been before. Anti-Jewish incidents already on record should have confirmed these suspicions by now. But we are told exactly the opposite. Everything is fine, nothing to report, the night is calm. Anti-Semitic acts committed in a period of manifest violence are but one expression, among many others, of a universal problem. Everyone is blowing up everyone else, and the Jews just happen to be living on the same planet as everyone else. Consequently, there is no cause for alarm.

★

In 1979, though, the main area of concern shifts over to neo-Nazism. The flame of a Hitlerian torch emerges out of the darkness of night. At first, the horror that it generates is so great that one sees only it. and entirely ceases to look beyond it. But afterwards, as it draws nearer, one discovers that it is held aloft by a pimply wimp who seems hardly intimidating or nasty. It therefore couldn't have posed a very serious threat. The apparent threat was merely an effect of focalization, and so was followed by decompression. Let us observe this in action.

Excessive focalization of concern on the neo-Nazis precludes any possible appreciation of the problem of anti-Semitism as a whole. Firstly, it makes too big an issue of the return of a sinister but well known phenomenon, one that was overcome long ago. Furthermore, Nazism implies structure. It can be located, encircled, trapped and destroyed, either through direct action, through action instigated by public officials or through pressure exerted by public opinion on these public officials. Nazism is detested, and everyone is fully aware of what it is capable of doing. Anti-Nazism, therefore, mobilizes communists, Gaullists, socialists and liberals, as it did in the days of the Resistance. This leads to two positive consequences. The Jews will not be left alone to face the bloodthirsty beast; and the beast will be destroyed, since all will step forward with celerity to crush it. The plague is well designated, identified, and catalogued. The infection is serious, but contained, and affects only a very small minority of the French. When one first sees it, Nazism is horrifying. But, paradoxically, it is from then on reassuring.

140

Although neo-Nazism explains many things, it falls far short of explaining everything. French anti-Semitism has underground roots and ideological foundations, and its public expressions and concrete demonstrations exceed and overflow the borders of Nazism. All of the Nazis are of course anti-Semites. But not all anti-Semites are Nazis, far from it. This is true, for example, of the anti-Semites of the Left, whether they disguise themselves as anti-Zionists or not. It is particularly true of the popular guises that contemporary anti-Jewish hatred wears and which we are highly accustomed to over-looking.

The effect of decompression, for its part, is best illustrated by the window test. A friend has just called to say that he saw a swastika on a wall. His call interrupted one's reading of a book on the Holocaust. The heart pounds, the mind reels. Images of atrocities begin to rush through the mind: they are back. Quickly, run to the window, throw aside the curtains, open it, lean out over the street . . . all is calm. No bellowing SS, no black automobiles from the Gestapo, only relaxed passersby and busy housekeepers. This verification can be performed at any moment of the day, however often one looks. There is no SS, no Gestapo.

This phenomenon is easily interpreted. In antiracist addresses and antiviolence lamentations, the relativization of anti-Semitism is achieved by lateral translation. Anti-Jewish acts are absorbed into two wider realms. The first of racist aggressions committed against immigrant workers, and the second is all of the violent acts committed in France. The evocation of Nazism, itself, leads to a relativization in depth. It invites a comparison of contemporary anti-Semitism to past anti-Semitism. Quite simply, it reduces the former to nil. A few desecrated cemeteries, a few samples of hastily scrawled graffiti, and a few anti-Jewish assaults are nothing compared to the ex-termination of six million people. Searching for any affinities between the two periods is just indecent.

As a result of the window test, the "we are not living in 1942" and the equally primitive "we are not living in 1929" arguments are introduced. Our memories of Nazism are so strong that they have occluded our recollection of its incipient stages, when anti-Semitism exists but is still limited and the movement is small but has the po-tential to grow. One too easily restricts oneself to a view that can only see all or nothing. If it isn't everything (the arrest of Jews by the police) then it is nothing (a few insignificant acts of graffiti).

Every attempt to conduct a comparative analysis runs up against a wall of nonacceptance that is not methodological. No one claims that one's documentation is insufficient (a technical objection) or that one hasn't the right to place two distinct historical junctures side by side (an objection on principles). They say "one cannot compare" as if this were their peremptory announcement of the results of a study that they have presumably conducted. One cannot compare them, since the two periods, before and now, offer no points in common. But their conclusion is as opaque as their research was nonexistent.

"We are not living in 1929" is not an objective statement but a dogmatic incantation whose success is easy to explain. Seen from our vantage today, the twenties and thirties look like an antechamber to the forties. Our recollection of them is indelibly associated with the horror that succeeded them. The inference is unconscious. To compare 1923 to 1983, most people think, is to assume that the Nazis will come into power in ten years. Historical reflection, which ought to be directed upon pre-Nazi Germany, is instead magnetically drawn toward Nazi Germany. This redirected focus is understandable. But the result is that any the comparison becomes absurd: it only takes the window test to assure oneself that there are no SS in the streets of Paris.

Our telescoping of the different decades wrecks any potential comparison. On a more sophisticated level, it warps and falsifies it. One might remember that FANE carried out a series of anti-Jewish assaults just before the Copernic explosion in October 1980. At that time, Robert Badinter, to bring things back into perspective, remarked that "Friedriksen is not Hitler nor even Doriot, and the handful of Nazi pests around him are truly unremarkable compared to the SA of Germany in 1930."[19] He is right, of course. But he is setting up a comparison between a French fascism that has scarcely begun its re-entry into the political arena and which has taken only the first halting steps along its new course, and a Nazism that, although not yet in power, was nonetheless already quite powerful. It is Germany in the twenties and not in 1930 that he ought to refer to. This reference, in any case, could not apprise us of the future course of events, nor could it authorize any predictive extrapolations. It would have, simply, the virtue of coherence.

Let us keep in mind, lastly, that in the twenties the phrase equivalent to "we are not in . . . 1929, 1933, 1938 and 1942" was "we are not in the Middle Ages." But the Middle Ages lasted for several hundred years, during which the Jews experienced persecutions, expulsions and massacres, but also knew periods of tranquility, progress and prosperity. Then a few more centuries slipped by. A German Jew, in

142

1929, could reasonably assert that we are no longer in the Middle Ages. Today, such an assertion is less self-evident. The distance that separates us from the disgraceful epoch is not five centuries, but fifty years. The interval is far too brief for us to be able to ascertain whether the Nazi genocide was definitive and final or whether it was perhaps just the first (and not the last) act in a new era of anti-Jewish outrage. In which case, of course, the forty years that have passed since the Liberation must be regarded as a simple respite following a particularly ruthless anti-Semitic eruption, and just one part of a cycle of acute, calm and transitional phases. The two formulae are therefore not commensurate. "We are not in the Middle Ages" was plausible in 1929. "We are not in 1929" is much less so in our time.

★

Let us complete this eclectic panorama of 1979. The CRIF makes an unintentional quip. After the attack on Medicis, it throws light on the "criminal intentions of its authors": "To spread panic among the Jews of France and to create the impression that their fellow-citizens are hostile towards them."[20] In other words, the anti-Semites set off bombs to "create the impression" that there is anti-Semitism in France.

The theme of unreal anti-Semitism is found again in the views of Jacques Attali, who denounces the dangers created by the media: "Also, speaking irresponsibly about anti-Semitism as a potential menace produces a real desire for a forbidden fruit, and all those who make their grandiose statements about anti-Semitism in order to increase their sales or their audiences, only channel society's growing need for a scapegoat towards the Jews: the Jew spurs sales in the media; the media might in turn devour the Jews."[21] Jacques Attali forwards an ancient thesis in modern parlance, one that arises from the strange conception that anti-Semitism does not exist from its own side. The poisonous plant only draws itself towards a source of illumination. It only grows because we are looking at it.

Gerard Israel envisages a scenario in which anti-Semitism is once again active: "There is no doubt that a large segment of the nation, as was the case during the Dreyfus Affair, would rise up against injustice, barbarism and racism." A few paragraphs earlier, in the same article, Israel gravely declares that "the French people did not rouse themselves en masse to prevent the occupying forces from arresting the Jews." The French, then, "rise up" for an officer unjustly accused of high treason, but do not "rise up" for thousands of Jewish children interned in the Velodrome d'Hiver in the heart of

143

Paris. The contradiction is not entirely lost on the author, for he concludes that "it would be wrong to cast aside all wariness."[22]

Scopus writes an editorial in the *Bulletin de l'ATJ* in September 1979, a piece whose ostensive goal is to dissipate the concerns expressed by Harris and Sédouy in their book *Juifs et Français*. Scopus, looking for an avenue of self-reassurance, could specify that we are not in 1942, nor indeed in 1930. But he instead opts for another method, one very similar to the bountiful talk about "our beautiful France" at the end of the last century. There is no anti-Semitism in France, he explains, because there never really was any. During the War, "the French people remained inert, overwhelmed by all that had happened to them, and unconscious of the responsibility that befell them." There were, of course, collaborators, but there were also the Resistance and Free France "whose actions were rooted in the history of France, and so preserved her honor." In addition, "incidents that, from the Dreyfus affair until the eve of the Second World War, disturbed people, not only very rarely led to violence (mini-pogroms in Algeria, an attack on Léon Blum), but have today entirely disappeared from the French scene."[23]

The key word in this retrospective is mini-pogrom. When the *Jewish Telegraphic Agency* reports the troubles in Constantina in its August 8, 1934 news bulletin, it headlines "Pogrom in Algeria."[24] When the *Bulletin de l'Agence Télégraphique Juive* recalls the same events in 1979, it employs a prettified expression (mini-pogrom), which aptly illustrates the idea that Scopus has of France.

The dominant approach is that of the CRIF. Its New Year's resolution, published in September 1979, is drafted in a lyrical style, but with care and dignity. "In these difficult times, the CRIF calls upon the organized Jewish community of France to keep unbreached its wall of solidarity with Israel, with the struggle of the Jews in the Soviet Union, and with the struggle for the liberation of the Jews in Syria. It exhorts it to act with resolution and composure, conscious of its rights and duties and also of its contributions to French society. Enlightened by the ordeals of its own history, it must be ready to face any upcoming crises, and to resist threats and pressures, no matter what their source, by opposing them with conviction and cohesion. . . ."[25] The references to Israel and to persecuted Jews sincerely express the feeling of unity and common destiny shared by the majority of Jews in France.

But CLESS suggests another course. Its proclamations concerning the "violent, profound and lasting character of the actual anti-Semitic crisis" assert that "the Jews of France have renewed their connection

144

with the traditional destiny of the exiled Jewish people." CLESS denounces the error of the community leaders who hold that "a Jewish future is possible in France. This is false." "The correct answer is offered by Zionism, our movement for National Liberation. Our future is not in France. It is in Israel, our own country. There, the cities and towns are Jewish. The schools are Jewish schools. . . . In Israel, our people liberates itself from the oppression of the Exile. It again becomes a free and independent people, master of its own destiny. This is the solution to the Jewish question, to the problem of assimilation as well as anti-Semitism. This is for us, the Jews of France, the only route. The route of courage, the route of aliyah."[26]

The "unbreached wall" of the CRIF, and the "route of courage" of CLESS. The settled community (Jews! Stay in France!) vs. the Zionist appeal (Jews! Return to Zion!). The classical debate that one might have thought dead and buried has been revived. Two programs, two futures, two solutions—adversaries once again.

The year draws to a close, however, on a distant note: "The FSJU launches an appeal on behalf of the Cambodian people," the *Bulletin de l'ATJ* headlines in December, 1979.[27]

★

After the Copernic bomb in October 1980, the theme of the insurgent evil conspiracy replaces the great apologia of crises past.

The evil conspiracy hypothesis, in fact, creates an entirely unique fusion of four different, major ideas. Anti-Semitism is not French: it comes from elsewhere. Anti-Semitism is not a popular current: the anti-Semites are a small bunch of bomb-planters. Anti-Semitism is instrumental: it is simply a means directed towards further ends. And, lastly, anti-Semitism threatens France as a whole and not just the Jews: all of the French must, and therefore will, mobilize. All of these themes are, of course, classical ones; one comes across them, in one form or another, throughout the twentieth century. But the evil conspiracy hypothesis, which is pure phantasmagoria, enables one to maximally exploit each of the four themes, viewed separately, and also optimizes their impact by weaving them all together. If the bomb is directed at democracy in general, and not just at the Jews in particular, the two dreaded specters, Jewish nationalism, on the one hand, and French indifference, on the other, can be simultaneously exorcised.

This chimera feeds on the terrorist, and thus secretive nature of the act. Nothing is known and so everything can be imagined about its authors. But in 1980, the Rhine is peaceful. The frontiers are calm and sirens announce the passage of ambulances and not the arrival of stukas in attack formation. The present state of Franco-German relations prohibits the Germanization of anti-Semitism. It is necessary to search elsewhere for the central command post that sends out the assassins and seeks to destabilize France.

But, even though there are multiple hypotheses concerning the origins of the attack, there is virtual unanimity of judgement about what the strategy of the assault is. And that is where the weak point of the entire theory lies. How could the mysterious central command post hope to destabilize all of France (the goal it aspires to) by staging anti-Jewish attacks (the method it employs)?

The crux of the matter is summed up in the editorial of the *Bulletin de l'ATJ*, which first reveals the "objectives" of the terrorists: "1. To provoke fear and terror amongst the Jews in order to push them towards extreme reactions and to escalate the spiral of violence. 2. To marginalize the Jews and cut them off from the nation, to make them a 'foreign' entity that is responsible for the malaise evident in the current economic and social crisis in France. 3. To unsettle the foundations of the State and endanger the governing democracy whose impotent response to terrorism might expose it as incapable of maintaining order or ensuring the safety of all citizens."[28]

This text is important, since it introduces a stratagem that will be an essential feature of every later analysis of anti-Jewish violence. It exposes people' fears (here: counter-violence, isolation of the Jewish community, passivity of the authorities), but only as transformed into the strategic intentions of the authors of the attacks. This tendency to displace and rationalize the nightmare will remain in effect long after the assault on Copernic.

"Today, the attack by our enemies has misfired, since its goal was to separate the Jewish community from the rest of the French nation," says Claude Chouraqui. "They sought to strike at the Jews, and then isolate them from the rest of the nation. The project is bold; the trap, obvious," Ady Steg also adds. The thesis of a great conspiracy often impels the leaders of the community to send out operational directives to the Jewish public, and especially to young people ready to rashly launch themselves into punitive action. And so, Henri Hajdenberg, president of the Renouveau Juif: "It would be clumsy to succumb to the provocation or the trap that those who wish to destabilize French society have extended toward us, by responding to violence with violence."[29]

Pierre André Taguieff develops the analysis further. The terrorists want to "divide and destabilize public opinion" after the ground work has been laid by ideological campaigns. "The objective is to provoke a Jewish self-defensive reaction, and so initiate a process of counter-violence destined to become unpopular because of its anti-Semitic tone (real or suggested), and so isolate the Jewish community within the French nation by pinpointing the former as the cause, by its mere presence, of a general climate of insecurity."[30] Robert Badinter professes an identical point-of-view in March 1983, recalling the "objective" of the authors of the assaults: "To destabilize France . . . and, at the same time, marginalize the Jewish community, by provoking within it a feeling of anguish and bitterness that will push it towards counter-violence, which will only further accelerate the process of destabilization."[31]

Goals, projects, traps, objectives. Not a single document, not a single police report, not a shred of proof—no concrete indications will, at any time, be presented in support of the theses advanced. But even when considered free of any concern for its adherence to reality, the anti-destabilization discourse is not entirely convincing. It establishes that anti-Jewish assaults could lead to reactions of retaliation and self-defense within the Jewish community. It does not quite establish in what way such reactions run the risk of destabilizing the country, and are thus eagerly awaited by the anti-French conspirators lying in wait, lurking in the shadows.

The sublimation of fear, that is, its transposition into the strategic intentions of the adversary and the "trap" into which one is consequently forbidden to fall, furnishes no information about the terrible conspiracy. But it says all there is to say . . . about fear itself. Being cut off from the nation, either voluntarily or as a result of a negative trend in public opinion, *that* is the danger so highly feared. It is, in the meantime, averted. "If the terrorists of rue Copernic wanted to marginalize us, isolate us or ghettoize us, they have failed," Bernard Attali announces triumphantly during a stay in the United States in November 1980.[32]

★

The popularity of talk about anti-destabilization during these times of peril (peril presumed and not real, but at the time perceived as real) demonstrates that many Jews feel anguish about being cut off from the French nation, of which they considered themselves members.

This reaction is not, however, universal: ". . . I regret the absence of the French flag from the march on the Champs-Elysées, led by the blue flag adorned with the Star of David," Raymond Aron writes in *L'Express*.[33] In fact, and quite spontaneously, the Jews who assembled in protest after an anti-Jewish attack did not brandish the

147

French flag, but quite simply and very logically . . . the Jewish flag. From the Jewish quarters, from the suburbs, from the youth movements, the Jewish demonstrators assembled and did not deem it necessary to hoist the tricolored flag. Their abstention showed that the concept of a break with the (French) nation had not seemed as insufferable to them as it had to their official leaders. In raising the Jewish flag, the Jewish masses gave evidence that they had withstood the shock. They performed an act of political maturity and human dignity.

Certainly, their logic was incomplete. In the last analysis, one's true and actual allegiance (the country in which one lives) must be in accord with one's chosen symbol of allegiance (the flag that one bears). If the affirmation is Jewish, then the country must also be. The return of the Jews of France to Israel lies at the end of a long road, a road along which only the very first landmarks were passed in October 1980.

★

The idea of a possible departure is, of course, not supported by all. *L'Express,* in October 1980, reports on a dialogue between a Jewish mother and her son. "Perhaps we will have to go away and leave the country," she said to her son. "No way," he answered her, "I'm staying here and I'm going to fight."[34]

"Run away? Not a chance," *Le Droit de Vivre* wrote on this topic in April 1938. "On the contrary . . . French like others, 100 percent French, that is what we are . . . we will fight like Frenchmen, on French soil, until death."[35]

"It has become clear to everyone that the future of the Jews of France is in France, no matter what declarations to the contrary are made by certain Jewish organizations," Richard Marienstras says after the Copernic demonstrations, thus engaging in polemics with the Zionist movements.[36]

"Nisht Emigratzie. Nor Kampf oifn Ort!" (Yiddish: "No emigration. Fight where we stand!") This slogan appears in the headlines of the *Unzer Shtimme,* the voicepiece of the Bund in France, in March 1939, a few months before the start of the Second World War.[37] This epithet condenses into a few words the fundamental ideological attitude of the Bund and other anti-Zionist elements within the Jewish community.

Another rejection: the idea of a return to the ghetto, the word here being used in its positive sense. "Some expressed an unconscious desire to return, not to the ghetto that is emblematic of the fearful, submissive and feeble Jew whom everyone pushes around, but to the ghetto that is bellicose, aggressive and proud. No ghetto!" exclaims Guy de Rothschild.[38]

He is only restating a point of view that was amply developed in the issues of the 18th and 25th of February, 1939, in the journal *Unzer Shtimme.* Two controversial articles, *"Zurick in Ghetto"* (Yiddish: "Return to the ghetto"), violently attack the Zionists and other Jewish nationalists who claim that the Jewish people have become more and more isolated and can therefore rely only on themselves and their own forces to safeguard their future. *Unzer Shtimme* warns against the unjustified "pessimism" that drives the partisans of the "return to the ghetto."[39]

The same theme was explored a few years earlier in Berlin. In November 1930, shortly after the legislatives in which the Nazis gain their first major foothold, there is another electoral campaign, this time internal to the Jewish community. Several important leadership posts in the Jewish community of Berlin must be filled. At stake is control over numerous educational, social and cultural institutions. But the confrontation is, more than anything else, ideological, and pits against each other the two great forces of German Judaism: the Liberals, who support the continuation of Jewish identity, but are also anxious to maintain the allegiance of the Jews to the German nation; and the Zionists, who are joined together in the Judische Volkspartei, which asserts that the Jews are offspring of the Jewish nation, and not the German one.

Although not anti-Zionist, the Central Verein decides to fully endorse the liberals against the Zionists. "They want to bring us back to a spiritual and political ghetto from which the emancipation liberated us after a struggle that lasted for generations," says an official edict of the *C.V. Zeitung* that calls upon the German Jews to vote against the politics of *"Rückkehr ins Ghetto"* ("return to the ghetto").[40] The appeal bears fruit. In the elections of November 30, 1930 in Berlin the Liberal party gains 54 percent of the vote as opposed to 33 percent for the Jüdische Volkspartei. The majority of voters (who are numerous, serving witness to the degree of organization and cohesion in German Judaism at the time) thus reject by their votes the temptation to return to the ghetto.[41]

In France today, the theme of the ghetto appears on different occasions. "The time of the ghetto is over," Adam Loss decides in 1980 before the Copernic bombing.[42] "The time for the return to the ghetto . . . seems to have forever passed," he says again in November 1982.[43]

But we already knew that. The news was announced by Bernard

149

Lecache in 1933: "The times when Jews had to confine themselves to the ghetto and found no relief other than their faith are no more."[44] It was confirmed by Raymond-Raoul Lambert in 1938: "But the days are over in which the Jews, when their brothers are mounted on the stake . . . flee back to their ghettos, passively awaiting a brighter future."[45] Lambert will be deported and burned a few years later, along with his wife and children.

Another classical theme rises once more to the surface. Let us listen to Isidore Loeb, on January 25, 1890: "Just as long as there remains a spark of biblical spirit in our hearts, we will side with the oppressed (among whom we ourselves are) against the oppressors, with those who would like to bring people together against those who divide them, with those who want to quell racial hatreds against those who stir them up. . . ."[46]

Israel Lévi, Chief Rabbi in France, has the very same thought several decades later. In a meeting called in protest of anti-Semitism in 1933, he affirms, in particular, that Judaism is "with all who are persecuted, against all who persecute." He adds: "If ever, God forbid, Christians were persecuted for their religion, we would be with them against their persecutors."[47]

"Judaism has always been, for me, a most urgent quest for human equality and human fairness. . . ." Guy de Rothschild states in a 1980 speech in which he advises the Jews of France to resist the impulse to return to the ghetto. "Our action against racism and anti-Semitism must be an action in defense of human rights, and not only the rights of Jews. The Jews should rise up to defend humankind wherever it is attacked, since we know so well what discrimination and racism can mean. It is within this context and within this context only that our actions will be accepted and understood."[48]

The generous idea (it pretends also to be efficacious, and not just generous) underlying his appeal is put forth at the same time in the Trotskyist weekly, *Rouge*. Bernard Cohen and Daniel Bensaid there likewise assert that "we must grant the fight against anti-Semitism, and against every form of racism its full militant dimension."[49]

(Their article is devoted to criticizing the slogan of CLESS: "Only one solution, the return to Zion.") One finds the following item in an interview given by Daniel Cohn-Bendit to *L'Arche* in 1978: "The cure for anti-Semitism will only be found in the complete transformation of the societies in which we live," he states to Victor Malka. "And in the meantime?" the journalist asks. "In the meantime, it is necessary to fight," decrees the intrepid revolutionary, who perceives neither the irony of the question nor the feeling of "déjà vu" that his reply evokes.[50])

Finally, Alain Geismar too, after Copernic, invents a new method for fighting anti-Jewish hatred. "It is most necessary and urgent that a movement of Jews and non-Jews be created joining different generations and sensibilities, whose sole objective would be to rid the streets of the danger of racist assassins along with their instigators and protectors," he proposes in *Le Nouvel Observateur.*[51] No sooner said than done. The Verein zur Abwehr des Anti-Semitismus, bringing Jews and non-Jews together, is created in Berlin in 1890. The League of Human Rights is created in France at the end of the nineteenth century. The LICA is born in 1927. In 1939, there is not a country in Europe in which Jews and non-Jews are not fighting anti-Semitism side by side.

★

But, by the way, where is the French anti-Semitism that we hear so much about at the end of 1980? In October, Annie Kriegel reports that "if fascist plague there be, it must have symptoms other than these assaults" and forwards the hypothesis of an attack of Palestinian origin.[52] Developments in the investigation will confirm that her conclusion was correct. In January 1981 she states: "The assault on rue Copernic was isolated: after it, the rash of offenses that were before being perpetrated against Jewish institutions abruptly diminished and practically disappeared."[53] There, she is mistaken. There weren't any major terrorist blows akin to the bombing on rue Copernic nor even any acts like the series of machine-gunnings of September. But many minor incidents nonetheless continued to take place in France.

Let us read the *Bulletin de l'ATJ* for October 10, 1980. "Over the last few days, there have been reported, both in Paris and the suburbs, a large number of malevolent acts directed at the Jews. The electronics plants of Claude Trigano were set ablaze in Paris. In many dwellings inhabited by Jews, unknown persons scratched out swastikas on the doors . . . in Romilly-sur-Seine, the shop-window of a Jewish tailor was smashed and the walls were covered with anti-Semitic slogans. In Montpellier, perhaps ten storefronts were found covered with swastikas. In Nice, a kosher butchery was ransacked. In Grenoble, an explosive device was thrown at a grocery bearing a Jewish-sounding name. . . ."[54]

Let us end this account by citing *Le Nouvel Observateur* of the 13th-19th of October, 1980, which says that "anti-Semitism is expressing itself all around us": "In Saint-Dié, where the synagogue is desecrated; in Bron, by graffiti . . . in Nice, In Fontaine (Isère) and

151

in Troyes, where Jewish stores served as targets; in the Paris-Enghien train, where a young Israelite was assaulted by three ruffians."[55] And let us push on into December. At Grosbiledersdorff (sic), a Jewish cemetery is profaned. In Marseille, a bomb is discovered in a restaurant belonging to a Jew. In Lyon, a young Jew is beaten by a taxi-driver. Another Jewish youth is assaulted in Paris. On October 29th, a student of the Yavneh school in Marseille is attacked and beaten by four youths. On the night of October 30th, the car of a Jewish physician in Montrouge is set on fire. On November 4th, shots are fired at two watchmen in front of a Jewish school in Paris. On Christmas Eve, the director of a Jewish institution in Strasbourg is roughed-up. Anti-Jewish inscriptions are found in Longwy, Lille, Roanne, Clichy-la-Garenne, Lyon, Marseille. . . .

These acts form the backdrop for all the debates and articles that speculate about the origins, the scale and the strategy of anti-French terrorism. If a murderous bombing is considered a serious act, then shots fired from automatic rifles must be more minor acts and profanations of cemeteries just unimportant trifles. The multitude of small anti-Jewish acts has lost any and all power to disturb people as their attention has been drawn towards larger, more spectacular attacks. The Copernic bomb was therefore diversionary—not by virtue of having been followed by a tenebrious maneuver on the part of the forces of evil, but rather, quite simply, because of having monopolized people's attention. By too assiduously scanning the horizons off towards Beirut, Moscow and Berlin, one all too easily loses sight of the French terrain: reassured by the reactions of the majority of the French towards the assault on Copernic, the Jews of France failed to accord the smaller incidents of the closing months of 1980 all the attention that was due.

★

Let us get back to the terrorists, whose swarthy complexions betray their Middle Eastern origins. The Palestinization of anti-Semitism attributes the sum total of anti-Jewish crimes to the PLO or to extremist Arab nations, like Libya. Roughly speaking, the guilty party is just Arafat himself.

True, Arab nationalists and Palestinian terrorists never hesitate to attack, by bomb or machine-gun, civilian targets in Israel or elsewhere. The examples are plentiful, and the presumptions one might make are strong. The PLO often condemns the assaults, but only truly guileless people still believe that the very existence of a denial that has been hurriedly transmitted to all the press agencies is ipso facto sufficient to exonerate a suspected organization. Cases have been known to happen in which the very same organization carries out an assault through its military arm, while, at the same time, it drafts a strongly-worded and indignant protest through its propaganda service. Not only that, but if rebel factions happen to be the ones who do the killing, even in the case of bona fide rebels who aren't craftily disguised members of a division of Fatah, the political responsibility still falls upon the PLO. They are no less implicated. The PLO is, whether one likes it or not, representative of the Palestinian movement as a whole.

However, not all the major anti-Jewish assaults in the world have been committed by the PLO. No one has access to any reliable sources of information about the relative weights of the two following categories. That of assaults committed and claimed by the PLO, committed and denounced by the PLO, committed by an affiliated splinter-group, committed by rebels split off from the PLO or committed by non-Palestinian groups having links with the PLO on logistical or ideological grounds. And, secondly, that of attacks perpetrated by groups who have absolutely nothing to do with events in the Middle-East, not even from afar. Above all, anti-Semitism does not show its true face in a few spectacular attacks, but rather in a multitude of acts that are far less grave but much more frequent than major terrorist bombings. The leaders of the PLO don't spend their nights scribbling "Death to the Jews!" on the walls of France.

The Palestinization of anti-Semitism is therefore unacceptable. While awaiting the day when peace will be established between Israel and all the peoples of the region, the Jewish State will continue to fight for its security. But, for the Israelis, self-defense does not require that the enemy be misrepresented. Self-defense does not require that acts which he is known to be innocent of be attributed to the enemy. Defending oneself does not require that one ignore the fact that those facing one are also men. Removed to France, these principles reduce to a single rule-of-thumb. The PLO must be attacked for its actions, indeed for all of its actions, but only for its actions. No more.

For the Jews of France it is also a question of clear-sightedness. The Palestinization of anti-Semitism is reassuring. The Jews of France do accept that they are victims, but only indirect and secondary victims of assaults that are manufactured abroad. There is an Israeli-Arab conflict, but there is no Jewish question in France: the Palestinian scarecrow chases all fears away.

The "destabilizing evil conspiracy" theory nurtures the symbiosis between Jews and French by establishing that an attack against the Jews is an attack against France. The "Middle-East Connection" fills in the remainder of the picture, by providing a conduit for the expression of the other major component of Jewish sentiment, that is, solidarity with Israel. If the anti-French terrorists were . . . members of the PLO, then everything would fall into place. The Jews of France are French and, at the same time, bound up with Israel. Their two referential totalities, France, the country in which they live, and Israel, the land to which they are filially tied, become harmoniously reconciled.

A noisome mist of small anti-Semitic acts will, as always, tarnish this radiant image. One cannot, in all honesty, attribute them to a resolution made by the Central Committee of the PLO, and one must also genuinely consider the possibility that they have a local, and not galactic, origin. But the Palestinian diversion engages precisely those elements in the Jewish community that are most militant. Their absolute indictment of the PLO propels the Jewish militants towards a truncated and therefore dangerous vision of the Jewish reality in France. The most activist persons and organizations devote their full energy to crossing swords with Yasser Arafat. They neglect the anti-Jewish opinions of Mr. Dupont who lives right next-door.

A new paradox must be comprehended. Pro-Israelism creates an obstacle to the perception of the dangers threatening Jewish life in Galut (Exile). It therefore drains vitality from the Jewish National movement and from an awakening of Jewish conscience that might lead to a return to Israel. Pro-Israelism vs. Zionism? The surprising antinomy is explained when one restores to each of these terms its proper sense.

★

Systems of self-reassurance all function in the same fashion. Bursts of ingenuity are deployed to expand the horizons of the battlefield. The true target, well, it's actually immigrant labor (racism), France as a whole and its democracy (neo-Nazism and/or international terrorism), or Israel (Palestinian terrorism). In none of these cases are the Jews of France found on the front lines. There is an expansion of horizons in the description of the victims. There is, conversely, a narrowing in the identification of the guilty, whose ranks are delimited to include only professional terrorists, nostalgic neo-Nazis, Palestinian commandos, or any combination of the three. Accent is placed on both the cliquish and international character of the phenomenon. When squeezed into these molds, anti-Semitism can be more easily handled. The State only has to react with force (neo-Nazism), or decide to close the Parisian Bureau of the PLO (Palestinian terrorism) in order to dispel the threat in a single blow.

The obfuscation of the true targets, who are shielded behind their many purported co-victims, is intended to put the Jews of France out of harm's way. The marginalization of the marksmen, who are at once diabolized and miniaturized, places the French people beyond suspicion's reach. Anti-Semitism is impossible. But, in order to really take hold, the discourse of reassurance must be energetic and rousing. When it arrives at the solution stage, its tones become magisterial. It dredges up the terrible past and the lessons that the Jews have never failed to extract from it. It sends out a compulsory triple appeal for unity, vigilance, and combat. It might conclude (this is discretionary) with mention of the solidarity of the Jews with the State of Israel. Words so grand must express an indomitable resolve.

Fractious rhetoric and reassuring explanations are combined to make the Jews forget their vulnerability. Anti-Semitism, in fact, is a lot of people (the non-Jews) who make trouble for a few people (the Jews). The ploy is to invert these proportions. A few people (a few thousand bad souls) attack everyone (democracy, immigrant laborers, victims of violence, France, and incidentally the Jews). The result of the scuffle is not in doubt and the Jews have nothing to fear.

Here then, barely caricatured, is a composite portrait of the typical anti-Semite, drawn from the diverse systems of self-reassurance that have flourished in France since the late seventies. He is a sinister-looking foreigner, clothed in a Nazi uniform that he procured in Libya. He lands in Paris, where he knows no one, or else only the third Undersecretary to the Soviet ambassador, who is secretly manipulating him. The fierce anti-Semite, on his very first night out, desecrates a Catholic church and a Protestant temple. That very night, in addition, a purely accidental blaze breaks out in a synagogue. The monster utters some racist remarks concerning immigrant laborers and attacks French democracy. But the admirable demeanor of the French people prevents him, just in the nick of time, from setting off a one kilo bomb with which he had hoped to destabilize France. He is unanimously rejected by public opinion, arrested by an efficient police force, and condemned by an intractable judge. Two days after his arrival in France, the ignominious beast is under lock and key: there is no anti-Semitism in France.

Anyhow, there isn't any anti-Semitism of this sort. Ten percent of the French consider the Jews not to be French like themselves and feel that they are too numerous in France. Ten percent of the French—that's a lot of people, people who don't correspond to the idealized prototype of the anti-Semite.

Ten percent of the French on the one hand, and on the other, a series of minor anti-Jewish incidents and offenses. Might there exist a link between the two? The supposition is bold, but is nonetheless worth a closer look.

Chapter Eleven
Interpretation

Some, as we have seen, have taken advantage of the episodic, repetitive and relatively harmless character of minor anti-Jewish acts to advance the claim that they don't even exist. Others have admitted their existence and have even been disturbed by them. But even these people have sometimes been mistaken in their analyses of the incidents. Let us read the report on racism and anti-Semitism in May 1981,[1] which provides a rather complete picture of anti-Semitic incidents. The figures are valid, on the whole, and the facts reported are precise.

But we must keep in mind two schematic figures that show us how the existence of a shadowy zone constrains our appraisal of this information. These figures have already been sketched out. The first is that of incidents that become centrally collated. It is compact and cylindrical, with assaults on top and graffiti on the bottom in relatively similar quantities. The other is that of incidents that actually take place, whether they happen to be called to anyone's attention or not. Its form is distinctly conical. Its peak (serious acts) is clearly defined. Its center (acts of middling importance) is already much larger. Its base (small, everyday forms of harassment) is a vast nebula whose contours are indeterminate. The famous recapitulatory lists are drawn up from the acts that were reported and catalogued and not, of course, from all those that actually took place. They therefore include all of the more important attacks, but display only a very small portion of the more benign incidents, since these are rarely reported. A quick scan of these lists might cause one to wonder at the relatively high number of the former and the relatively low number of the latter. The road to misinterpretation is wide open, and the authors of the report have themselves wandered onto it.

"The aggressions are almost exclusively directed at important figures, institutions or symbols and are only rarely simple street incidents," they write, forgetting that there might be few street incidents on the list yet many in the streets that never find their way onto the list. Why do the authors of the report ignore the fact that it is not sufficient to simply inspect catalogs of events, but necessary as well to ask oneself what portion of the problem they reflect and what portion they completely miss? When the subject is racism aimed at immigrant laborers, however, reason prevails: ". . . offenses that are the work of isolated individuals, inflammatory graffiti, and denials of service or employment are infinitely more numerous than aggression that are claimed (by terrorists)." Further on, they recall "the traditional racism of the average Frenchman." Actual racism thus far exceeds the bounds of known racism.

Their selective neglect of the shadowy zone (as concerns anti-Semitism) leads the authors to an encouraging finding: "it anti-Semitism is much more often the work of ideologically motivated activist groups than the result of more or less spontaneous incidents resulting from popular racism." From whence they draw the conclusion: "The greater part of all desecrations and offenses are signed. They seem to be committed by small commando groups trained in terrorist acts, who almost always utilize the same techniques and arms and follow the same plan. Their signatures, which vary little, designate splinter-groups that couldn't possibly possess sufficient means, by themselves, to have such widespread impact on the country or be able to act in different regions at the same time. One might conclude, since they are not supported by the public, that they must obtain their backing through ties within the State apparatus that assure their protection, or from a national network that is unknown and well-structured, or as part of an international terrorist network; these different hypotheses are not even mutually exclusive."

The greater part of all desecrations and assaults are signed: false, as we shall see. The trained commandos almost always utilize the same weaponry: what a farce. . . . They operate throughout French territory, although they are only little splinter-groups: take care, the entire line of reasoning could tumble over this stumbling block. The authors of the report therefore forward three additional hypotheses. Political complicity (the Hitlero-Giscardian thesis). The "unknown" national network (the pure neo-Nazism thesis). The international terrorist network (the "enemies-of-the-French" thesis).

Their assessment only lacks the hypothesis of a Palestino-Soviet plot. But one can appreciate their tour de force analysis nonetheless. The omnipresence of anti-Jewish incidents is not negated. On the contrary. It is used to support the idea that two or three mysterious conspiracies are interconnected, this being the sole rationale for how anti-Jewish inscriptions could appear at the same time on the walls of Avignon and Rouen, or how a synagogue can be profaned in Toulouse and another be profaned, a few days later, in Strasburg. The existence of secret networks, national or international, whose activities the authors of the report have disclosed with such exemplary sagacity, confirms that the French people themselves, en masse, are not anti-Semites. They are so little anti-Semitic that, if threatening letters are to be sent out within the same month to Jews in Dijon and Jews in Paris, a clandestine coordination of guerilla operatives is indispensable. The multiplicity of anti-Jewish incidents serves as proof of the nonexistence of anti-Semitism in France!

★

A gang of French youths desecrates a Jewish cemetery in the Moselle. A citizen of Lille scribbles "Death to the Jews" on the margins of a billboard. A person from Bordeaux expresses his regret: "Hitler did not kill enough!" A Marseillean carefully seals threatening letters that he addresses and dispatches, from time to time, to a few Jewish organizations. A Jewish office is dynamited in Paris. There is a very simple explanation for the simultaneity of all these operations, carried out all over the country. Here it is. The French people live in all four corners of the land. And one Frenchman in ten feels that there are too many Jews in France. Therefore, in all four corners of the land, there is one Frenchman in ten who feels that the Jews are too numerous in France. Out of this total there are a few, here and there, who want to give their point-of-view more concrete expression, each in his own fashion.

The large majority of known aggressions (and the near sum of committed aggressions) are simple acts of individual initiative and local origin whose execution requires neither complex planning nor perfected logistics. Telephone threats, anonymous letters, and bomb-alerts are solo operations. Graffiti is planned and carried out on the spot. In order to write "Death to the Jews" on a wall, it is not necessary to have ultra-secret instructions from a large international headquarters. It is enough to know how to form and line up the letters and to buy a felt-tip marker in any stationery shop. Many markers are "made in Germany." One should not assume though that Nazi agents secretly introduced them into France. A painted inscription implies; the purchase of some materials in a hardware store and the formation of a small gang. The same group might push their point further, right up to the doors of the synagogue and, if there is one, the Jewish cemetery. There, hammers and crowbars might be utilized to destabilize, not French democracy, but a few Jewish tombs. Iron bars are rather easily obtained. They aren't parachuted over from Berlin, Moscow, Tripoli or even Paris. Likewise, fuel for incendiary concoctions is available in every service station and bottles are not in short supply anywhere in the vicinity.

Individual offenses are of many kinds. An abuse or injury often arises from a trivial confrontation (between car drivers, for instance, or between neighbors) that degenerates into a dispute. More serious are disputes that result in fist fights. More serious still are cases in which a group of "toughs" attacks one or more Jews. In 1981, about ten cases of this type were reported, although we don't really know how many actually occurred. Here is one that took place towards the end of September, shortly before the detonation of the bomb on Copernic. In Marseille a young Jew is attacked by a gang of youths. They blindfold him, force him to kneel down, and tear off the Star of David hanging from his neck.

Attacks using explosives obviously have a more elaborate genesis and require an organizational infrastructure of a certain degree of sophistication. But the preparation of bombs of the size used in France is technically speaking, very simple. It requires an artisan's methods and know-how. Since 1974, a few dozen attacks have been directed at Jewish targets or antiracist targets in general. This frequency divulges neither the presence of a single tentacular monster nor the existence of a great subterranean laboratory like the ones in James Bond films (which are probably best appreciated by the followers of the conspiracy theories of anti-Semitism).

A young woman, say, is called a "dirty Jew" in the metro. She wears glasses, but the abuse isn't a matter of anti-bifocular racism. She is a brunette, but brunettes as a class have nothing to fear. The young Jewess is the victim of an anti-Jewish insult, benign, limited, and at most disagreeable, but anti-Jewish nonetheless. And the aggressor is not a dangerous international terrorist who travels in second class so that he may more effectively destabilize French society. He is a man who is returning home after a hard day's work. He is not part of the Berlin-Paris connection, via Chypre. He is on the Porte d'Orléans-Porte de Clignancourt line, and he changes at Châtelet.

★

Confusedly, two images of Nazism are drawn together in questions that are raised about these anti-Jewish incidents.

The first is that of the Nazism of the late twenties. Already quite strong, it is a popular, mass movement, noisy and active, that involves itself in gatherings, meetings and street marches. It is recalled

160

to mind in the late seventies in order to demonstrate that "we are not living in 1929," that is to say that there is no political party on the horizon that might be able to overturn democracy and renew the persecution of the Jews. The second image is that of the Nazism that survived after 1945. It is organized through escape conduits leading in Latin America, and later on in the fifties, into Arab countries. In this case, the structure is truly clandestine and the capture of Eichmann by the Israeli Secret Service in 1961 only reinforces it underground character. This image reemerges in every theory that seeks to explain the various anti-Jewish incidents and assaults by referring to an obscure plan set into motion by one or more secret but influential organizations.

The first image suggests that there is no Nazi danger, since we don't see any SA parading around in the street. The other explains that a Nazi danger does exist, since desecrations of synagogues are happening all over; satellites from the Nazi networks must already be at work in every city of the country. There are no Nazis since we don't see them, some say. We don't see them, therefore they are Nazis, say the others.

Let us try to penetrate further. One Frenchman in ten feels that there are too many Jews in France. Out of this mass of people emerge the persons implicated in anti-Jewish incidents of lesser import, such as disputes and insults. One Frenchman out of a hundred feels that the extermination of the Jews was a salutary measure.[3] From this fringe are recruited the activists (very few, though) who launch themselves into violent assaults of more serious import.

Who are these people? Three categories can be sorted out from police reports and court records. The first is that of the psychopathic anti-Semite who usually operates alone. "The Hitler of l'Aube is a night-watchman," we read in *Le Matin* on April 7, 1981.[4] The fellow specialized in the delivery of Nazi texts to Jews. The second is that of human debris left over from the collaboration, from the Waffen SS and all the other structures of its type. With few exceptions, this group isn't characterized by an excess of activity. The third is that of new recruits, generally quite young, the number of whom exceeds that of the first two groups combined. Some belong to fascist organizations, like the youth of twenty-one years sentence in 1982 to two years in prison with one year's probation. He had clubbed a Jewish couple at the close of a public meeting in Paris in April 1980.[5] Others don't belong to any groups, like the twenty-one year old teacher arrested in 1979 for having drawn anti-Semitic inscriptions on the walls of a synagogue in Lyon.[6]

The madman, the brute and the greenhorn. They don't trouble themselves with the subtleties of the official Far Right and don't read the publications of the New Right. The have no concern for refined distinctions between anti-Zionism, which is a very good thing, and anti-Semitism, which is a bad one. They detest the Jews of France and the State of Israel indiscriminately. They have no use for Faurisson's demonstration that the genocide of six million never occurred. They know very well that it did and are very gratified knowing it. This rabble therefore identifies with Nazism. Hitlerism, the expression of absolute anti-Semitism, serves as a fascinating reference for them that proves that nothing is impossible.

But the organizational structure of this contingent is not Nazi, and it neither reproduces the prototypes of the twenties (noisy and enthusiastic street marches) nor echoes the movements of the fifties (clandestine conduits and secret bases). Let us review the litany of acronyms that it goes by in the late seventies.

The "Group for the Defense of Europe" blows up the Saint-Germain drugstore on the eve of Rosh Hashanah in 1974. The "Free European Legion" hands out anti-Jewish pamphlets in Sarcelles in 1975. The "French Neo-Nazi Party" covers the walls of Lille University with inscriptions in January 1977. "The Iron Guard" calls for the liquidation of the Jews in Marseille in 1978. The "German National-Socialist Pary—Baden Province" sends out threatening letters in Paris in March 1978. Anti-Semitic tracts are distributed in February 1979 by the "International League against Jewish Racism." The "League of French Fighters against the Jewish Occupation" takes credit for several attacks. The "Odessa Organization" takes credit for the attack against the car of Beate and Serge Klarsfeld in July. The "Neo-Fascist Autonomous Organization" claims a bombing in November 1979. In January 1980, the "French Liberation Front," which rails against the "the Jewish dictatorship that is corrupting France" claims to be responsible for the bomb that goes off in front of the Pompidou Center in Paris. The Front in question is rather anemic. It is as much a "front" as the others are leagues, legions, guards, collectives, organizations and parties.

The followers of the great conspiracy theses, of course, see in this multiplicity of appellations a supreme form of camouflage implemented by the diabolical center whose whereabouts they have not yet discovered. Others hold the view that, on the contrary, the organizational quality of the current is inconsistent and fragmentary, given the profusion of preposterous signatures it uses. The organizational titles are drawn from a prestigious catalog of names and terms (prestigious in the eyes of those who employ them), whose strong words are supposed to charismatically win over partisans and cause dismay for the enemy, Jew or Liberal, who hears in them the most distressing resonances.

Decompression is, as a result, inevitable, as these two examples will demonstrate. "An anti-Semitic campaign has been brewing in Dijon for a month" writes the *Bulletin de l'ATJ* on January 10, 1978.[8] It surfaced in several isolated episodes of harassment, anonymous telephone calls to the leaders of the local Jewish community, threats against Jewish businessmen, and writings on the walls. On January 12, the news becomes more dramatic: "According to some sources, these campaigns have been launched by the French division of the Odessa International" movement which is best known for its escape network that aided Nazi criminals after the War."[9] This time, the Nazis are there. Did the signature "Odessa International" appear on a threatening letter or on a wall? If it did, it was surely taken at face value. By January 16th, though, the monster has disappeared. The president of the Jewish community states to the ATJ: "We must remain vigilant without, however, becoming too alarmed, for according to our most recent information, and after over a month of investigation, all of the incidents appear to trace back to a single individual. . . ." At this stage, the true nature of the threat posed by Dijon's Odessa has been understood, and the inclination now is to downplay it—perhaps event to an extreme, since a small informal group could just as easily be responsible as a single individual. But let us listen to the description that the president of the community gives of the individual in question: ". . . he expresses himself well, but with a light German accent, and seems a bit paranoid."[10] Very interesting. Either he is from the Odessa network and his German accent fits the bill. Or else he is a Dijonnais, involved in pathological anti-Semitism, ans so ought to speak French without a foreign accent. The second version is much more convincing, but in the passage from one interpretation to the other an element of the first has been retained, since the individual has a "light" German accent.

Another example of decompression. The desecration of the Jewish cemetery in Bagneux on the night of Friday, April 25, 1981 is signed by the New Nazi Front. On the tombstones are painted the following slogans: Nuremburg, soon to return, death to all the Jews, etc. The aggression stirs up the indignation of the Jewish community, which organizes a protest rally with almost five thousand demonstrators.[11] Soon afterwards, the police apprehend the culprits. "The Nazis' of

Bagneux cemetery: hooligans" we read in *Le Quotidien de Paris* on May 10, 1981.[12] There are two of them. One is 16 years old. The other is 18. The New Nazi Front does not exist. The news is naturally greeted with relief by activists in the Jewish organizations, and for many Jews the two young bullies of Bagneux will serve as absolute proof of the absence of anti-Semitic danger in France.

Nobody went to the trouble of looking up the average age of those who desecrated Jewish cemeteries in Weimar Germany. In May 1927, 16 graves in the Jewish cemetery of Bopfingen in Wurtemberg are destroyed. The guilty parties are easily identified. They are a group of 16 year old girls.[13] At Fulda in March 1928, eight Jewish graves are overturned by a gang of 12 year old brats.[14] These two cases are of course extreme; in general, the defilers are between 18 and 20 years old.

★

In France, in the eighties, one fears dangerous Nazis and finds young children. One direction of research might be to dissociate harmless acts, which are symptoms of an ordinary social pathology whose spontaneous character is well known and easily dismissed, from bombings, which are the result of planned actions by underground networks. The first are inoffensive. The second are dangerous, but a good police operation ought to be able to locate the headquarters that issues the commands and the specialized commandos who carry them out. The dichotomy that is here suggested is thus a practical one. It takes into account the facts about anti-Semitism that have been discovered by the police, whose typical profile of an anti-Semite turns out to be that of an awkward adolescent or an inveterate Petainist rake. And it maintains intact the needed thesis that secret groups, divorced from the public-at-large, are continually going about their dirty business.

This contemporary theory is much improved over the "we are not living in . . . " thesis, a truism most reflection on anti-Semitism in France has traditionally limited itself to. In spite of this, it is still way off the mark. The sea of anti-Jewish incidents is in fact an organic whole whose waves differ in degree but not in kind. The many acts appear to be spread out over time, although there are definite strong and weak phases. They are universally present in French territory, with no clear demarcation between regions of bombings and regions of graffiti. On the contrary, all the different sorts of incidents are found pell-mell. The wave is endemic.

There is a continuum of motivation at work behind graffiti on the door of a synagogue, an inscription scrawled on a wall, an attempted

164

break-in, a successful break-in accompanied by looting of religious artifacts, an incendiary bottle thrown in the night, and a bomb. There is a continuity of design in a threatening letter received by a Jewish merchant, a rock thrown through a shop-window, a burning of a store and an arson of a major industrial plant belonging to a Jew. There is continuity between an anti-Jewish insult shouted in a school, a telephone harassment campaign and a street attack.

There is also continuity of personal involvement. A fellow who specializes in sending out anonymous letters might end up joining forces with a more hardened gang. The youth who goes along with a few cronies and profanes a synagogue might go on to more serious acts, either with the same crowd or as part of a more stable configuration he might later join. Activist groups are not born readymade. They are constituted. They take shape, lose shape, and reshape. Their favorite recruitment base is precisely those, both young and not so young, but mostly young, who have already practiced anti-Jewish activism on their own.

Dangerous Nazis, on the one hand, and young persons, on the other, do not live, in fact, separated by an impenetrable barrier. The former are not extraterrestrials who disembark from their flying saucers under cover of darkness on a cold winter's night. They are born and raised right here, caught up in social, political and historical circumstances. And for a social force to grow, it must enlarge its ranks and recruit new adherents, sympathizers, and voters. These are not just fools who can be enticed by shiny new boots and cowed by a rousing remonstration. They think, act, reason and militate under the same conditions as all other citizens. They might prove refractory to the anti-Jewish message, but they might well heed it. At that point, when the young begin to cross over the line, the Nazis become dangerous.

★

What is most surprising about the strange anti-Jewish tremors felt on the margins of French society is their relatively low degree of structuration. This sector has discovered neither its organizational coordinator nor its ideological spokesman. The proliferation of local individual and group initiatives has not given rise to a movement or movements openly professing anti-Semitism. A few stable elements have anchored themselves in this tide, but groups like FANE, which began operating well before 1974, have not changed much in composition or undergone significant expansion since their inception.

Until 1983, the many activist elements had not coalesced. The various leagues, guards, legions and so on have not united into a central organization. They all resemble one another in basic composition, in style of assault and in ideological content. But they are not united. The current has remained multipolar even at its highest structural level where dozens of small local cells operate randomly, edit tracts under some ephemeral and terrifying masthead, strike several blows against Jewish targets and then disband, parting only to reunite later on, and then disperse once more.

But dispersion, for a social movement, can signify two different things. As time goes by, what was once powerful can come apart, leaving only a few surviving and embittered castoffs who vegetate for a few years before finally becoming extinct. Splintering, here, is a sign of decrepitude. But there are dispersion that reflect the first stirrings of a new force that is trying to find itself. It is very small, its components are ignorant of one another and it has yet to perceive itself as a single entity.

The anti-Semitic current in France in our time has two essential characteristics. The many individual acts have not yet coalesced into a single political formation, but in practice they have still manifested as a relatively violent wave. Silence on the superstructural level tells us that the mental block that has protected the Jews since the Second World War is still solid enough to contain the hatred. The multiplicity of anti-Jewish acts, however, disclose the force of the thrust. The organizational and ideological weakness of the current indicates the strength of people's opposition to anti-Semitism. The quantity of offenses is revelatory of the pressure behind them. In the modern history of the French Jews, the years 1975–1980 will be seen as a time when anti-Semitism continued an earlier trend, one in which the memory of the Holocaust was still fresh enough to forbid anyone speaking ill of the Jews in Parliament. But they will also be seen as a time when it embarked on a new course, when the recollection of the past no longer stayed the defilement of synagogues.

Chapter Twelve
Desecrations

The Commission of Assessment, on the basis of figures provided by LICRA, came up with a total of 100 synagogues and 27 Jewish cemeteries attacked or defaced between 1975 and 1980. Another compilation listed a total of about 30 cemeteries and commemorative monuments, but only about 60 synagogues. The imprecision of the figures is due to the absence of any unified system of information gathering. It is precise enough, nonetheless, to indicate the scale of activity involved.

Sixty synagogues and thirty cemeteries. Is this a lot, or a little? Who is responsible? What is the significance of such acts? To answer these questions, one must have something else to measure these acts against. Marc Lévy, in 1978, stated on this subject that "these desecrations are executed in the same spirit as those committed during the 'Night of Broken Glass.'"[1] The direction is a good one. One must look towards Germany. The period indicated, however, is not so good. It is ten years further back, ten years before the Night of Broken Glass, where one might find the needed indicators.

The event transpires at night. We are in Germany in the twenties or France in the seventies and eighties. A small group of young people enters a Jewish cemetery and defaces the stones. If they had the foresight to equip themselves with the right materials, they proceed to destroy the tombs: some of them, if the act is meant to be symbolic, or if time is running short; all of them, if the demolition is systematic. The group, in full stride, goes over to the nearby synagogue. There also, they scribble on the walls and the portals. But they might also break down the entrance, make their way inside and deface the premises. They might also smash windows and stained-glass. The team then puts the finishing touches on its night's activities by blackening a few walls in town with its slogans. They work at random, though with a predilection for Jewish stores and shops. All these operations must be done quickly so as not to be detected by the police.

Weimar Germany, today's France. The techniques cannot be compared. There, one generally moves about on foot and uses cans of black paint. Here, one travels by car or bicycle and employs colored aerosol sprays. The signs painted cannot be compared. Sure enough, in both cases there are swastikas. But, over there, the symbol is a new one. No one—scribblers, Jews or anyone else—foresees what horrors it will one day signify. It is well-known, in France. The accompanying slogans cannot be compared either. *"Juda verrecke,"* "Jew perish," sounds medieval. "Jews in the oven" was unknown, for obvious reasons, in the twenties.

The figures can be compared. In Germany, from 1924 to 1930, the number of cemeteries and commemorative monuments profaned is ninety-one. In France, 1975 to 1980: twenty-seven. Still, one must recall that in Germany the Jewish settlements are much older and more spread out. In France, they have only recently reached large numbers and are primarily urban. There were therefore many more Jewish cemeteries in Germany to profane, all over the country, than there are today in France. If half of all the desecrations of cemeteries that occur in France today are in the Eastern Regions, the Germanic origin of the population there is not at fault. What is decisive is the antiquity of the Jewish presence in lands like Alsace, where, consequently, a large number of old Jewish cemeteries are located.

As for synagogues, their total number depends not so much on the antiquity of the Jewish settlement, but on the number of Jews living in the country at any given time. There are 600,000 Jews in Weimar Germany, who form a little less than one percent of the total population. There are 600,000 in France today, representing a little more than one percent of the country. It is thus safe to assume that the number of active synagogues does not differ considerably from one country to the other. And what are the figures for desecrations? In Germany, from 1924 to 1930, about 30 cases are reported. In France, from 1975 to 1980, about 60. France takes this round over Germany.

More synagogues and fewer cemeteries desecrated in France. The inverse in Germany. Record keeping is clearly better in Germany. Each offense is described in great detail in *Der Schild* or in the *C. V. Zeitung*. Moreover, cumulative lists are often published. *"Tafel der Schmach"* ("the balance-sheet of disgrace"): on June 27, 1927, *Der Schild* gives the names and dates of 39 cemeteries that have been profaned since 1923.[2] The Central Verein prints several brochures devoted to the subject. They are illustrated with statistical tables that allow one to trace the development of the phenomenon. If shadowy region there be, it is much, much smaller in Weimar Germany than in contemporary France. Let us return, however, to the crucial point: *roughly speaking, the two waves have similar amplitudes.*

Both Jewish populations are confronted with a problem that is in sharp contrast with their most recent experience. There have always been desecrations, but their quantity was virtually negligible. Neither nineteenth century or early twentieth century Germany, on the one hand, nor France in the thirties or after the War, on the other, ever had to face such a frequency of offenses, which, although not dramatic, is nonetheless far out of the ordinary. The two communities react in very different ways. One takes matters very seriously and organizes (or at least tries to organize) itself accordingly. The other accepts events with a "let it be" attitude. The one? The other? Let us take a look at them.

★

First, the Jewish community of France. When it doesn't just outright deny the existence of the problem, the Jewish community elaborates a series of self-protective myths. The legend of synagogue "thieves," who also indiscriminately burglarize temples and churches, has a brief tenure in the spotlight between 1978 and 1980. The story of "atheism" expanding within French society also spreads for a time. The two tales are quickly withdrawn from circulation, however, when they are unable to account for the increase in profanations or for the curious habit those "pillagers" and "atheists" have of writing "Death to the Jews!" at the scenes of their exploits. Even so, it takes a certain amount of time for the evidence to be gathered and the truth to be discovered: it is not hatred for tombs but rather hatred for Jews that inspires the despoilers of Jewish cemeteries. Burning a synagogue could be the work of an incurably unbalanced mind. The probability is great, however, that the act is anti-Jewish. Many synagogues have burned in Europe over the course of the 20th century and in most cases anti-Semites, and not pyromaniacs, have been at the source of the flames.

Myths based on ecumenicism (these days all creeds are victims of detestable banditry) give way to another form of palliation, this time concerning the desecrators themselves, of whom two portraits are drawn. The first is that of professional Nazis. This tiny minority, active despite being cut off from society, dedicates itself to carefully premeditated destruction, working within the framework of a vast conspiracy. The thesis is reassuring in light of the numerical weakness and marginal character of the criminals. The second portrait is that of the innocent youth. Ruffians keep themselves amused on

Saturday night by overturning Jewish tombs or breaking windows in synagogues and Jewish offices. The dramatization, here, plays up the non-political nature of the act and the imbecility of the actors. The two versions are, of course, mutually exclusive, but no effort has been made to take the analysis any further.

The desecration of the cemetery in Bagneux, in April 1981, gives rise to a protest demonstration. Why? Bagneux is the largest Jewish cemetery in Paris, and many Jews in the capital have parents or relatives buried there. The act arouses their indignation, whereas the destruction of a far-off provincial cemetery goes unnoticed, aside from possible mention in the Jewish press. The anti-Jewish significance is, however, the same. If the deed is serious in Bagneux, then it is equally serious anywhere else. The desecration of the cemetery of Bagneux provokes an emotional reaction that is explained by family ties and geographical proximity. The totality of desecrations of synagogues and cemeteries has not, however, captured the attention of the Jews of France.

★

The German Jews, for their part, react with courage and vigor. On the 20th of May, 1927, when the gauge shows as eleven the number of synagogues and forty the number of cemeteries affected, the Central Verein sends all of its divisions and staff members a circular memorandum reminding them of their duties. In the event of another desecration, they are to telegram the central headquarters, and later send a complete report, including all available press clippings. They are to call the police immediately. They should block the entrance of unknown persons onto the site to keep them from disrupting the investigation. They must apprise the local press, and eventually the provincial press, and also provide them with photos. They must exert constant pressure upon the local authorities to ensure that all possible methods for apprehending the guilty parties are explored.[3]

Often, apart from the measures mentioned in the text of May 20, 1927, the communities offer financial recompense to any person who is able to assist the police action by furnishing information. The proposed figure is generally about 100 marks, a large sum at that time. It rises to 500 marks in certain unusual cases, such as after the destruction of the stained-glass windows of the synagogue of Crefeld on the night of October 1, 1928. To understand the magnitude of this compensation, one should remember that a Phaeton Citroen imported from France is sold for 4,250 marks, in cash, in 1928.[4]

"The disgrace of Germany!" This is the headline of *Der Schild* on August 8, 1927. The Jewish cemetery of Cologne has just been desecrated and 71 tombs within it destroyed. The police officer in charge of the investigation states that he has never before seen, in the course of his long career, such a "destructive rage" and the local divisions of the RJF and Central Verein decide to coordinate their activities in order to find the vandals.[5] Other desecrations are announced in a somewhat less dramatic fashion but the tone is always serious. "Another forty tombs destroyed. The 42nd cemetery desecration": this one is at Essen, in August 1927.[6]

The campaign against desecrations seeks, first of all, to mobilize the Jews, but also tries to influence public opinion in general. The press agency of the Central Verein provides all the newspapers with detailed descriptions of each desecration and letters of protest written by both Jewish and non-Jewish personalities. News accounts and position papers are published in abundance.

In March 1926, after the desecration of the Erfurt cemetery (which is the twenty-fifth), Lenka von Koerber exclaims: "The hideous Erfurt affair ought to mobilize us all, Jews and Christians, to liberate Germany from this opprobrium." Walter von Molo quarrels with those who say: "What do the dead matter to us?" He emphasizes to them the moral danger that these "maniacs" who prowl at night represent.[7] "Hyenas": that is how Marie Elisabeth Lüders, deputy of the Reichstag, labels the desecrators in 1928. She adds, speaking of the sixty-two cases on file when she publishes her article: "This has not happened under Neron or in the Middle Ages, during the persecution of heretics. It has taken place between 1924 and today. It has not occurred among savages, but in Germany. The culpable are not escaped lunatics, but ordinary citizens."[8]

Another dimension of positive action is pressure upon the authorities. The Central Verein sends the list of desecrations to all the Ministers of Worship, Interior and Justice in the different German States. Twenty-five responses arrive in June and July, 1927, from all the States. Some are detailed and show specific concern for cases that took place in their region. Others are more general and reaffirm that the authorities are doing everything in their power to find those responsible for the crimes.[9] The Ministers' intentions are sincere and their efforts praiseworthy. But the very nature of the desecrations—their nocturnal, anonymous and unpredictable character—makes their repression impossible.

There can be no good campaign without public meetings. The principal meeting takes place in Berlin on October 18, 1928. On this date the Republic is solid. In the elections of May 1928, the Nazis collected only 2.6 percent of the popular vote. The meeting of the

Central Verein is similar to all others held in that period on anti-Semitism. Its unique feature is that it is devoted to the problem of desecrations.[10]

Brodnitz presides. He reviews all that is known of the cemetery desecrations. The year 1924 yields 16 cases. The year 1925 brings with it four new cases of grave site desecrations. The year 1926 brings 11 cases. The year 1927, 17 cases. In all, there are 62 cases he speaks of, including the partial figures for the year in progress. "We would like to understand this terrible phenomenon down to its very foundations and, once this is done, to fight it with force and dignity." Levi, a Rabbi from the community of Mainz, speaks of other anti-Jewish incidents, including threatening letters sent to Jewish merchants in his town. Our liberty and our salvation will arrive "when we have understood that the lessons of the past must be learned."

The speaker is now Koch-Weser, Minister of Justice, who has come as the representative of the government. "The government of the Reich, in whose name I now speak, shares the outrage you are feeling towards the events you have assembled to protest." The President of the Executive of the Jewish community of Berlin, Gerson Simon, expresses his solidarity. There were not, in the capital, either degradations of synagogues or desecrations of cemeteries, but the Jews of Berlin stand ready to fight by the sides of the rest of the Jews of Germany. Bruno Weil punctuates his address: "Any attempt to terrorize us . . . by means of monstrous crimes against our dead, will come up against our iron-hard resistance." The president of the Prussian parliament, Bartel, affirms: "I know that the large majority of the German people consider themselves on your side in this battle." The Secretary of State to the Prussian Minister of Justice offers an account of the juridical measures that have been put to work to end the desecrations. Bernhard Weiss, vice president of the Berlin police force, treats the problem of anti-Jewish incidents from the point-of-view of police suppression. We are protesting as Jews, Julius Bab says, but also as Germans. "These transgressions are a symptom of the internal decomposition of the German people," he intuits.

★

It is now ten years later, November 1938, in Paris. A man presents himself at the German Embassy and asks to speak with a diplomat. He shoots the third Secretary, von Rath, who dies a short time later of his wounds. Hershl Grynspan is a young Jew whose parents, residing in Germany, were cruelly deported to the Polish frontier, along with several thousand other Jews. "I did not act out of anger or in a spirit of vengeance, but out of love for my parents and my people, who are being unjustly treated," he later says. "It is not a crime to be Jewish. We are not dogs!"[11]

At once, the German authorities seize the event as a pretext for setting a series of simultaneous pogroms against the Jews of the Reich into motion. On the night of November 9, 1938, rioters break the windows of Jewish shops all over the country, from whence the name "the Night of Broken Glass." A few dozen Jews are killed. Thousands are arrested and deported.

Here is a witness' testimony on the situation of the Jews in Germany in Autumn 1938. "Fasanenstrasse: a small store selling accessories for dogs. There was an old, sick Jew just sitting there, resigned. They insult him, drag him outside across the shards of broken glass, so he comes out covered with blood. They stomp on him and step on his head. He is dead. I saw that. Soon after, I hear a growing clamor: a hundred men are running, and, in front of them, there's this human rag, his face entirely covered with blood. The poor guy runs right into another squad of Nazis who are coming on from the opposite direction, he is grabbed, knocked down, and trampled, but gets up bleeding heavily and flees towards a passing taxi. But the driver of the taxi gets out and gives him a hard kick. Until the day I die, I will always see that dusty and bloody face, those eyes already over the edge of madness. In a narrow alleyway, they run off, leaving a young Jew there whose lower jaw was completely torn away."

And here is another testimony, offered by Albert Bayet. "I'm not going to specify the location because I don't want to provoke any "new reprisals." The Jewish men are driven out of town into a quarry. The women and children are left behind. They are rounded up and enclosed in a neighborhood which the Nazis encircle. A warning is made to all the "Aryans" forbidding them from helping the Jews in any way. After a few hours, the infants start crying and howling with hunger. Their panic stricken mothers try to break out of the cordon of troops, to go find their children some milk. They try to crawl out at the feet of the Nazis. The Nazis push them back with blows from their rifle-butts. The hours go by. One infant dies, then another, then a third."[12]

Autumn 1928. Autumn 1938. Anti-Semitism ignores every rule of linear progression. It advances by sudden leaps. Three or four synagogues are desecrated each year during the twenties. Hundreds are destroyed in a single night ten years later.

★

The material that the German Jews have left us concerning the desecrations contains not only precise statistical data, but also declarations and theoretical analyses. The time is right for us to apply the wise principle that the lessons of the past must be absorbed.

In March 1929, Brodnitz takes stock. Of all the cemetery desecrations that have occurred since 1923, guilty parties have been discovered in 17 cases. Their affiliations are as follows. In six cases, they belong to nationalist organizations (the Nazi party, in three of those cases). In nine cases, they are students or minors without political affiliation. In addition, one young communist and one person whose political affiliations cannot be identified have been arrested. Out of 24 synagogue desecrations, again since 1923, ten cases have been cleared up. Four are blamed upon non-political youths and six upon members of extremist groups (the Nazi party, in four of these cases).[13]

The desecration of Gladbeck in January 1929 provides us with a piece of information that deserves to be noted down. The two guilty youths are caught in February. Their trial reveals that they had left the Nazi party shortly before their transgression. They upbraided the movement for not being radical enough.

From this, we make an initial observation. There are *some* Nazis among the desecrators, but they act on their own initiative. It is not *the* Nazis who direct the operations. They are not guided from on high, by the national, regional or local branches of the party, as the following example will show. In the entire state of Bavaria, there are only two desecrations of cemeteries in 1924, two in 1925, two in 1926, four in 1927, four again in 1928, three in 1929, and six in 1930. As for synagogues, very few profanations crop up. The most noteworthy case is the synagogue in Munich on whose doors swastikas are painted towards the end of April 1927. This takes place, however, in a region that has, during the twenties, 102 Jewish cemeteries and 204 houses of worship, belonging to a total of 206 communities.[14] It also happens in a region where the Nazis have always been strong, even when they have been all but nonexistent on the national level.

If the party, then, had wanted to organize the systematic desecration of all possible targets, if it had included this "action" within the framework of its overall objectives, it would have at no time had any difficulty sending out its rural and urban Bavarian divisions to desecrate en masse the sum total of all synagogues and cemeteries within their reach. And that, as often as it liked. What is striking, in fact, is the very small number of desecrations that occurred in light of the facility with which the Nazis could have carried them out.

There exists, nonetheless, a basic link between the wave of desecrations and the anti-Semitism that rises in the twenties and crests in the thirties. It is not a direct or causal link, since the desecrations are not, for the most part, Nazi undertakings. Might it be, then, an environmental link? In other words, the Nazis, who devote themselves to an unbridled anti-Jewish campaign, influence young and impressionable minds. The mobs then "spontaneously" begin to attack cemeteries and synagogues, although the responsibility for these acts really belong to the Nazis. The thesis appears to be logical. But it isn't. Pushed to its limits, it must fall back on the presupposition that Germany luxuriated in philosemitism until 1919, the fateful date when a certain Austrian corporal landed on her shores. This diabolical being was able, by the sheer force of his demagoguery, to transform a gentle Germany into a hell for the Jews. . . . But the truth has already been disclosed. German anti-Semitism predates Nazism. Behind it are a thousand years of savage history that have been recorded in the Memorbücher, those endless chronicles of anti-Jewish persecutions. German anti-Semitism experiences a revival at the end of the last century, when some of its themes are brought up to date and tailored to the realities of contemporary Germany. At this stage, it is no stronger than French anti-Semitism, which is going wild over the Dreyfus Affair. But it grows steadily after the First World War under the dual influence of nationalist frustration and economic and political crisis. Nazism clearly does not, therefore, create German anti-Semitism. It is its most intransigent political expression. Desecrations also spring forth its depths. Although not life-threatening in themselves, they reflect the fertility of the soil in which Nazism will later bloom.

The wave is strong enough to arouse the indignation of German Jews, and also strong enough to disturb them. They judge the frequency with which it batters them to be abnormal. The care (which, in the twenties, might have seemed paranoid) with which the desecrations are labelled and numbered bears witness to the anxiety that the Jews felt about deciphering the enigma. Furthermore, the phase-shift is astonishing: The desecrations are lurid and shocking after the paucity of anti-Semitic agitation that prevailed in the early years of the Weimar Republic. Further, they seem to increase most in those years when democracy is gaining strength, the far Right is losing members, the tumults are dying down and everything is returning to normal. But what intrigues the German Jews most of all is the outdated and ancient character of the acts themselves.

In 1978, Marc Lévy conjures up Nazi Germany in order to style the "spirit" of the desecrations of his day. The Jews of pre-Nazi Germany, in 1928, also look back upon an abhorred period of the past for a reference or a clue. But they are not content to say "it's medieval," in the way others today say "it's Hitlerian." Working more methodically, they undertake research into the past in order to determine whether their apprehensions are well-founded. To that end, they use the word "medieval" in its precise historical sense and not in its derivative, pejorative sense, connotative of brutality and barbarism. They seek to discover what really took place in that era. Letters and articles on this topic in Jewish journals of the twenties will help us trace their investigation.

"Item si christianus cimiterium judeorum quacumque temeritate dissipaverit aut invaserit, in forma judicii moriatur et omnia sua perveniant carriere duci quocumque nomine nuncupentur." Quid? one might well ask. It is the fourteenth paragraph of the protective statute Duke Frederick accords to the Jews of Austria in 1244. It punishes by death any Christian who destroys a Jewish cemetery. The benevolent measures are extended to the Jews of Bohemia in 1254. The arch-Bishop of Cologne condemns the destruction of Jewish cemeteries in 1266. The theme is taken up again in the pontifical directive *Sicut Judaeis* dating from the beginning of the twelfth century and later reconfirmed by numerous Popes.[15]

Two conclusions force themselves upon us. Firstly, if the Jews are accorded protective statutes, it is because they are in need of protection. Statutes appear, not in periods of calm, but in periods that are already troubled, periods when anti-Semitism has manifested or is manifesting itself in full force, without having become exterminatory, for then judicial barriers would no longer serve much purpose. Secondly, if, here and there in the texts, prohibitions against desecrations are mentioned among the provisions for safeguarding the Jews, it is because they are frequent and are posing a problem to the Jewish communities of the day. A very rough correlation is thus established between restless times and desecrations.

How did the desecrators proceed, in those obscure times? One might imagine them coming out at night and acting swiftly, to avoid being spotted by patrolling archers. Their instruments are simple, mallets, crowbars, and stakes, but good enough to break open the tombs and unearth the stones. Do they then make their way into the synagogue? It's quite plausible. What is certain, in retrospect, is that they were not members of the German National-Socialist Workers'

Party (NSDAP), since it did not exist at that time. There is no question. The profaners are inhabitants of the region, town, borrough, or neighboring countryside. The act is local.

Local, but not harmless. Synagogue and cemetery play a crucial role in the establishment of a Jewish community. When a feudal lord, an ecclesiastical authority, or a commune grants the two tracts of land where the first will be erected and the second plotted out, the Jews have gained the right of permanent residence. Owning the land legitimizes their presence. Desecrations therefore strike grievously at the Jews in their two most vulnerable and sacred areas, but, worse than that, they strike at right of the Jews to be living where they are living. In times of heated anti-Semitism, when the crusaders go by, when the clergy becomes hostile, or when disturbances erupt, the Jews are killed or expelled, their synagogues burned and cemeteries destroyed. In times of mild anti-Semitism, when the Jews are protected, before or between catastrophes, the attacks are furtive and limited. Synagogues and cemeteries are profaned.

The Jews of Weimar therefore wonder about this surprising resurgence—in the twentieth century!—of a medieval rite. They are amazed to see young Germans rediscovering a gesture whose significance was born so long ago. The youths come in small bands, break in, despoil, destroy, and leave. This cycle of action they reproduce blindly, without realizing its historical import or perceiving its final direction. Are their acts cryptic signs of a new rupture in an ancient pact, and are their desecrations ceremonies of initiation in which the youth of Germany is rediscovering how to brandish the sword? This question ought to engage our interest in two texts, both filled with precise citations, both catching a fleeting glimpse of something but failing to totally illuminate it, and both relying on the same glimmer of intuition. An article by Heinrich Kuhn, in May 1929, in *Der Schild,* sees in the desecrations the expression of a will to cut the Jews off from "the rights to their native-land and the feeling of belonging to it."[16] A letter by Michael Fraenkel asks in 1928: "Must we not fear a return of medieval times?"[17]

Who are Heinrich Kuhn and Michael Fraenkel, and what became of them after 1933? Perhaps they made their way to Eretz-Israel along with several tens of thousands of other German Jews and participated in the establishment of the State. Or else they won their way to England and the United States. They might have emigrated to France, but in that case would have been turned over to the Nazis again a few years later. They might also have stayed where they were. If so, were they paraded around in the streets to the laughter of the crowds, were they interned at Dachau, were they humiliated, beaten and tortured? The one and the other followed one of these routes, like so many other comrades of the *Reichsbund Judisher Frontsoldaten.*

Their two brief writings, printed in Gothic characters, reveal a precept. The lessons of History are to be learned from the history books. And a warning. Desecrations are not to be taken lightly.

Chapter Thirteen
False Accusations

The first profanation of a Jewish cemetery mentioned in the lists of the Central Verein is in Schneidemuhl, a small town in Posnania with a few hundred Jewish residents. On three occasions, January 27, February 6, and February 9, 1923, more than fifty graves are destroyed there. The police are unable to identify the criminals.[1]

This information would not merit special attention if, more than twenty years earlier, the same town of Schneidemuhl had not been the subject of a short article in the *L'Univers israélite.* "Schneidemuhl. The hairdresser—having placed in his shop window a picture portraying so-called scenes of ritual murder, was sentenced by the mayor to pay a fine of 20 marks. The convicted man issued a subpoena to the mayor to appear before the municipal tribunal. The tribunal then sentenced the hair-stylist to a fine of 30 marks; our dissatisfied barber lodged an appeal; he was then fined 60 marks."[2]

Bringing these two news items together is not, of course, an attempt to prove that the hair-stylist—the anti-Semite who was sentenced in 1900, lay in wait for 23 years, then, sensing that the time was ripe, took his vengeance in 1923 upon the crypts in the Jewish cemetery. However, bringing them together does bring out the bond that has existed throughout the history of anti-Semitism between desecrations, on the one hand, and false accusations, on the other.

This bond was forged far back in time. An edict by Pope Innocent IV dating from September of the year 1253 prohibits both the "carrying out of offenses against Jewish cemeteries" and the ascription to the Jews of "the use of human blood in their rites."[3] Desecrations of cemeteries and false accusations are tied together in the protective writ. This is because they must also have been tied together in the realities of the thirteenth century as they will again be in the harsh reality of the twentieth.

★

The theme of treachery is found throughout history. The Jews are accused of betraying Christianity at the behest of the Moslems in the eighth century, and of delivering arms to the Mongols in the thirteenth. In the nineteenth century, the French accuse them of acting in the service of Germany. In 1918, the German Jews are blamed for delivering the stab in the back that led to the victory of the French. Later on, the Jews are treated as Bolshevik agents by the one and as Imperialist spies by the other. In the early fifties, the Rosenbergs are electrocuted in the United States for performing acts of espionage for the Soviet Union, while in the "People's Democracies," many "Zionists" are liquidated for taking part in antisocialist conspiracies.

The theme of Jewish poison operates on two levels. There is, first, the accused individual, like the criminal Jewish doctor or the poisoner who acts on his own. Léon Poliakov mentions a Muslim legend attributing the death of Mohammed to a Jew.[4] The poisoning doctor is met with in Moscow at the end of the fifteenth century. He is found again in the Soviet Union in 1953. But "Jewish poison" also has a collective dimension. In the fourteenth century the Jews of France are accused of poisoning the wells. Worse still, from 1347 on, with the onslaught of the Black Plague, a rumor spreads that the Jews brought about the scourge.

The theme of sexual abuse also haunts the centuries. It is found in the writings of the anti-Jewish polemist, Agobard de Lyon, in the ninth century.[5] Much later, Pope Gregory IX accuses the Jews of kidnapping Christian children and selling them into slavery.[6] The theme flourishes anew in the modern breeds of anti-Semitism propounded by Drumont and then Céline. The anti-Jewish brochure *Je vous hais!* ("I hate you"), published in April 1944, says that "white-slave trafficking is a flourishing industry, perfectly organized, whose essential workings are generally managed by the Jews."[7]

The accusation of blood sacrifice is another form of false accusation. Among all, it is the most frequent and the most typical. Its scenario varies in an infinite number of ways but always reproduces the same fundamental structure. Jews are accused of having kidnapped one or several non-Jews, preferably infants or young girls, for the purpose of drawing their blood to use in various ways. The accusation is "factual." It accuses specific Jews of a specific action. Anti-Jewish hatred here abandons its vague and indeterminate ways (of the sort: the Jews killed Christ) in order to concentrate on specific Jewish persons and on a specific crime (as in: Such and such Jew killed so and so Christian yesterday in the small wood behind the village). But the murder is ritualistic. It is dictated by the religion or by the very nature of those presumed guilty. This is the subterfuge by which the accusation can reascend from the particular instance to the general case, from which it was momentarily disconnected. The story is perverse. It highlights the bloodthirsty character of the Jew and the demoniacal essence of Judaism, and this weighs heavily upon people's spirits and arouses their wrath. Usually, the affair is local. It is initiated from the base (lower clergy, minor nobility, common population) of society, generally without any encouragement from on high. The accusation of ritual crime combines mystery with proximity. It is, one might say, decentralized.

Hence, its incredible repetitiveness. After a few isolated cases in the first centuries of the Christian era, it develops anew at the turn of the twelfth century. It starts up in England in Norwich (1144) and Gloucester (1168). It flourishes in Germany in the thirteenth century, especially in Fulda (1236), Weissemburg (1270), Mainz (1238) and Munich (1285). In 1298, the Rottingen affair spurs a series of massacres in Franconia. Still more cases unfold in England until the final expulsion of the Jews from the country in 1290. In the fourteenth century, false accusations mount and lead to the great exterminations that decimate the Jewish communities of Europe.[8]

★

In France, the principal anti-Jewish calumnies were already in circulation before the year 1000 (treachery, poison, sorcery, sexual abuse).[9] The millennium had scarcely passed when a sombre accusation struck the Jews of Orléans. They were castigated for sending a secret letter to the Moslem authorities in Jerusalem, inciting them to destroy the Church of the Sepulcher.[10]

The first accusations of ritual murder, in the strict sense, appear in the latter half of the twelfth century. The Janville affair is mentioned but no precise date is given. The only certainty concerning it is that it precedes the Blois affair. The case of Pontoise, which makes an issue of the kidnapping by some Jews of a child named Richard, is variously dated. References are also made to cases in Epernay and Loches-sur-Indre near Tours.[11]

The Blois affair is very widely recounted in Jewish and French chronicles. In the Spring of 1171, a Jew, Itzhak ben Eleazar, is transporting untanned hides. His bundle accidentally falls into the Loire. A Christian servant observes the scene and reports to his master that he saw a Jew cast the cadaver of a non-Jewish child into the water.

The rumor gets around very quickly. It comes at a time when the local political situation is volatile. An ongoing struggle for influence with Theobald of Blois had, in fact, pitted his Jewish mistress, the lady Polcelina, against his spouse, supported by a faction of the regional aristocracy. The occasion is used to settle an old score. Several dozen Jews are arrested. On May 26, 1171 (20th of Sivan, in the year 4931 of the Hebrew calendar), thirty-one Jews, men and women, are burned alive. The memory of the Blois martyrs has been preserved to this very day in the Jewish tomes.[12]

Considerable emotion is felt within the Jewish communities upon hearing of the massacre. The Jews of Orléans, the nearest to the danger, are immediately alerted. They record the incident in a missive that they dispatch to the other Jewish communities, most notably the one of Paris, whose leaders plead for the intercession of the King of France. The letter from Orléans recounts the courageous deaths of the Jews of Blois, who remained loyal to their faith despite their tortures.[13] Other surviving texts that carried this news include a letter from Paris and a message delivered to the Jewish communities of the Rhineland by the Jews of Troyes.

The Blois affair marks an important date in the history of false accusations in France. The rumor is powerful enough to ignite flames, but the reactions of the central authorities, especially the King, who are alerted by the Jewish community are strong enough to circumscribe the burnings.

The case of Bray-sur-Seine, in March 1192, augurs the deterioration of the Jews' position in France. The new king, Philippe Auguste, hears in his residence of Saint-Germain-en-Laye that Jews hanged a Christian during the Purim festival. He makes his way to the spot and has more than eighty Jews put to death.[14]

In the thirteenth century, the separation of the Jews from the rest of feudal society widens. Economically, the appearance of a local bourgeoisie and a class of artisans banishes the Jews from the trades that they have hitherto practiced and relegates them to the extreme periphery of the tertiary professions, that is to say, to purely financial occupations. Politically, because of the increasing centralization of power, policies towards the Jews, whether benevolent or hostile, are more uniformly practiced. Ideologically, anti-Judaism becomes even more militant. The Talmud is burned in Paris in June 1242. Philippe le Hardi forbids the establishment of new synagogues and Jewish cemeteries.

The end of the century has two famous cases of false accusations. Thirteen Jews are condemned in Troyes, in 1288. They are offered the chance to convert to Christianity and thereby save their lives: they refuse.[15] In Paris in 1290, a Jew is accused of having stolen a communion wafer in order to defile it. He is burned alive, and a chapel is erected to commemorate the event.

On the whole, the circumstances of the Jews in France becomes increasingly dire. Small-scale local expulsions are reported in several parts of France at the end of 1290. In April 1291, the ban on Jews from residing in villages and small communities is more heavily enforced. With restrictions piled upon restrictions (some are of local origin, while others are initiated by the central authorities, but all enjoy growing popular approval), the stage is set for the decrees of Summer 1306.

The order is given in a Mandate from Philippe le Bel to his Seneschals, bailiffs and other provincial representatives. He enjoins them to keep silent until the very date of execution. The operation is directed by Guillaume de Nogaret. Armed men arrest the Jews all over the realm on the 22nd of July. Men, women and children who are imprisoned are given notice that they have one month to leave the country, leaving all their property behind. The exodus of August 1306 is of a vaster scope than the one of 1182. The crown has influence over a wider realm and central authority is more consolidated. The measure thus affects a very significant portion of French territory and tens of thousands of Jews who live within it. Where do they go? England is closed to the Jews. Some make their way down South into the Mediterranean regions. The majority move East. Some find refuge in Germany.

Louis X allows the Jews to reenter France in 1315, but the respite is short-lived. The fourteenth century is full of false accusations of all sorts, which very often, much more than in the twelfth and thirteenth centuries, degenerate into persecutions. There is a carryover from an accusation of ritual murder in Chinon in 1317 to an accusation of another type, that of conspiring with the lepers to poison the wells, which peaks in 1321. One hundred and sixty Jews are burned alive in Chinon as a result. A similar process unfolds during the same period in Velay.[16]

By the end of 1320, the Jewish community has already been severely tried: the Pastoureaux, the rebelling peasants of the South, massacre the Jews of Bordeaux, Toulouse, Castelsarrasin. . . . In all, 100 communities are destroyed. In 1321, the Jews are collectively suspected of conspiring with the lepers to infect the wells, encouraged and abetted by the kings of Tunis and Grenada. In Touraine and in Berry, Jews are put to death. Everywhere, they are imprisoned or levied heavy fines. In 1322, they are forced to leave once again. The link is immediate, this time, between the false accusation and the expulsion.

Anti-Jewish massacres take place in Alsace in 1338. Similar to those committed by the Pastoureaux in 1320, their origin is popular and they are reproved by the authorities. They are less extensive, of course, than the massacres of the Black Plague that will sweep over Europe in 1348 and 1349. Jews blamed for the plague are killed in Provence, Savoy, Dauphiné and Alsace. In Strasbourg, even though some non-Jews oppose it, two thousand Jews are burned. Here, the false accusation leads directly to mass murder.

The Jews of France are called home in 1359. In 1380, a popular riot in Paris strikes out at the Jews of the capital. In 1382, the insurrection of the Maillotins chases the Jews out of the city. On September 17, 1394, Charles VI uses crimes committed by the Jews against the sacred faith as a pretext for their expulsion from the kingdom. The act is decisive. The Jews abandon France. "They will not return there until the very eve of the Revolution," writes Isidore Loeb.[17]

In the outlying regions, expulsions and massacres abound in the fifteenth century. Le Dauphiné rids itself of its Jews at the end of the century. In Savoy, persecutions increase. Students and seasonal workers massacre the Jews in Carpentras, Avignon, Tarascon, Arles. . . .

An accusation of ritual crime brings Raphael Lévy to the stake in Metz in 1670. In Nancy in 1761, Jews are killed under the pretext that they have desecrated the Holy Host, used sorcery, and performed sacrilege. "When one reads of the proceedings in those two affairs, one can scarcely imagine that they came to pass only thirty years before the Revolution, in the same country in which Father Gregoire would launch his campaign in favor of the emancipation of the Jews and for mutual tolerance—if not respect—and one cannot help but consider what a boon for the people of that generation—despite its imperfections—the Revolution of 1789 was."[18] These lines form the conclusion of an article in the *Revue des Etudes Juives* by Jacques Godechot, dedicated to the terrible affairs in Nancy in the mid-eighteenth century. His study was published in 1930, ten years before the adoption of the *Statut des Juifs* by the French State.

★

In the meantime, accusations of bloodletting continue. Clusters of such accusations strike the Jews of Poland in the seventeenth and eighteenth centuries. It is observed in Russia in the early nineteenth century and in Damascus, Syria in 1840. The movement catches on widely again after 1880.[19]

The first major incident is in Tiza-Eszlar, Austria-Hungary. In

1882, Jews are accused of having kidnapped a young Christian girl. The suspects are acquitted by a tribunal. Many important figures in the world take a stand against the accusation of bloodletting. The cases multiply after 1886. They touch all of Central and Eastern Europe, and some countries of the Mediterranean basin as well.

The Xanten affair in Germany in 1891 provokes a considerable outpouring of emotion. "No sensible man would have believed that in an enlightened country like Germany an accusation of ritual murder could still be raised in our time," the *Bulletin de l'Alliance Israélite Universelle* charges in its report on the affair. Anti-Jewish uprisings explode after the death of a five-year-old boy. The event is so shocking that pastor Stoecker (who is to German anti-Semitism what Drumont is to its French counterpart) finds it necessary to distance himself from those hurling the accusation of ritual murder. "I have never used this term and I have pleaded with my friends not to avail themselves of it. I openly state that it seems to me incomprehensible that some maintain that the Jews make use of blood for ritual purposes," he states during a parliamentary debate.

Later on, the Polna affair in Bohemia (1899) stirs up international protest once again. The Konitz affair in Prussia ends with the anti-Jewish slanderers being sentenced to severe prison terms.

Whenever there is a trial, the Jews always succeed in proving their innocence. In those instances when the incident does not come before a Judge, the agitation generally dies down of itself, as shown by an incident reported in 1899 in Cracow. Two Christian women enter the store of Hermann Statter. One is accompanied by a young girl for whom she is buying sweets. Soon after, the mother returns, crying that her daughter has disappeared. Let us read the testimony of Hermann Statter: "A large crowd gathered in front of my house; it was exactly the hour when the workers were returning home from work. The crowd heeded the cries of the woman and became menacing. It was only thanks to the intervention of some other citizens who knew me personally that I was able to escape injury." The young girl, who simply wandered off on the road home, is soon found.

In the late nineteenth century, false accusations are generally greeted with indignation. In most cases, social structures resist, authorities intervene, liberal forces stand up and intellectuals vehemently protest.

Perhaps as a result of this reassuring response, few perceive the premonitory character of the phenomenon. Let us listen to Nordau, in the fourth Zionist Congress, London, August 1900. Anti-Semitism is spreading, he explains, like a forest fire. "It strikes country after

185

country and threatens the Jews even in the countries where they once felt most secure. It is taking forms that even the most extreme pessimist could not have envisaged. All the specters of the Middle Ages have left their tombs and are raging about in broad daylight. The monstrous legend of blood sacrifice is reaching a wider audience. The cases of Tiza-Eszlar and Xanten were warnings that have already been forgotten. Polna and Konitz are heart-rending cries of alarm, towards which the Jewish people must not turn a deaf ear."[20]

But the message of Nordau and the Zionist movement convinces only one part, and not the whole of the Jewish people. In any case, the wave of false accusations soon dies down once more, and anti-Semitic agitation as a whole diminishes except in Russia and a few Eastern countries. One last major trial for ritual murder angers Jews and liberals the world over the way the Dreyfus Affair did a few years earlier: the Beilis affair, in Russia, concludes with the acquittal of "the man from Kiev" in 1913. The verdict confirms the final victory of progress and reason over the prejudices and fanaticism of another age.

★

"It is not in our blessed France, thank God, that we find such fearful aberrations," the *L'Univers israélite* writes on May 1, 1881.[21] In 1890, Drumont pens the preface to a book devoted to ritual murder. He sees in it an "ethnic nervous disorder, one of the most striking manifestations of the atavism bringing to life again, in the universally outlawed Jew, the semitic lust for blood."[22] This abstract theme is oft repeated in the anti-Semitic tirades of the period.

It becomes more concrete in the Ingrandes affair. On March 20, 1892, some young men who are fishing in a brook catch sight of a bag bobbing in the water. They discover in it the mutilated trunk of a child whose head has been cut off and limbs torn out. An investigation begins, but on March 27th, *Le Journal d'Indre-et-Loire* opens its own campaign: "Here we are going to startle all the free thinkers and people who consider themselves "tolerant." Here, in any case, is our profound conviction. We find ourselves confronted with a ritual murder performed by the Jews: everything corroborates it . . . the victim's throat was slit and his blood drained, the only procedure enabling the collection, while the victim is still living, of the blood necessary for the preparation of the unleavened bread. And Passover is fast approaching."[23] But the accusation is quickly squelched when the police discover the true criminal, none other than the child's mother, who is sentenced to twenty years of hard labor.

186

In 1892, French anti-Semitism turns towards another type of false accusation. *La Libre Parole,* the new daily edited by Drumont, publishes from May 22–24 a series of insulting articles about "Jews in the army."[24] A Jewish captain, Crémieu-Foa, challenges Drumont to a duel. They do battle on the 1st of June and inflict minor injuries on each other. A second duel pits Crémieu-Foa against the journalist Lamaze. But a third contest opposing the Jewish officer, Mayer, and the anti-Semite Morès concludes on a tragic note. Mayer is killed on June 23, 1892.[25]

The news arouses considerable emotion in the country. It isn't the first duel in which Jews and anti-Semites have squared off, but it is the first to have ended in the death of one of the combatants. "The disastrous work undertaken by the handful of anti-Semites who dishonor France has borne its poisoned fruits," the *Archives israélites.* write. The journal, which gives a detailed account of the duels, points out that: "The death of this brave officer has provoked an intense response from the public that has reverberated through all the channels of the press, with one or two exceptions."

In the Chamber of Deputies, on June 25th, Camille Dreyfus challenges the Minister of War. Freycinet answers, solemnly, to the applause of the Parliamentarians: "Sirs, in the army we know not Jews, Protestants or Catholics: we know only French officers, with no regard to origin." The Chamber passes a motion in support of the Minister's declaration. The vote is unanimous, Left, Right and Center.[26]

Not until 1980 will we again find parliamentary unanimity in the aftermath of an anti-Jewish act. After the October 7th Copernic bombing, the National Assembly votes for postponement of its session to allow the Deputies to attend the great demonstration. All of the Deputies vote yes.[27]

The funeral of Armand Mayer takes place on Sunday, June 26, 1892. An enormous crowd, estimated at a hundred thousand people, is in attendance. The military honors are carried out by a company of infantrymen and a squad of swordsmen from the Polytechnic School. Let us read the *Archives israélites:* "The moment the funeral procession begins to move forward, the drums beat and the bugles sound . . . the Central Consistory, the Consistory of Paris, and all of the Jewish administrations are represented. Deputies, Senators, most newspaper editors and a large number of officers from all branches of the military and cadets from the Polytechnic School are present in the great procession. . . . All along the length of the cortege, crowds line the road, visibly impressed by this grand march. At

Montparnasse cemetery, the congestion is enormous. It is only with difficulty that the cortege is able to make its way through." In his eulogy, the Chief Rabbi of France declares: "The cruel lesson to be extracted from such a deplorable event, has been understood: witness the general desolation, the unanimity of regret that has been voiced from one end of our country to the other."[28]

The breadth of the protest reinforces people's belief that anti-Semitism has captured only a small minority of the country. This conviction is supported by, among other things, two electoral results. In the Municipal elections of Paris, on April 27, 1890, the anti-Semite candidates turn in a very weak showing: "Anti-Semitism is beaten all across the board; more than beaten, erased," the *L'Univers israélite* editorializes on May 1st.[29] In the municipal elections of 1892, the tendency is even more plain, as Henri Prague writes in the *Archives israélites* on June 2nd: "The results of the ballots of May 1st and May 8th and the elections of Mayors and their deputies have sounded the death knell of the anti-Semitic faction."[30]

The Dreyfus Affair explodes onto the scene in late 1894, a little over two years after the stirring unanimity of 1892. It involves the most famous false accusation of the 19th century. It touches off violent anti-Jewish demonstrations all over the country in 1898. It divides the country in two. But it comes to an end with the triumph of Justice and the knowledge that anti-Semitism, this time, has truly died.

Isaie Levaillant chants its funeral dirge in a conference held on April 14, 1907. "How, after reaching its apogee with the Dreyfus Affair, how is it that anti-Semitism died precisely as a result of the Dreyfus Affair? The downfall of anti-Semitism began when, cast into the limelight, its true character and its true aims became apparent to the whole country. . . . And the fight was no longer between anti-Semitism and the Jews, but between anti-Semitism and the ideas of the Revolution. It was consequently inevitable that anti-Semitism be defeated and quelled."[31]

In France, as elsewhere, the twentieth century finally began.

★

"We are living in the twentieth century," Hans Reichmann emphasizes in the *C.V. Zeitung* in November 1928. "Ritual murders are fables which men of the twentieth century laugh at, the way they laugh at superstitions. . . ." However, Reichmann writes, the Nazi *Stürmer* dares to launch a campaign on that very theme after the death of a schoolboy in Gladbeck.[32]

In late March, 1929, the Manau affair bursts onto the scene. A child is dead under mysterious circumstances. The Nazis seize the opportunity to hold a series of meetings denouncing the Jews. The reply from the Jewish community is immediate. *"Kampf dem Mittelalter!"* ("Fight against the Middle Ages!") the *C.V. Zeitung* writes on April 5, 1929. The Rabbinical Council of Bavaria issues a statement condemning the campaign of hatred.[33] A debate is held in the Prussian parliament. Linneborn, speaking for the Catholic Zentrum, rejects the criminal accusation and concludes his remarks to the applause of the majority of Deputies: "The German people are too serene to become excited by anti-Semitism."[34] Goldenberger, Minister of Worship for the State of Bavaria, also condemns the false accusation before the Bavarian Landtag. The Minister articulates measures that have been taken, within the schools of Franconia for instance, to neutralize anti-Jewish foment. He quotes reassurances from Catholic and Protestant officials on the matter. "Concern for justice ought to preclude the possibility that, in the twentieth century, such accusations be cast at our Jewish fellow-citizens," he concludes.[35]

On May 6th, the Wurzburg division of the Central Verein organizes a protest meeting. Between 1500 and 1800 people participate, but 300 to 400 Nazis, most quite young, find their way into the hall. Rosenthal denounces the fable of ritual murder. Pastor Rudolf Wintermann condemns the accusation from a Christian perspective. The Nazis in attendance constantly interrupt his speech. After him, Alfred Wiener of the Central Verein speaks, and then the Mayor of Wurzburg, who tells of having encountered a false accusation of the same type thirty years earlier, when he was just beginning his municipal career. He calls upon the Germans to reject the lie. The rest of the meeting degenerates into a free-for-all in which Nazis and anti-Nazis alternately take the podium. The police end it by evacuating the hall.[36]

In the meantime, in the Gladbeck affair, the Nazi Ley is convicted of anti-Jewish defamation for accusing the Jews of committing a ritual murder. A meeting of the Central Verein in Cologne, assembling 2000 people, rejoices over the verdict. One of the orators, Rosenthal, speaks of "the irony and the tragedy" of the situation. Long ago, Popes and Emperors were familiar with the deceitful nature of the accusation. Today, in July 1929, a German tribunal is still needed to condemn a man for spreading such slander.[37]

Some affairs are staged by the Nazis, but others are spontaneous. A significant indication of the receptivity of the German public to false accusations is offered by Bernhard Weiss in a *C.V. Zeitung* article on April 12, 1929: "How rumors of ritual murder are born: Weiss discusses an event that occurred two years before in the capital. A woman complains to police inspectors that she heard the cries and screams of children and claims that they must relate to a Jewish ritual murder. A brief investigation demonstrates the falsity of the accusation. The rapid action taken by the police halted any possible development of the incident before the anti-Semitic press knew anything about it and was able to exploit it."[38]

Ten years later, in May 1939, *Der Stürmer* issues a special edition devoted to ritual murder. The anti-Semitic journal already published one like it in 1934. But the one of 1939 mentions the tenth anniversary of the "murder" of Manau, which a vast official assembly also serves to commemorate. *Der Stürmer* offers a nostalgic retrospective of the events of 1929, recalling, notably, how the meeting of the Central Verein in Wurzburg was disrupted by the Nazis of Franconia.[39]

★

In France, the new anti-Jewish wave of the thirties is accompanied by a renewal of false accusations. Most of them are voiced in the Right-Wing and Far Right press and in specialized anti-Semitic literature, whose circulation swells in prewar France, returning to the level it attained at the end of the nineteenth century. Some circulate by word-of-mouth. And so, in March 1938, *Le Droit de Vivre* reports a calumny that accuses Jewish vendors of livestock of spreading foot-and-mouth disease.[40]

Other vilifications appear during the anti-Jewish uprising of Autumn 1938. In Nancy, on September 26, a man named Ourdi accuses the Jewish merchant Silberstein of having a direct telephone line to Hitler in his cellar. "A crowd gathered in front of the store and, hearing Ourdi's accusations, took his side. The windows were blown apart, the store was sacked and the merchandise stolen."[41]

In Dijon, on October 1, 1938, word gets around that a woman named Mrs. Lerner cried: "We want war!" The anti-Semite Lhuillier says to a friend: "You see, they're Jerry stores, we've gotta break their necks and their stores." A crowd gathers. "Those are Jerry Yids," Lhuillier cries to several hundred roused Dijonnais. Let us read the account of the *La Tribune juive:* "Overcome with fear, the Lerner family closed the lobby door and locked it to be safe. The metal screen of the second store was forced open and the show-windows shattered into a thousand pieces. Mrs. Lerner opened the window of her dining room, yelling: Help! Then the crowd, seeing her, roared: Wait, we will kill you. . . . The police brought trucks around with guards, and pulled the unfortunates into the bed of the truck to protect them. The crowd, at that moment even more incensed, ran after the truck, yelling: Death to the Jews, they must be killed."[42]

★

Thirty years later, another French city experiences turbulence. On May 31st, 1969, tension is high in Orléans. Groups gather in the doorways of Jewish stores. The rare clients who risk entering are escorted. The Jewish shopkeepers are frightened.

For several days, word has been going around that young girls are drugged in the dressing-rooms, then kidnapped and transported to distant prostitution havens. The rumor originates among female teenagers. Then, after May 20, it spread into the adult world, to parents, friends, and indeed everyone. Teachers warn their students against Jewish shops. The rumor swells in late May, thriving on seemingly corroborative details: why don't the police arrest the criminals? Why is the press silent? It's because the police and the press have been bought out by the Jews.

The rumor reaches a fever-pitch the morning of May 31st. Let us read Edgar Morin: "Housewives from all strata of Orléans society are alarmed and outraged. Mobs form around nearby stores. . . . Customers are few to none on this big sale day. Licht feels surrounded by the hatred. He feels the hostile glances there in the street, in the cars that slowly roll past his shop front. He hears or imagines abusive shouting going on. He imagines or hears "Don't buy anything from the Jews!" In Sheila's boutique, Jeannette Buki . . . feels like she is under siege and waits for the pack to break in. . . . Are we on the verge of an explosion, is only the igniting spark missing?" Or else: "When the crowds gather around Dorphé, is this not already like the first phase of a possible pogrom?" As for the Jews: "What arise in them are feelings of isolation, distress and fear. People are gathered in mobs in front of three stores this morning of the 31st of May, and are staring at them. Others slowly pass them in cars and stare at them."[43]

But nothing comes of it. The pogrom never takes place. The very next day, the rumor begins to decay, drift apart and disappear. The authorities, political parties and antiracist organizations, who were alerted days earlier by various militant Jews (whose activism is in marked contrast with the passivity of the official Jewish community officers) finally intervene. Everything returns to normal.

Other rumors, on identical themes, turn up in Amiens (1970) and

191

a few other cities in France during the seventies. They are more restrained and unfold under differing circumstances, but follow the same pattern.

Let us review some of the characteristics of the rumour. It is *sudden* (it travels quickly), *widespread* (many people believe it), *inventive* (it constantly feeds on new elements) and *violent* (Morin uses the expression "cyclonic region" to describe the atmosphere of May 31st). It is, first and foremost, *spontaneous*. The first inclination of militant Jews and antiracist activists is to look for conspirators, and their search for a conspiracy takes one of two directions: plots by competitors, or fascist enterprises. Their incapacity to accept the popular and self-generated nature of the rumor of 1969 is an early indication that they will be unable to comprehend the sporadic, multifarious and yet consistent character of the anti-Semitic crisis of the late seventies. They look for specific criminals having complex strategic goals, since it seems unthinkable to them that such slander could be born of itself (in the case of rumors) or that such acts could be locally committed, without planning by a secret headquarters (in the case of desecrations).

★

To what referential totality should the rumor of Orléans be linked? Those who think that everything that happens in 1969 has its source in 1969, and not earlier, do not see in these events anything more than a sociological oddity, one that brings collective hallucinations out into the open and is best interpreted in terms of mass psychology.

Others turn towards the past. But there are two manners of doing so. One, not too elaborate, consists of rehashing a few vague concepts about accusations of ritual murder: in the Middle Ages, they burned Jews accused of having kidnapping and killing Christians. In 1969, both the theme (prostitution) and the outcome (dissolution) of the accusation are different The Orléans rumor is regarded as both an enigmatic resurgence of, and a benign deviation from the model case. From this angle, Blois (1171) serves as a counterpoint to Orléans (1969): geographical proximity only heightens its sense of foreignness, while differences of content create a clean breach between the distant past and the present.

One might turn towards the past in another way, this time being prepared to study it. The significant whole to which the Orléans rumor belongs is no longer, in that case, the Middle Ages, but the interim period of the closing 19th century and dawning twentieth century. From 1880 to 1905, several dozen affairs of this nature are recorded in Europe. Some are accusations of ritual murder, in the traditional sense of the term. Others are accusations of kidnapping young girls, and are aimed at Jewish merchants.

Thus, in 1886, a young girl found unconscious near a bridge on the railway tracks leading into Budapest claims to have been kidnapped by Jews. In 1889, the Jewish merchant Leibowicz, living in the Rumanian town of Maila, is accused by a mob of intending to kidnap a young girl who came to buy some cheese. In 1898, in Yamboli, Bulgaria, an eleven-year-old school boy tells his school principal that Jews tried to kidnap him. In Cracow, in 1899, a crowd gathers in front of David Buchner's store; he is accused of child abduction. The same scene is reenacted in the same city, that same year, around the store of Hermann Statter, as mentioned above.[44]

The false accusations of this past century have often led to rioting, but they have all eventually melted away. In every country the Jews have always been able to prove their innocence when placed before a tribunal or under public scrutiny. Is the rumor of Orléans, in 1969, really over and done with? Yes, true, but so were all those episodes three-quarters of a century ago.

The events that followed them confirmed that the false accusations in question were not harmless. Their emergence was indicative of rising hatred. Their anachronistic quality was symbolic of the unity underlying the two periods of anti-Semitism. The bygone one, whose terrible memory is preserved in Jewish memoirs to this very day. And the new one, whose appearance was foreseen by only a few hardened pessimists. The Orléans affair (France, 1969) is a member of this series. It seems to come from afar, but it is really close at hand. It is no more medieval than the Konitz affair (Germany, 1900), which was in Nordau's words, a "heart-rending cry of alarm."

★

And what of Schneidemuhl? As we recall, Schneidemuhl was the site of the trivial affair of the anti-Semite hairdresser sentenced in 1900 for posting up images of ritual murder. Our recollection of this incident can be completed with the addition of another noteworthy date.

"On March 12, 1940, the 160 Jews of Schneidemuhl were deported on freight trains and taken towards the region of Lublin. Other convoys were waiting there. The deportees were forced to abandon all of their possessions. They were not even allowed to bring handbags along. The women had to leave their purses behind. Some of the deportees were forced to remove their coats, especially those who wanted to wear several layers in order to protect themselves from the cold. . . ." These lines are extracts from document NG–2490 of the archives from the Nuremberg trials.[45]

The case of Schneidemuhl, in particular, and the many false accusations of the end of the last century, in general, demonstrate that a number of years can slip by from the moment when a sign first appears, and is quickly and solidly quashed, until the time when the phenomenon it discloses reaches full maturation. In the *Histoire des Juifs en France,* published in 1972, one is overjoyed to read that: "Anti-Semitism was shown to have limited appeal during the Orléans affair, when slanderous accusations of white-slave traffic were levelled at Jewish merchants." The affirmation is soothing, but forgets to look back (it ignores the recent past) and up ahead (it neglects the problem of dynamic evolution and gradual fermentation).

Epilogue

The Next Crisis

On the Jewish New Year of 1983, the *Tribune juive* publishes a series of statements by public figures from the Jewish community and the world of French politics. Théo Klein, the new president of the CRIF, asserts: "Even though it seems to present itself, by its choice of targets, as anti-Semitic, terrorism is, in reality, a new form of subversion working against Democracy." At the end of a long and convoluted argument he concludes that "anti-Semitism hence constitutes a METHOD utilized in terrorist activity and is not the actual GOAL of this activity." He adds, furthermore: "Of course, this is only an analysis and I don't have access to any previously unreleased information that would lend further support to my reflections."

One wouldn't doubt it for an instant. Exploring the facts would actually undermine his demonstration, as, for example, this banal incident reported a few pages further on in the *Tribune juive* shows: "Around seven o'clock in the morning, as usual, Mr. Leon Gehler, a teacher in Strasburg, and his son Michel make their way to the synagogue on rue Kageneck. They notice three boys and one girl painting graffiti onto the facade of a large warehouse. Swiftly, the group rushes towards the two bystanders and peppers them with insults like "Dirty Jews!" Mr. Gehler has no time to react before one of the assailants strikes him, breaking his glasses, and runs off."[1]

Four young people of Strasburg did not succeed, it seems, in making a clear distinction between anti-Semitism as an end and anti-Semitism as a means.

★

It is not only in Strasburg, moreover, that people remain deaf to this argument. A municipal by-election is held in Dreux after the annulment of the results from March. In the first round, on September 4, 1983, the slate of the Front National, a formation of the Far Right that runs a campaign against immigrant laborers, carries off 16.7 percent of the vote. In the second round, it is incorporated into the opposition slate, which takes the election and brings Dreux back over to the Right.

The alliance forged in the second round is tacitly or even explicitly approved of by the leaders of the two major factions of the French Right. It is overwhelmingly ratified by the moderate electorate of Dreux, which guarantees the victory of the joint slate. They are sharply rebuked. The alliance with the Far Right is in fact dictated by the logic of the bipolar system (all of the Left vs. all of the Right) that governs the functioning of French political institutions. The Right, in order to come back into power, is in need of votes from the Far Right, and the latter, of course, knows it. In exchange for what it contributes, it regains the legitimacy it lost during the Second World War and, on a smaller scale, at the end of the Algerian War. This regained legitimacy procures for it an enlarged zone of influence, which in itself is enough to make future alliances of this type very likely.

Naturally, 16.7 percent remains a minority, and one French city is not all of France. The resurgence of French fascism would require a conjunction of objective circumstances (a grave social crisis and a Nationalist thrust) and subjective facts (an ideological renewal) that are, for the time being, lacking. The opening carved in Dreux, however, reveals an aspect of France that has been forgotten. It shows the electoral vitality of a Far Right that many were content to believe had been marginalized once and for all.[2] It also demonstrates the responsiveness of the French people to xenophobia and racist agitation, which in Dreux did not drive away the voters of the Neo-Gaullist and Liberal Rights.

In all of that, anti-Semitism hardly appears. Jewish officials who comment on the affair most often emphasize the exclusively racist, and not anti-Jewish, character of the Front National's campaign. Many speak of the pressing need to strengthen the fight against racism and to redouble vigilance. At heart, they are only reassuring themselves: the foul wind is not blowing towards the Jews.

Their illusions will not last long. Shortly before the vote, the Jews are mentioned furtively, almost hesitantly, in speeches given on television by an agitator of the Far Right.[3] The Jewish question is, however, extensively debated during a "French Friendship Day" at the Mutualité in Paris on October 16, 1983, sponsored by several Nationalist organizations emboldened by the auspicious surprise in Dreux. Several thousand people attend.

One orator runs through the list of "Jewish Ministers in Mauroy's government" and states matter of factly that "it is therefore Judaism that inspires all or most of their policies." He asserts that "the Jews are at two poles of contemporary society: (they are) promoters of financial capital as well as its most vehement detractors." Another speaker criticizes a television broadcast on Christians and Jews before 1789: "If I had heard it in a Zionist broadcast on television in Tel-Aviv, I would have understood it. But I heard it in a Catholic broadcast on national television!" Another speaker is equally indignant: "There are those who do not allow for integration in France . . . for whom the interests of Judaism are superior to those of French society." He adds: "The International of assassination, the Communist International, was composed mainly of Jews. . . ."[4]

The Day of Friendship is held in 1983, and not 1938. On that date, as strange as it may seem to the proponents of the "we are not living in 1938" thesis, French anti-Semites often found it difficult to express their views in public. In January 1938, *Le Droit de Vivre* reports that a reception for Darquier de Pellep in the IVth ward of Paris is disrupted by militants from the LICA.[5] In February, a major meeting organized by the same Darquier is called off through the intervention of the LICA.[6] In March 1938, antiracists sabotage an anti-Jewish meeting held by the fascist Jean-Charles Legrand.[7]

Let us also compare styles of presentation. The pages of *Le Droit de Vivre* in 1938 overflow with combative rhetoric. In 1983, its account of the gathering complains that "it has been quite a long time since the Far Right was last able to bring together so many people in one crowded place to chant slogans reeking of fascism, collaboration and racism."[8] On the whole, the tone is melancholy.

Is it any wonder? The meeting of October 16, 1983 marks a turning-point in the history of anti-Semitism in France; it is the day when the movement regains, in a modest fashion, the use of speech. An underground passage that has endured from Orléans in 1969 on through the sundry desecrations and attacks of the late seventies has finally broken through to the surface.

★

Rumors and desecrations of Jewish cemeteries and synagogues: the telltale signs have already been signalling to us for several years. Of course, those well-documented events are harmless. If they were otherwise (that is to say, if the persecutions had already restarted), no one would have to ask himself what the future holds in store. The dispute between pessimists and optimists would already have been settled in favor of the former. A precursive sign is benign, by definition. In medicine, one has to keep one's eye on a small disagreeable tumor that has manifested on otherwise unblemished skin. In seismology, one must keep track of several small tremors that have registered on one's measuring apparatus. In anti-Semitism, one must follow along after a few advance troops who write "Death to the Jews!" on the walls of a synagogue.

The advance indications of a phenomenon should not be confused with the phenomenon itself. They are not at all alike. The early sign is not terrible in itself. Compared to the dreaded tragedy, it is ridiculous. Compared to the present tranquility, it is incongruous. To top off the bad run of luck, those who already take it seriously quickly become disillusioned. It reveals very little information about the manner in which, later on, the crisis might transpire. A synagogue desecration today teaches us nothing about the form, the actors, or even the timing of the next anti-Jewish uprising. The narrow beam of light cast by the precursive sign is incapable of piercing the opacity of the future. At best, used in conjunction with other elements of analysis, it helps us catch a fleeting glimpse of the vague contours of the coming crisis.

★

Around what issues will it revolve? An anti-Semitism campaign always raises whatever issues are necessary to its polemical and literary viability; at the same time, it grasps at any immediate pretext for provoking riots or unleashing persecutions. A range of anti-Jewish themes has accumulated over the centuries, proving itself not to be limited by the inventive capacities of any particular people, but just by their aptitude for rediscovering old ideas and applying them in new ways. The French are by no means an exception to this rule.

The uncertainty that hangs over the form also occludes the degree. Some anti-Jewish thrusts are verbally high-powered but physically effete. Others are accompanied by acts and exactions that are serious enough to unsettle the routine existence of the Jews in a given country, but not serious enough to put an end to the existence of that Jewish community. Still others, finally, partially or totally destroy that Jewish community. Hatred that hollers, hatred that unsettles, and hatred that kills. Within this range of possibilities, where will the next crisis be situated?

First major indication is furnished by the very nature of the relationship between Jews and non-Jews in modern society. Emancipation implies the complete integration of the Jews into all domains of national life. It thus goes beyond the forms of tolerance, benevolence and protection that Jewish communities in the Diaspora have enjoyed on many occasions in all countries and epochs. This, of course, is not the first time the Jews have felt themselves to be living in a Golden Age, confident that their tribulations have finally come to an end. But it is the first time their confidence has been accompanied by such a grand overture on the part of society-at-large, the first time society has viewed relations between Jews and non-Jews on the model on complete equality of rights and duties.

But, the same causes that led to the Emancipation (secularization of political life, progress in science, advent of democracy and liberalism, growth of industrial society, rise of modern nationalism) also led to profound mutations in anti-Semitism itself. Its themes became racial, and no longer religious, outflanking the difficulty created by the secularization of contemporary society. It fully profited from the advantages offered by modern technology: speed of dissemination of ideas, rapidity of formation of tides of opinion and mass organization. In its final, most exacerbated stages, all of the perquisites of the centralized State work in its favor, and it thereby attains a concentrated destructive power greater than what could ever have been imagined in the darkest stages of pre-Emancipatory history.

Medieval statutes acted as a screen. They discriminated, in times of tranquility, and blocked the introduction of the Jews into mainstream society. But in troubled times they protected, and regulated the rhythms of the degradation. In modern society, the transition from one state to another is more rapid and more brutal. When all goes well, the integration is complete. When all goes badly, the deflagration is total.

The expectation of future violence is supported by the anti-Semitic spasm of the late seventies and early eighties, which was characterized by the emergence of diffuse, but aggressive anti-Jewish agitation. Its virulence can be explained by the circumstances surrounding its appearance: in a period of constraints on its ideological superstructures, anti-Semitism can dump its excess charge through individual or group activism. But this violence could also be a rehearsal on a small scale of what French anti-Semitism will later attempt on a larger scale, and so might expose an irrevocable, ingrained quality of French anti-Semitism.

Will the wave be devastating? In theory, it's quite possible. Some people might want to suggest that every century knows its fair share of evil, but their argument is not corroborated by the lessons of Jewish history. Some centuries turn out to be particularly murderous and catastrophic. Such is the case, for example, with the 14th century. It is also true of the seventeenth for the Jews of Poland. And it is unquestionably the case for the twentieth century. The Russian pogroms of 1905 do not prevent the Ukrainian massacres of 1920, which in turn do not have any influence on the Hitlerian genocide. The present century is therefore a century of high risk, and there is no magical reason why this characteristic should have disappeared in 1945.

Practically speaking, however, it is unlikely that the next crisis will be absolute. It isn't that the French people have changed: changes in the attitudes of non-Jews towards Jews, in one direction or another, are transitory. Benevolence and oppression have alternated so often that neither can be regarded as definitive or final. The movement varies in duration and amplitude, but it is indeed cyclical. It isn't that the Jews have changed: they have remained a fragile and threatened minority, dependent on the good will of an environment that is by turn welcoming and hostile, capable of extending its hospitality to the point of total integration, but also its hostility to the point of systematic massacre.

If extermination seems to be ruled out, it is as a result of a new fact that has transformed—partially and not totally, but considerably all the same—the parameters of the Jewish problem. That is to say, the reestablishment of the sovereign Jewish State after two thousand years of Jewish history in Exile.

The existence of Israel, per se, obviously cannot suppress a serious anti-Jewish crisis in another country. It has not altered the dependent condition of every one of the Jewish communities that live outside its frontiers, which remain prey to the same hazards and constraints that every branch of the Jewish people in Galut (Exile). The creation of Israel has not put an end to either anti-Jewish hatred or to the vulnerability of Jews who are entrenched on foreign soil.

On the other hand, it limits the damage. It has resolved what was, during the thirties, the primary problem of the Jewish people: growing anti-Semitic pressure, universally restrictive immigration policies, and a British policy of refusing Palestinian entry permits. The Law of Return guarantees Israeli citizenship to every Jew who desires it. What's more, as we well know, the Israelis are not content to wait passively on the docks for the arrival of the boats. When serious anti-Semitic trouble threatens a Jewish community abroad, the Jewish State intervenes, as it has already done on numerous occasions in a number of different countries. The Jewish State has recourse to diverse diplomatic and organizational channels, as well as to all the needed human and material infrastructures. Its capacity for action is not negligible.

200

It must not, for that matter, be overestimated. The only sure answer it offers is to an anti-Semitic policy of expulsion, when the Jews of a given country are forced to leave (as was the case, for example, with German anti-Semitism until the end of the thirties). But it cannot deal effectively with the opposite case, that of an anti-Semitic policy of retention that forces Jews to stay. Many examples, past and present, ought to demonstrate that this eventuality should not be discarded.

The option of leaving (where the situation has become bad, but conditions are such that it is still possible to leave) does not only apply to Israel, and some, because of doctrinal anti-Zionism, or for more pragmatic reasons, might try their luck elsewhere. They will quickly discover that the choice they have made is far from simple. Anti-Semitism, in fact, is rarely isolated. A wave that is rising will be visible in a whole group of countries, even if in some of these it comes to a halt at a relatively harmless and, all in all, tolerable level. There is a risk, then, that the refugees' reception there will be quite cold, and above all, quantitatively limited.

★

When will the crisis occur? No mathematical formula (multiplying the cube root of the number of desecrations over a given stretch of time by a coefficient expressing the force of the resistance of political structures to the development of a new anti-Jewish wave) can give the precise date X when the explosion will be set off. The emancipation of the Jews of France was consolidated in the ten or fifteen years following 1789. The 50th Anniversary of the occasion was celebrated with the pogroms of Alsace, in 1848. The one-hundredth anniversary was marked by the violence and the chant of "Death to the Jews!" of the Dreyfus Affair. The one-hundred-and-fiftieth anniversary was celebrated under circumstances that are well known to us all. At this pace, the approach of the 2nd centenary of the Declaration of the Rights of Man and Citizen presages nothing very promising. . . . When we look over a more extended span of time, we might also notice that the ends of centuries tend, more often than not, to be heated times in the history of the Jews of France. Such was the case for the eleventh, twelfth, thirteenth, fourteenth and nineteenth centuries. The rule is by no means absolute. There have been particularly favorable ends to centuries, like that of the eighteenth, when the Jews were granted civilian and political equality. And there are hearts of centuries that are devastating, like that of the fourteenth (black plague) or the twentieth (brown plague).

Sophisticated algorithms, infernal spirals and dangerous promontories: the phenomenon is far too complex for us to force into a prefabricated intellectual collar. Somewhere ahead, however, there awaits a certain moment which, though seen only hazily through the mists of time, heralds the end of French Jewry.

The history of the Jews, in fact, provides us with a dual lesson. On the one hand, the Jewish people as such is indestructible. But, on the other, its various scattered communities, each alone and in its own time, are mortal. As strong, prosperous and creative as they may be, they finally disappear. All delude themselves with the same illusion, confusing the provisional with the final, and all experience the same fate.

Sometimes the fall comes at the end of an evolutionary process, studded with both pauses and sudden leaps, that lasts for a very long time. A century elapsed between the anti-Jewish massacres of Spain in 1391 and the final expulsion of 1492. Sometimes the tumble is sudden. German Judaism is at the height of its power in the twenties. It collapses in the thirties. A Galut is extinguished through forced conversion, assimilation, massacre, or departure: and the many avenues do not exclude one another.

The French Galut will experience the fate of all the great Jewish communities, a fate that was already once its own, during the Middle Ages. But this long term perspective, infallible in its prediction of the event, is powerless to fix a date for it. Is it three decades from now, or three centuries? Familiarity with the ironclad laws of Jewish history enables one to espy the final outcome, but not to situate it in time. No analysis is capable of indicating whether the next anti-Jewish crisis in France will be the last, or whether, on the contrary, it will be followed by a new lull, a new abatement of the threat that might or might not itself endure for a long time.

For now, our reflection must be concerned with the day when the Jews of France will cease to be protected. Today, they still are. Not by the bulletins of the CRIF. Not by the antiracist analyses of the MRAP. Not by the laws, the police, or the demonstrations. Not by their own self-defense. The Jews of France are protected by a sentiment felt by the large majority of the French, one that associates anti-Semitism with the memory of the Hitlerian occupation. We can use an arbitrary expression to name this sentiment: the Holocaust Barricade.

Its existence is well known to the apologeticists. They devote much effort to shoring it up by elucidating past events (or by repeating over and over that they should be elucidated, which in practice amounts to the same thing), hoping that once these events are well enough understood, they will never again be reproduced.

Until now, the Holocaust Barricade has had to withstand two major assaults. One sought to twist its way around the obstacle by attributing to a demoniacal "Zionism" the defects and crimes traditionally ascribed to the Jews. And so, anti-Zionism tried to get around through word-substitution (international "Zionism" in the place of international Judaism) and image-alteration (the bloodthirsty Jew becomes the bloodthirsty Israeli). It also practiced symbolic role reversal, applying key concepts reminiscent of Jewish martyrdom (pogrom, ghetto, camp, genocide) to fantasized analyses of the Arab-Israeli conflict. The other offensive tried a frontal assault, with Rassinier in the lead, Faurisson flanking him on the Right and Thion on the Left, by outright denying the very existence of the Nazi genocide.

However, the true threat to the Barricade is not the offense of the lie, but the desertion of memory. Its effect is slow but steady. It doesn't attack openly on the surface, but goes about undermining the Barricade using a weapon of attrition that cannot be counteracted. A nation's memory is, in effect, two-levelled. It has erudite, bookish memory, reposited in libraries and history courses, in which past events, great and small, are hoarded together; and it also contains recent memory, that of dramas that are still torrid, that of wounds that are still open. The first, dead memory, stores up facts. The second, living memory, dictates behaviour.

How does an event switch over from living memory to dead memory? The war from 1914–18 was a terrible one. It cut down an entire generation in its prime, it galvanized nations and it threw Europe into disorder. It traumatized an entire generation to the degree that all political life in the twenties and thirties was organized with reference to that one event. Today, the Great War is lost in the darkness of years. Its memory still makes a few decorated veterans of the trenches tremble; but for the most part it has become assimilated into the long list of things which we know took place but towards which we no longer feel anything: neither enthusiasm nor revulsion.

It will soon be the same for the Second World War. Its memory will never disappear from the pages of the history texts. But it will lose its emotional impact and its political message, which links anti-Semitism to barbarism. Its dedramatization will come about naturally with the passing of the War and postwar generations. Or else it will happen brusquely, in the wake of a national or international crisis. The more time passes, the more accurately the disappearance of the

Holocaust Barricade can be foretold. Will it give way with one shove, or will it crumble away by bits and pieces? In either case, the Jews of France will find themselves, once again, out in the open.

★

"The French people remember the Dreyfus Affair. They would turn aside a second wave of anti-Semitism . . . " Bernard Lecache writes in 1932.[9] Much later, in 1978, Scopus concludes an editorial in the *Bulletin de l'Agence Télégraphique Juive* by running through, without realizing it, the same, timeless argument. This time, the French remember Vichy, and no longer the Dreyfus Affair. "The postwar generations are astounded by what was done by some of their elders. . . . Anti-Semitism no longer has a future in France."[10]

Let us venture, in light of these twin citations, towards a less optimistic prognostication.

The path to the coming crisis will not be rectilinear. It will have its feverish times and its interludes of relapse. Each fever will give rise to concerns that a few aggressive speeches should prove enough to dispel. Each relapse will confirm that anti-Semitism is definitely in decline. When the crisis, properly speaking, springs up, it will take all by surprise. It will have been, after all, unforeseeable.

Foreword: Zola's Smile

1. *Le Temps,* January 19, 20, and 21, 1898.
2. Joseph Reinach, *Histoire de l'Affaire Dreyfus,* vol. III, Paris, 1903
3. *Le Temps,* February 13, 1898.
4. *The American Monthly Review of Reviews,* March 1898.
5. See: Robert F. Byrnes, *Antisemitism in France. The Prologue to the Dreyfus Affair,* New York, 1969 (2nd edition).
6. Edouard Drumont, *La France juive devant l'opinion,* Paris, 1886.
7. Edouard Drumont, *La France juive. Essai d'histoire contemporaine,* Paris, 1886.
8. Edouard Drumont, *La France juive devant l'opinion,* Paris, 1886.
9. Edouard Drumont, *La dernière bataille (Nouvelle Etude psychologique et sociale),* Paris, 1890.
10. Edouard Drumont, *Le testament d'un antisémite,* Paris, 1891.
11. *La Libre Parole,* January 22, 1898.
12. Nordau's speeches in Max Nordau, *Sheelat HaYehudim VePitrona. Mivh'ar Neumim VeMaamarim,* Jerusalem, 1960.
13. Quoted in: Michel Ansky, *Les Juifs d'Algérie. Du décret Crémieux à la Libération,* Paris, 1950.
14. Alliance Israélite Universelle, general assembly of April 29, 1903.

Chapter One: Jews and non-Jews, United!

1. *Bulletin de l'ATJ,* October 6, 1980.
2. *Bulletin de l'ATJ,* issues of September 1980.
3. *Bulletin de l'ATJ,* October 6, 1980.
4. *Bulletin de l'ATJ,* October 8, 1980.
5. *Droit et Liberté,* October 1980.
6. *Le Figaro,* October 6, 1980.
7. *Vorwärts,* issues of June 24 to July 6 1922.
8. Count Harry Kessler, *Walter Rathenau. His life and Work,* London, 1929.
9. *Israelitisches Familienblatt,* July 6, 1922.
10. *C.V. Zeitung,* June 30, 1922.
11. *C.V. Zeitung,* July 13, 1922.
12. *C.V. Zeitung,* September 28, 1922.
13. *C.V. Zeitung,* October 12, 1922.

14. *C.V. Zeitung,* October 19, 1922.
15. Leaflet of the Comité juif d'action, circulated in 1979.
16. *Le Nouvel Observateur,* October 13 to 19, 1980.
17. *Naie Folkszeitung,* March 16, 1936.
18. *Naie Folkszeitung,* March 17, 1936.
19. *Naie Folkszeitung,* March 21, 1936.
20. *Naie Folkszeitung,* March 18, 1936, March 20, 1936.
21. *Naie Folkszeitung,* March 18, 1936.
22. *Naie Folkszeitung,* March 19, 1936.
23. *Naie Folkszeitung,* March 20, 1936.
24. *Le Nouvel Observateur,* October 13 to 19, 1980.
25. *L'Arche,* November 1980.
26. *Le Droit de Vivre,* April 1933.
27. *Le Droit de Vivre,* May 1933.
28. *Le Droit de Vivre,* May 1934.
29. *Le Droit de Vivre,* February 22, 1936.
30. *Le Droit de Vivre,* July 11, 1936.
31. *Le Droit de Vivre,* July 18, 1936.
32. *Le Populaire,* June 8, 1936.
33. *Le Droit de Vivre,* June 10, 1936.
34. Interview in the *Tag.* Quoted in the *Bulletin de la Fédération des Sociétés juives d'Algérie,* January 1935.
35. Quoted in: Henri Amouroux, *La grande histoire des Français sous l'occupation,* vol. V.
36. *Le Droit de Vivre,* April 1, 1939.
37. Quoted in: Henri Amouroux, *op. cit.,* vol. II.
38. See: Marc Sadoun, *Les socialistes sous l'occupation. Résistance et collaboration,* Paris, 1982.
39. *Le Droit de Vivre,* November 26, 1938.
40. *Le Droit de Vivre,* June 24, 1939.
41. Annie Kriegel, *La Résistance communiste,* in Centre de Documentation Juive Contemporaine, *La France et la question juive. 1940–1944.* Paris, 1981.
42. Quoted in: Auguste Leçur, *Le Parti communiste français et la résistance Août 1939–Juin 1941,* 1968.
43. *Le Nouvel observateur,* October 13 to 19, 1980.
44. *La persécution des Juifs en Allemagne. Attitudes des Eglises chrétiennes des Etats-Unis d'Amérique, du Canada, de France, de Grande-Bretagne, des Pays-Bas, de Roumanie, de Suisse et de Syrie.* September 1933.
45. *Le Droit de Vivre,* March 5, 1938.
46. *Le Droit de Vivre,* April 30, 1938.
47. *Le Droit de Vivre,* November 26, 1938.
48. *Le Droit de Vivre,* February 18, 1939.
49. Jean-Marie Mayeur, *Les Eglises devant la persécution des Juifs en France,* et Danielle Delmaire, *Le Cardinal Lienart et la persécution*

des Juifs de Lille, in Centre de Documentation Juive Contemporaine, *La France et la question juive. 1940–1944,* Paris, 1981.
50. *L'Arche,* November 1980.
51. *Le Droit de Vivre,* July 1935.
52. *Le Droit de Vivre,* May 7, 1938.
53. *C.V. Zeitung,* December 11, 1931.
54. *L'Arche,* November 1980.
55. *L'Arche,* January 1983.

Chapter Two: Appealing to the State

1. *Les Juifs en France,* Histoire, no. 3, November 1979.
2. *L'Univers israélite,* July 16, 1887. See also, for other mentions of the problem, the same paper on February 1, 1888, July 16, 1892. . . . See also the article by Isidore Cahen in *Archives israélites* of June 2, 1892.
3. *Le Droit de Vivre,* April 29, 1939.
4. *Le Droit de Vivre,* May 27, 1939.
5. *Le Droit de Vivre,* June 24, 1939.
6. *Les délits racistes. Compte rendu du Colloque Juridique organisé par la LICA le 18 novembre 1978 au Palais de Justice de Paris,* Cahiers de la LICA, November 1979.
7. World Jewish Congress (British Section), *Protection Against Group Defamation. Present Law and its Extension,* London, September 1944.
8. F.S., *Der Antisemitismus der Gegenwart und seine Abwehr. Ein Weckruf an die deutschen Juden,* Mülheim-am Rhein, 1895.
9. About legal action against antisemitism in Germany before the first World War: Dr Maximilian Parmod, *Antisemttismus und Strafrechtspflege,* Berlin 1894 (Zweite Auflage); Ismar Schorsch, *Jewish Reactions to German Anti-Semitism 1870–1914,* Columbia University Press, 1972; Sanford Ragins, *Jewish Responses to Anti-Semitism in Germany 1870–1914,* Cincinnati, Ohio, 1980.
10. About legal action from 1918 to 1933: Ludwig Foerder, *Antisemitismus und Justiz,* Berlin, 1924; Alfred Hirschberg, *Kollektiv-Ehre und Kollektiv-Beleidigung,* Berlin, 1929; Dr. Rudolf Callmann, *Zur Boykottfrage,* Berlin, 1932; Ambrose Doskow and Sidney B. Jacoby, *Antisemitism and the Law in pre-Nazi Germany,* in *Contemporary Jewish Record,* September-October 1940. See also note 1, chapter IV.
11. *C.V. Zeitung,* June 17, 1927. See also *Deutsches Judentum und Rechtskrisis,* Berlin, 1927.
12. On the problems of collective defamation, see for instance: *C.V. Zeitung,* September 28, 1922.
13. *C.V. Zeitung,* June 17, 1927.
14. *Der Schild,* July 4, 1927.
15. *C.V. Zeitung,* July 31, 1927.
16. *C.V. Zeitung,* September 23, 1927.

17. *Der Schild,* October 17, 1927.
18. *Der Schild,* August 2, 1929.
19. *Der Schild,* October 11, 1929.
20. *C.V. Zeitung,* November 8, 1929.
21. *C.V. Zeitung,* September 5, 1930.
22. *Israelitisches Familienblatt,* April 26, 1932.
23. *Cahiers de la LICRA,* no. 3, November 1981.
24. *Le Nouvel Observateur,* September 4, 1982.
25. *Vorwärts,* September 17, 1931.
26. *Vorwärts,* September 13, 1931. *C.V. Zeitung,* September 18, 1931. *Der Schild,* September 24, 1931.
27. *Le Droit de Vivre,* April, 1933, July-August 1933.
28. Texts in: Serge Klarsfeld, *Vichy Auschwitz. Le rôle de Vichy dans la solution finale de la question juive en France. 1942.* Paris, 1983.
29. Leaflet of the Renouveau juif, circulated in 1980.
30. See: Robert Chazan,*The Blois Incident of 1171: a Study in Jewish Intercommunal Organization,* American Academy for Jewish Research, Proceedings 36, 1968.
31. *Bulletin de l'ATJ,* October 9, 1980.
32. *Bulletin d'information bimensuel du Bureau de Presse et de Documentation de la LICA,* May 21, 1938.

Chapter Three: Education

1. *Le Monde,* October 25, 1980.
2. *C.V. Zeitung,* October 14, 1927. The book is *Les pogroms en Ukraine sous les gouvernements ukrainiens (1917–1920),* edited in Paris by the "Comité des Délégations Juives."
3. Bernard Lecache, *Au pays des pogromes. Quand Israël meurt...,* Paris, 1927.
4. *Tribune juive,* January 12 to 18, 1979.
5. In: Henri Dagan,*Enquête sur l'antiséamitisme,* Paris, 1899.
6. Maurice Vernes, *Antisémitisme et méthode historique,* Paris, 1898.
7. Léonce Reynaud, *Les Juifs français devant l'opinion,* Paris, 1887.
8. Le groupe des ESRI de Paris, *Antisémitisme et sionisme. Rapport présenté au Congrès révolutionnaire international (Paris 1900) par le groupe des Etudiants socialistes révolutionnaires de Paris,* Paris, 1900.
9. Anatole Leroy Beaulieu, *L'antisémitisme,* Paris, 1897.
10. Jacques Prolo, *La caverne antisémite,* Paris, 1902.
11. *Le Droit de Vivre,* April 8, 1939.
12. *Le Droit de Vivre,* May 7, 1938.
13. *Centre de Documentation et de Vigilance. Bulletin d'information,* January 13, 1939, February 10, 1939, May 17, 1939.
14. In: *Au service de la France. Les immigrés juifs dans les journées de septembre.* Edited by the Union des Sociétés Juives de France, December 1938.

15. *Paix et Droit,* June 1936.
16. Press clippings—File PC2 at the Weiner Library.
17. *Bulletin de l'ATJ,* April 5, 1979.
18. *Bulletin de l'ATJ,* September 11, 1980.
19. Communiqué of the CRIF.
20. *Tribune juive,* October 10 to 16, 1980.
21. *Bulletin de l'ATJ,* October 6, 1980.
22. *Le Journal des Communautés,* October 1980.
23. *L'Arche,* November 1981.
24. *Les Cahiers de l'AIU,* October 1980.
25. *Le Nouvel Observateur,* August 14 to 20, 1982.
26. *Les Nouvelles Littéraires,* August 19 to 25, 1982.
27. *Les Nouveaux Cahiers,* Spring 1983.
28. Ahad HaAm, *Ktavim Nivharim,* Tel-Aviv.
29. *Le Nouvel Observateur,* October 13 to 19, 1980.
30. *L'Univers israélite,* July 19, 1935.
31. *Le Populaire,* November 22, 1938.
32. *Le Droit de Vivre,* January 7, 1939.
33. *Le Nouvel Observateur,* October 13 to 19, 1980.
34. *Le Droit de Vivre,* December 26, 1936.
35. Zadoc Kahn's letter to the *Temps* is reproduced in *L'Univers israélite,* February 1, 1890.
36. *L'Arche,* December 1981.
37. Irène Harand, *Son combat. Réponse à Hitler,* Bruxelles et Vienne, 1936.
38. *Le Droit de Vivre,* April 1, 1939.

Chapter Four: The Combat Front of the German Jews

1. On the fight of German Jews against antisemitism and nazism: Hans Reichmann, *Der drohende Sturm. Episoden aus dem Kampf der deutschen Juden gegen die nationalsozialistische Gefahr 1929 bis 1933,* in *In zwei Welten. Siegfried Moses zum Fünfundsiebzigsten Geburtstag,* Tel-Aviv, 1962; *Entscheidungsjahr 1932. Zur Judenfrage in der Endphase der Weimarer Republik,* Ein Sammelband herausgegeben von Werner E. Mosse unter Mitwirkung von Arnold Paucker, Tübingen, 1965; Arnold Paucker, *Der jüdische Abwehrkampf gegen Antisemitismus und Nationalsozialismus in den letzten Jahren der Weimarer Republik,* Hamburg, 2.verbesserte Auflage, 1969.
2. *C.V. Zeitung,* April 20, 1928, April 27, 1928, May 11, 1928, May 18, 1928. See the Central Verein brochure: *Wahlen 1928.*
3. *Anti-Anti. Tatsachen zur Judenfrage,* Philo-Verlag (several editions). See also: *Waffen im Abwehrkampf,* Berlin, 1921; Stern, *Angriff und Abwehr. Ein Handbuch der Judenfrage,* Berlin, 1924.

4. *C.V. Zeitung,* May 25, 1928. Posters and tracts of the Central Verein for the elections of 1928 in: Arnold Paucker, *op. cit.*
5. Anecdote told by Hans Reichmann, *op. cit.*
6. Electoral results analyzed in: *C.V. Zeitung,* May 25, 1928, June 1, 1928.
7. *C.V. Zeitung,* May 25, 1928.
8. *Der Schild,* May 31, 1928.
9. *C.V. Zeitung,* September 14, 1928.
10. See: *C.V. Zeitung,* November 9, 1928.
11. *C.V. Zeitung,* September 28, 1928.
12. For instance, *C.V. Zeitung,* October 26, 1928.
13. *C.V. Zeitung,* November 16, 1928.
14. *C.V. Zeitung,* February 15, 1929.
15. *C.V. Zeitung,* April 5, 1929.
16. *C.V. Zeitung,* April 19, 1929.
17. On the problem of methods of propaganda, see for instance: *Grundlagen und Formen politischer Propaganda,* Von Professor Dr. S. Tschachotin und Dr. C. Mierendorff, Bundesvorstand des Reichsbanners Schwarz-Rot-Gold, Magdeburg, 1932.
18. *Alarm (Kampfblatt gegen alle Feinde der Republik. Für wahre Demokratie und sozialen Fortschritt),* July 28, 1932.
19. *C.V. Zeitung,* January 3, 1930.
20. *Schafft Aufklärung. Ein Leitfaden für Ortsgruppen,* Handbüerei für Ortsgruppenvorstände, Herausgegeben vom Central-Verein Deutscher Staatsbürger jüdischen Glaubens. Berlin (several editions).
21. *C.V. Zeitung,* January 10, 1930, February 7, 1930, March 21, 1930, April 11, 1930.
22. *C.V. Zeitung,* February 21, 1930.
23. *C.V. Zeitung,* January 17, 1930, January 24, 1930.
24. *C.V. Zeitung,* January 17, 1930.
25. *C.V. Zeitung,* May 16, 1930.
26. *C.V. Zeitung,* May 23, 1930, June 6, 1930, June 13, 1930, June 20, 1930.
27. *C.V. Zeitung,* July 25, 1930.
28. *C.V. Zeitung,* August 8, 1930.
29. *C.V. Zeitung,* August 15, 1930.
30. Reproduced in the Central Verein brochure: *Hitler Deutschland? Wahlen 1930.*
31. *C.V. Zeitung,* August 22, 1930.
32. *C.V. Zeitung,* August 29, 1930.
33. *C.V. Zeitung,* September 12, 1930.
34. *C.V. Zeitung,* August 29, 1930.
35. *C.V. Hauptgeschäftsstelle an Ortsgruppen. 29 August 1930,* in Arnold Paucker, *op. cit.*
36. *C.V. Landesverband Rheinland an Ortsgruppe Neuwied. 3 September 1930,* in Arnold Paucker, *op. cit.*

37. *JTA Bulletin,* September 19, 1930.
38. *C.V. Zeitung,* September 19, 1930.
39. *Der Schild,* October 9, 1930.
40. For instance: *Der Schild,* August 14, 1930, and *Der Schild,* June 28, 1929.
41. *C.V. Zeitung,* October 17, 1930.
42. *C.V. Zeitung,* January 23, 1931.
43. *C.V. Zeitung,* February 13, 1931.
44. On the fight against antisemitism among youth, see: *C.V. Zeitung,* January 8, 1932, March 11, 1932, April 1, 1932. . . . On educational and propaganda work: Dr. Julie Meyers, *Anti-Defamation Work in pre-Hitler Germany,* Published by the Jewish Labor Committee, New York.
45. On the Jewish vote in Weimar Germany, see: Arnold Paucker, *Jewish Defense Against Nazism in the Weimar Republic,* Wiener Library Bulletin, vol. XXVI, 1972.
46. *Aufruf des C.V. von Anfang 1932,* in Arnold Paucker, *Der jüdische Abwehrkampf. . . , op. cit.*
47. *C.V. Zeitung,* January 22, 1932. *JTA Bulletin,* January 18, 1932. *Paix et Droit,* January 1932.
48. *Wir deutschen Juden,* 1932.
49. The headlines of the *Völkischer Beobachter,* reproduced in *C.V. Zeitung,* February 6th.
50. *C.V. Zeitung,* March 18, 1932.
51. *Der Schild,* March 24, 1932.
52. *C.V. Zeitung,* April 8, 1932.
53. *C.V. Zeitung,* April 15, 1932.
54. *Der Schild,* April 14, 1932.
55. See for instance: *C.V. Zeitung,* July 8, 1932, July 29, 1932.
56. *JTA Bulletin,* June 20, 1932.
57. *C.V. Zeitung,* July 1, 1932.
58. *C.V. Zeitung,* July 15, 1932.
59. *C.V. Zeitung,* July 8, 1932.
60. The *C.V. Zeitung,* of August 5, 1932 gives an account of all activities.
61. See: Curt Riess, *Joseph Goebbels,* New York, 1948.
62. *C.V. Zeitung,* June 3, 1932.
63. *C.V. Zeitung,* August 5, 1932.
64. *C.V. Zeitung,* July 15, 1932.
65. *C.V. Zeitung,* July 22, 1932.
66. *C.V. Zeitung,* July 29, 1932.
67. *C.V. Zeitung,* October 7, 1932.
68. For instance: *C.V. Zeitung,* November 18, 1932, December 2, 1932.
69. *C.V. Zeitung,* December 23, 1932.
70. *Der Schild,* December 22, 1932.
71. *C.V. Zeitung,* January 26, 1933.
72. *Der Schild,* January 26, 1933.

73. *Jüdische Rundschau*, January 12, 1932.
74. *JTA Bulletin*, February 1, 1933.
75. *Der Schild*, February 9, 1933.
76. *Ibid.*
77. Quoted in: Leonard Baker, *Days of Sorrow and Pain, Leo Baeck and the Berlin Jews*, New York, 1978.
78. *Jüdische Rundschau*, April 4, 1933.

Chapter Five: Demonstrations and Meetings

1. *JTA Bulletin*, March 21, 1933, March 24, 1933, March 29, 1933.
2. *JTA Bulletin*, March 29, 1933, *Der Moment*, March 26, 1933, March 28, 1933, March 29, 1933. On the Bund's decision not to participate in the National Committee and to launch a separate campaign, see: *Naie Folkszeitung* March 27, 1933.
3. See, for the months of March, April and May: *JTA Bulletin, Le Droit de Vivre, Jewish Chronicle, Der Moment, Naie Folkszeitung*, etc.
4. *Jewish Chronicle*, March 31, 1933.
5. *JTA Bulletin*, April 20, 1933, April 26, 1933.
6. See for instance: *Special Bulletin issued by the Jewish Telegraphic Agency*, April 28, 1933.
7. *Le Droit de Vivre*, June 24, 1939.
8. Here, the meetings organized or supported by the LICA. Source: *Le Droit de Vivre*, of the corresponding dates.
9. Jacob Kaplan, *Les temps d'épreuve. Sermons et allocutions*, Paris, 1952.
10. *Bulletin de l'ATJ*, October 6 and 7, 1979.

Chapter Six: Self-defense

1. *Le Monde, August 12, 1982.*
2. *Minute*, August 28 to September 3, 1982.
3. *Le Monde, April 15, 1981.*
4. *For a complete anthology of Jewish self-defense, see: Sefer HaGvura, Anthologia Historit Sifrutit.* (Edited by Am Oved in 1951. Fourth part edited by the Israeli Defense Ministry in 1980.)
5. Quotations from: *Archives israélites*, vol. IX, 1848.
6. *JTA Bulletin*, July 1,2, 7 and 8, 1931.
7. *JTA Bulletin*, May 13, 1933.
8. *Bulletin de l'ATJ* October 2, 1980.
9. *Le Droit de Vivre*, May 30, 1936.
10. *Le Droit de Vivre*, August 1934. *JTA Bulletin*, August 7, 8, 9 and 10, 1934.
11. *Le Droit de Vivre*, May 2, 1936.

12. *Le Populaire,* May 28, 1936.
13. *Le Droit de Vivre,* July 4, 1936.
14. *Bulletin de la LICA,* March 1931, April 1931.
15. *Bulletin de la LICA,* October 1931.
16. *Le Droit de Vivre,* November 1933.
17. For instance: *Le Droit de Vivre,* May 1934.
18. *Le Droit de Vivre,* June 10, 1936.
19. *Le Droit de Vivre,* December 12, 1936.
20. *Le Droit de Vivre,* July 1935.
21. *Le Droit de Vivre,* January 1934.
22. *Le Droit de Vivre,* June-July 1934.
23. *Le Droit de Vivre,* April 30, 1938.
24. *Le Droit de Vivre,* October 1, 1938. *Le Populaire,* September 25, 1938.
25. *Le Droit de Vivre,* October 1, 1938.
26. *Le Droit de Vivre,* October 8, 1938.
27. *Le Droit de Vivre,* October 1, 1938.
28. *Le Droit de Vivre,* October 15, 1938.
29. *Le Droit de Vivre,* December 3, 1938.
30. *Le Droit de Vivre,* October 15, 1938.
31. *Le Populaire,* November 11, 1938.
32. *Le Populaire,* October 3, 1938. *Le Droit de Vivre,* October 8, 1938.
33. *Le Nouvel Observateur,* August 14 to 20, 1982.
34. *Naie Folkszeitung,* March 18, 1936.
35. Source: Leonard Rowe, *Jewish Self-Defense: A Response to Violence,* in *Studies on Polish Jewry 1919–1939,* YVO, New York, 1974.
36. Bibliographical references on Zionist Self-Defense in prewar Poland found in: Emmanuel Ringelblum, *Polish-Jewish Relations during the Second World War,* Jerusalem, 1974.
37. *Naie Folkszeitung,* March 18, 1936.
38. Quoted in: Trunk, *Der ekonomisher antisemitizim in Poïlen zwishen di zwei weltmilhoumes,* in *Shtudies vegn Yden in Poïlen, 1919–1939,* YVO, New York, 1974.
39. Yakov Lestshinsky, *Erev Hurban, Foun Ydishen leben in Poïlen 1935–1937,* Buenos Aires, 1951.
40. *Le Nouvel Observateur,* October 13 to 19, 1980.
41. The January 1919 appeal is reproduced in *Der Schild,* July 5, 1929. On the history of the RjF, see: Ruth Pierson, *Embattled Veterans. The Reichsbund jüdischer Frontsoldaten* Leo Baeck Institute, Yearbook XIX, 1974; Ulrich Dunker, *Der Reichsbund jüdischer Frontsoldaten 1919–1938. Geschichte eines jüdischen Abwehrvereins,* Düsseldorf, 1977; Carl Jeffrey Rheins, *German Jewish Patriotism 1918–1935,* Ann Arbor Mich., 1979; and the chapter *The Jewish Response to Anti-Semitism* in Donald L. Niewyck, *The Jews in Weimar Germany,* Baton Rouge and London, 1980.
42. On the trial: *C.V. Zeitung,* May 22, 1924. *Der Schild,* June 1, 1924.
43. Ulrich Dunker, *op. cit.*

44. Ruth Pierson, *op. cit.*
45. On Goebbel's first years in Berlin: Curt Riess, *Joseph Goebbels,* New York, 1948; Erich Ebermayer and Hans Otto Meissner, *Evil Genius. The Story of Joseph Goebbels,* London, 1953; Victor Reimann, *The man who created Hitler. Joseph Goebbels,* London, 1977.
46. For instance: *Der Schild,* March 28, 1927.
47. *Der Schild,* April 11, 1927.
48. *Der Schild,* May 23, 1927.
49. *Der Schild,* October 5, 1928.
50. *Der Schild,* September 24, 1931. For the Central Verein's reaction, see: Arnold Paucker, *Documents on the Fight of Jewish Organizations against right-wing Extremism,* in *Michael. On the History of the Jews in the Diaspora,* II, The Diaspora Research Institute, Tel-Aviv, 1973.
51. *C.V. Zeitung,* January 26, 1933.
52. *Der Schild,* Sonderausgabe, 1924.
53. *Bulletin de l'ATJ,* October 1, 1980.
54. *Le Droit de Vivre,* September-October 1933.
55. *Le Droit de Vivre,* September 26, 1936.
56. *Tribune juive,* March 26 to April 1, 1982.

Chapter Seven: Before and Now

1. *Bulletin de l'ATJ,* October 2, 1980.
2. *Le Droit de Vivre,* September-October 1933.
3. *Bulletin de l'ATJ,* February 11, 1980.
4. *Le Droit de Vivre,* May 1935.
5. *Le Figaro,* October 6, 1980.
6. *Le Droit de Vivre,* January 1933.
7. *Le Monde,* September 30, 1980.
8. *Le Droit de Vivre,* June 1933.
9. *Le Matin,* September 29, 1980.
10. *Le Droit de Vivre,* April 30, 1938.
11. *L'Arche,* September-October 1980.
12. *Bulletin de l'ATJ,* October 6, 1980.
13. *Le Monde,* October 25, 1980.
14. *JTA Bulletin,* February 22, 1933.
15. Jacob Kaplan, *Les temps d'épreuve. Sermons et allocutions,* Paris, 1952.
16. *Le Droit de Vivre,* May 1933.
17. *Le Droit de Vivre,* June 1933.
18. *Le Droit de Vivre,* February 15, 1936.
19. *Le Droit de Vivre,* October 15, 1938.
20. *Le Droit de Vivre,* February 25, 1939.
21. *JTA Bulletin,* May 3, 1933, May 19, 1933.
22. *Naie Folkszeitung,* March 18, 1936.

23. *Naie Folkszeitung,* March 19, 1936.
24. *Le Droit de Vivre,* June 19, 1937.
25. *Le Droit de Vivre,* May 29, 1937.
26. *Le Droit de Vivre,* November 19, 1938, November 26, 1938.
27. *Le Droit de Vivre,* February 25, 1939.
28. *L'Arche,* May 1983.
29. *Le Droit de Vivre,* May 1935.
30. See for instance Michel Mayer's article in: *Combat pour la Diaspora,* 1st trimester, 1981.
31. Tribune juive, June 20 to 26, 1980.
32. *Bulletin de l'ATJ,* October 6, 1980.
33. *Jüdische Front,* May 15, 1936.
34. Manès Sperber, *Ces temps-là. Le pont inachevé,* Paris, 1977.
35. *JTA Bulletin,* June 22, 1932.
36. *JTA Bulletin,* June 27, 1932.
37. *Jüdische Front,* December 29, 1932.
38. *JTA Bulletin,* March 18, 1933.
39. *Jüdische Front,* December 29, 1932.
40. *JTA Bulletin,* June 12, 1935.
41. See:*Jüdische Front,* March 1, 1936.
42. *Jüdische Front,* April 17, 1936.
43. *Jüdische Front,* February 1, 1937.
44. *Jüdische Front,* May 15, 1937.
45. *Jüdische Front,* July 1, 1937.
46. *Jüdische Front,* February 3, 1938.
47. See the *JTA Bulletin,* for March, April and May 1938.
48. William Shirer, *The rise and Fall of the Third Reicht.* New York ,1960.
49. *Le Droit de Vivre,* June 11, 1938.
50. Quoted in: Georges Wellers, *L'étoile jaune à l'heure de Vichy,* Paris, 1973.

Chapter Eight: Apprehensions

1. *L'Arche,* March 1979.
2. *La Tribune juive,* April 3, 1936.
3. Quoted in: *The Zionist Idea,* A Historical Analysis and Reader by Arthur Hertzberg, New York, 1972.
4. *The Jews and the Crusaders. The Hebrew Chronicles of the First and Second Crusades,* Translated and edited by Shlomo Eidelberg, The University of Wisconsin Press, 1977.
5. Gilles Lambert, *Operation Hazalah,* Paris, 1972.
6. *L'Arche,* January 1983.
7. *L'Arche,* July 1983.
8. *Bulletin de l'ATJ,* October 31, 1980.
9. *L'Arche,* March 1983.

Chapter Nine: Description

1. Eric Benmergui, *La résurgence de l'antisémitisme en France*, Université de Droit, d'Economie et des Sciences d'Aix-Marseille. Institut d'Etudes Politiques d'Aix-en-Province, 1981.
2. Sources: *Bulletin de l'ATJ* and *Survey on Antisemitic Events* (1978).
3. *Die Stellung der National sozialistischen Deutschen Arbeiterpartei (NSDAP) zur Judenfrage.* Eine materialsammlung vorgelegt vom Centralverein deutscher Staatsbürger jüdischen Glaubens E.V., Berlin.
4. *Le Droit de Vivre*, June 10, 1936.
5. *Le Canard Enchâné*, October 8, 1980.
6. Commission chargée d'établir le bilan de la situation de la France, *La France en mai 1981.* *T.V: L'Etat et le citoyen*, La Documentation française, December 1981.
7. Annie Kriegel, *Israël est-il coupable?*, Paris, 1982.
8. Anti-Defamation League of B'nai B'rith, *1980 Audit of Anti-Semitic Episodes*, December 1980.
9. *Le Droit de Vivre*, January 1977.
10. See: *Unsere Massnahmen zur Bekämpfung der Friedhofsschändungen in Deutschland Mit einer Liste der Synagogen schändungen*, Eine vertrauliche Denkschrift des Centralvereins deutscher Staatsbürger jüdischen Glaubens E.V., 1929; *125 Friedhofsschändungen in Deutschland 1923–1932. Dokumente der politischen und kulturellen Verwilderung unserer Zeit*, Zusammengestellt vom Central-Verein deutscher Staatsbürger jüdischen Glaubens E.V., 1932 (several editions).
11. Text reproduced in: Beth Lohameî Hagettaot, *Dapim LeH'eker HaShoa VeHaMered*, February 1952.
12. Sources: *Le Droit de Vivre, Droit et Liberté*, from the years 1958, 1959 and 1960.
13. Sources for 1976: *Bulletin de l'ATJ*, and *Survey on Antisemitic Events*.
14. On anti-Jewish attacks in France during the War: Jacob Kaplan, *La communauté juive française sous l'occupation*, Conférence donnée à la Societé des Etudes Juives, Rapport dû à M. Maurice E. Moch, *Revue des Etudes Juives*, Vol. 130, April-December 1971; Philippe Bourdrel, *Histoire des Juifs de France*, Paris, 1974.
15. *Le Quotidien de Paris*, August 12, 1982.
16. Public opinion polls on antisemitism in: *Sondages*, Revue Française de l'Opinion Publique, 1967 no.2 (IFOP); *Le Matin de Paris*, May 12, 1977, May 13, 1977 (Louis Harris France); *VSD*, 1978 (IFOP) in *Bulletin de l'ATJ*, February 13, 1978; *L'Express*, October 11 to 17, 1980 (Louis Harris France).
17. *L'Arche*, June 1977.
18. *L'Arche*, September-October 1979.
19. *Jewish Chronicle*, January 8, 1982.

Chapter Ten: Reactions

1. The *Bulletin de l'Alliance Israélite Universelle* in the year 1898 illustrates quite well the mitigative attitude. It deals abundantly with antisemitism in Russia, Yemen, Greece and Morrocco, but remains silent upon the Dreyfus Affair . . . in France.
2. Sources: *Bulletin de l'ATJ* and *Survey on Antisemitic Events* (1979).
3. See the Central Verein brochure: *125 Friedhofsschändungen in Deutschland 1923–1932, op. cit.* About Arnsberg: *C.V. Zeitung,* April 12, 1929.
4. *L'Arche,* September-October 1979.
5. *Tribune juive,* December 29, 1978 to January 5, 1979.
6. *La Tribune juive,* August 24, 1928.
7. *La Tribune juive,* November 30, 1928.
8. *La Tribune juive,* December 7, 1928.
9. *Le Monde,* September 21, 1979.
10. *Bulletin de l'ATJ,* October 6 and 7, 1979.
11. *Le Nouvel Observateur,* September 17 to 23, 1979.
12. On xenophobia in France before 1940, see: Raymond Millet, *Trois millions d'étrangers en France. Les indésirables, les bienvenus,* Paris, 1938; Jacques Saint-Germain, *La grande invasion,* Paris, 1939.
13. *Le Monde juif. Revue du Centre de Documentation Juive Contemporaine,* October-December 1981.
14. *Droit et Liberté,* April 1979.
15. *Droit et Liberté,* October 1980.
16. *Le Monde,* August 26, 1982.
17. *La Tribune juive,* December 29, 1978 to January 5, 1979.
18. See the editorial in *L'Arche,* December 1979.
19. *L'Arche,* November 1980.
20. *Bulletin de l'ATJ,* April 5, 1979.
21. *Le Monde,* November 3, 1979.
22. *Ibid.*
23. *Bulletin de l'ATJ,* September 24, 1979.
24. *JTA Bulletin,* August 8, 1934.
25. *Le Monde,* September 26, 1979.
26. *"Juifs agissons: rentrons en Israël,"* tract circulated by CLESS in September and October 1979.
27. *Bulletin de l'ATJ,* December 3, 1979.
28. *Bulletin de l'ATJ,* October 6, 1980.
29. *L'Arche,* November 1980.
30. *Droit et Liberté,* November-December 1980.
31. *L'Arche,* March 1983.
32. *Bulletin de l'ATJ,* November 17, 1980.
33. *L'Express,* October 11 to 17, 1980.
34. *Ibid.*

35. *Le Droit de Vivre,* April 16, 1938.
36. *Le Nouvel Observateur,* October 13 to 19, 1980.
37. *Unzer Shtimme,* March 10, 1939.
38. *L'Arche,* November 1980.
39. *Unzer Shtimme,* February 18, 1939, February 25, 1939.
40. *C.V. Zeitung,* November 28, 1930.
41. *C.V. Zeitung,* December 5, 1930, December 12, 1930.
42. *L'Arche,* September-October 1980.
43. *L'Arche,* November 1982.
44. *Le Droit de Vivre,* April 1933.
45. *L'Univers israélite,* April 29, 1938.
46. *Revue des Etudes Juives,* Vol. 20, 1890.
47. Comité français pour la protection des intellectuels juifs persécutés, *La protestation de la France contre les persécutions antisémites,* Paris, 1933.
48. *L'Arche,* November 1980.
49. *Rouge,* October 10 to 16, 1980.
50. *L'Arche,* June 1978.
51. *Le Nouvel Observateur,* October 13 to 19, 1980.
52. *Le Journal des Communants,* October 1980.
53. *L'Arche,* January 1981.
54. *Bulletin de l'ATJ,* October 10, 1980.
55. *Le Nouvel Observateur,* October 13 to 19, 1980.

Chapter Eleven: Interpretation

1. Commission chargée d'établir le bilan de la situation de la France, *op. cit.*
2. *Bulletin de l'ATJ,* October 1, 1980.
3. See the public opinion poll by IFOP in 1966, in *Sondages,* Revue Française de l'Opinion Publique, 1967, no. 2.
4. *Le Matin,* April 7, 1981.
5. *Le Matin,* April 28, 1982. *Jewish Chronicle,* May 7, 1982.
6. *Le Monde,* September 16–17, 1979.
7. Sources: *Bulletin de l'ATJ,* and *Survey on Antisemitic Events.*
8. *Bulletin de l'ATJ,* January 10, 1978.
9. *Bulletin de l'ATJ,* January 12, 1978.
10. *Bulletin de l'ATJ,* January 16, 1978.
11. *Bulletin de l'ATJ,* April 28, 1981. *Le Monde,* April 28, 1981 and May 2, 1981.
12. *Le Quotidien de Paris,* May 10, 1981.
13. *Der Schild,* June 20, 1927.
14. *Unsere Massnahmen zur Bekämpfung. . . , op. cit.*

Chapter Twelve: Desecrations

1. *Les délits racistes. Compte rendu du Colloque Juridique organisé par la LICA le 18 novembre 1978 au Palais de Justice de Paris,* Cahiers de la LICA, November 1979.
2. *Der Schild,* June 27, 1927.
3. *Unsere Massnahmen zur Bekämpfung der Fried hofsscha:ndungen in Deutschland Mit einer Liste der Synagogenschändungen,* Eine vertraulische Denkschrift des Centralvereins deutscher Staatsbürger jüdischen Glaubens E.V., 1929.
4. *C.V. Zeitung,* March 30, 1928.
5. *Der Schild,* August 8, 1927.
6. *Der Schild,* August 22, 1927.
7. *Unsere Massnahmen zur Bekämpfung...,* op. cit.
8. *La Tribune juive,* October 26, 1928.
9. *Unsere Massnahmen zur Bekämpfung...,* op. cit.
10. *C.V. Zeitung,* October 26, 1928.
11. *Le Populaire,* November 9, 1938.
12. Quoted in Suzanne Normand, *Sous le masque du racisme,* Paris, 1939.
13. *Unsere Massnahmen zur Bekämpfung...,* op. cit.
14. See: *Pinkas HaKehilot, Germania-Bavaria,* Yad VaShem, Jerusalem, 1972.
15. On desecrations in the Middle Ages, see: Otto Stobbe, *Die Juden in Deutschland während des Mittelalters in politischer, socialer und rechtlicher Beziehung,* Dritte Auflage, Berlin, 1923; James Parkes, *The Jews in the Medieval Community,* London, 1938; Guido Kisch, *The Jews in Medieval Germany,* New York, 1970; Salo Wittmayer Baron, *The Jewish Community. Its History and Structure to the American Revolution,* Philadelphia, 1942 (t. II).
16. *Der Schild,* May 31, 1929.
17. *Der Schild,* November 23, 1928.

Chapter Thirteen: False Accusations

1. *Unsere Massnahmen zur Bekämpfung der Fried hofsscha:ndungen in Deutschland Mit einer Liste der Synagogenschändungen,* Eine vertraulische Denkschrift des Centralvereins deutscher Staatsbürger jüdischen Glaubens E.V., 1929.
2. *L'Univers israélite,* October 19, 1900.
3. Quoted in: Salomon Reinach, *L'accusation du meurtre rituel,* in *Revue des Etudes Juives,* Vol. 25, 1892.
4. See: Léon Poliakov, *Histoire de l'antisémitisme,* Paris, 1981 (new edition).
5. Quoted in: Jules Isaac, *Genèse de l'antisémitisme. Essai historique,* Paris, 1956.

6. See: Salomon Grayzel, *The Church and the Jews in the XIIIth Century,* New York, 1966 (Revised Edition).

7. *Je vous hais!,* April 1944.

8. For the most complete listing of blood accusations: Herman L. Strack, *Das Blut im Glauben und Aberglauben der Menschheit,* Leipzig (numerous editions).

9. See for instance Jules Isaac, *op. cit.*

10. See *Gallia Judaïca,* by Henri Gross, about Orléns.

11. Shalom Spiegel, *MiPitgamei HaAkeda: Srufei Blois VeHith'adshut Alilat HaDam,* Sefer HaYovel Lih'vod Mordeh'ai Menah'em Kaplan, New York, 1953; Robert Chazan, *The Blois Incident of 1171: a Study in Jewish Intercommunal Organization,* American Academy for Jewish Research, Proceedings 36, 1968.

12. See the names in: *Das Martyrologium des Nürnberger Memorbuches,* Berlin, 1898.

13. Abraham Habermann, *Sefer Gzerot Ashkenaz VeTsarfat,* Jerusalem, 1945.

14. Robert Chazan, *The Bray Incident of 1192: Realpolitik and Folk Slander,* American Academy for Jewish Research, Proceedings 37, 1969.

15. Arsène Darmesteter, *L'Autodafé de Troyes (24 Avil, 1288),* in *Revue des Etudes Juives,* Vol. 2, 1881.

16. Israël Lévi, *Une cause des persécutions des Juifs au Moyen Age,* in *Revue des Etudes Juives,* t. 24, 1892.

17. Isidore Loeb, *Les expulsions des Juifs de France au xiv siècle,* Extrait de la "*Jubelschrift*" publiée à Breslau pour le 70 anniversare de la naissance de M. le Professeur Dr Graetz. *31 octobre 1887,* Paris, 1887.

18. Jacques Godechot, *Deux Procès de sorcellerie et de sacrilège à Nancy au xviii siècle,* in *Revue des Etudes Juives,* Vol. 89, 1930.

19. Sources: the best record of false accusations of the end of the XIX'th century and the beginning of the XX'th century, in *Bulletin de l'Alliance Israélite Universelle,* of this period.

20. *Vierter Zionisten Kongress. Bericht über den Zustand der Juden auf der ganzen Erde, von Dr Max Nordau.*

21. *L'Univers israélite,* May 1, 1881.

22. Préface to Henri Desportes, *Tué par les juifs. Histoire d'un meurtre rituel,* Paris, 1890.

23. *Le Journal d'Indre-et-Loire,* March 27, 1892.

24. *La Libre Parole,* May 23, 1892.

25. See: Ernest Crémieu-Foa, *La campagne antisémitique. Les duels. Les responsabilités. Mémoire avec pièces justificatives,* Paris, 1892.

26. Quotations from: *Archives israélites,* June 30, 1892.

27. *Bulletin de l'ATJ,* October 8, 1980.

28. *Archives israélites,* June 30, 1892.

29. *L'Univers israélite,* May 1, 1890.

30. *Archives israélites,* June 2, 1892.

31. *Revue des Etudes Juives,* t. 53, 1907.
32. *C.V. Zeitung,* November 2, 1928.
33. *C.V. Zeitung,* April 5, 1929. *Der Schild,* April 12, 1929.
34. *Der Schild,* April 26, 1929.
35. *Der Schild,* May 10, 1929.
36. *C.V. Zeitung,* May 10, 1929, May 17, 1929.
37. *C.V. Zeitung,* August 2, 1929.
38. *C.V. Zeitung,* April 12, 1929.
39. *Der Stürmer,* May 1939, no. 20.
40. *Le Droit de Vivre,* March 19, 1938.
41. *Le Droit de Vivre,* October 8, 1938.
42. *Le Droit de Vivre,* October 8, 1938. *Le Populaire,* October 3, 1938. The quotations are from *La Tribune juive,* October 21, 1938.
43. Edgar Morin, *La rumeur d'Orléans,* Paris, 1970.
44. Source: *Bulletin de l'Alliance Israélite Universelle,* of the corresponding dates.
45. Quoted in: Léon Poliakov, *Bréviaire de la haine (Le III Reich et les Juifs),* Paris, 1951.

Epilogue: The Next Crisis

1. *La Tribune juive,* September 7 to 15, 1983.
2. The Front National gets nine percent of the vote at Aulnay-sous-Bois in November 1983, and 12 percent in December in the Morbihan. The results all are waiting for are those of the European elections, in June 1984.
3. *Le Nouvel Observateur,* September 2 to 8, 1983.
4. *Le Monde,* October 19, 1983.
5. *Le Droit de Vivre,* January 8, 1938.
6. *Le Droit de Vivre,* February 19, 1938.
7. *Le Droit de Vivre,* March 19, 1938.
8. *Le Droit de Vivre,* November 1983.
9. *Le Droit de Vivre,* April 1932.
10. *Bulletin de l'ATJ,* November 22, 1978.